Eyre

The Small Scale Raiding Force

www.brianlettauthor.com

Other books by the same author:

SAS in Tuscany
Ian Fleming and SOE's Operation Postmaster

The Small Scale Raiding Force

'Shall we have a bash?'

Brian Lett

Pen & Sword
MILITARY

For Valerie

First published in Great Britain in 2013 by
Pen & Sword Military
an imprint of
Pen & Sword Books Ltd
47 Church Street
Barnsley
South Yorkshire
S70 2AS

Copyright © H.B.G. Lett 2013

ISBN: 978-1-78159-394-3

The right of Brian Lett to be identified as author of this work has been asserted by him in accordance with the Copyright, Designs and Patents Act 1988.

A CIP catalogue record for this book is available from the British Library.

All rights reserved. No part of this book may be reproduced or transmitted in any form or by any means, electronic or mechanical including photocopying, recording or by any information storage and retrieval system, without permission from the Publisher in writing.

Typeset in 11pt Ehrhardt by
Mac Style, Beverley, E. Yorkshire

Printed and bound in the UK by CPI Group (UK) Ltd, Croydon, CR0 4YY

Pen & Sword Books Ltd incorporates the Imprints of Pen & Sword Aviation, Pen & Sword Family History, Pen & Sword Maritime, Pen & Sword Military, Pen & Sword Discovery, Wharncliffe Local History, Wharncliffe True Crime, Wharncliffe Transport, Pen & Sword Select, Pen & Sword Military Classics, Leo Cooper, The Praetorian Press, Remember When, Seaforth Publishing and Frontline Publishing.

For a complete list of Pen & Sword titles please contact
PEN & SWORD BOOKS LIMITED
47 Church Street, Barnsley, South Yorkshire, S70 2AS, England
E-mail: enquiries@pen-and-sword.co.uk
Website: www.pen-and-sword.co.uk

Contents

List of Illustrations vii
Introduction 1

Chapter 1   Return to England 3
Chapter 2   Gubbins, March-Phillipps and Appleyard 9
Chapter 3   The Future 16
Chapter 4   Anderson Manor 21
Chapter 5   The Old and the New 25
Chapter 6   Training 39
Chapter 7   Sink the *Tirpitz* – Operation Frodesley 43
Chapter 8   Operation Barricade 48
Chapter 9   Operation Dryad 56
Chapter 10   Operation Branford 67
Chapter 11   Operation Aquatint 72
Chapter 12   The Survivors 80
Chapter 13   Adam Orr 83
Chapter 14   Graham Hayes 87
Chapter 15   André Desgranges 97
Chapter 16   After Aquatint 101

Chapter 17	Operation Basalt	105
Chapter 18	Operation Facsimile	125
Chapter 19	Expansion	128
Chapter 20	Operation Fahrenheit	131
Chapter 21	Operation Batman	141
Chapter 22	Operation Witticism	143
Chapter 23	Huckaback, Backchat and Pussyfoot	145
Chapter 24	Confusion in North Africa	153
Chapter 25	Geoffrey Appleyard	161
Chapter 26	La Galite	165
Chapter 27	Pantelleria: Operation Snapdragon	168
Chapter 28	Sicily: Operation Chestnut	173
Chapter 29	Anders Lassen on Crete	176
Chapter 30	Anders Lassen on Simi	181
Chapter 31	Lake Comacchio	188

Appendix A: Leslie W. 'Red' Wright – the Man Who Was Not There 194
Appendix B: Captain J. E. O. Evans 199
Acknowledgements 205
Sources 207
Index 211

List of Illustrations

1. Anderson Manor
2. MTB 344, 'The Little Pisser'
3. Major Gus March-Phillipps DSO, MBE
4. Major Geoffrey Appleyard DSO, MC
5. Captain Graham Hayes MC
6. Major Anders Lassen VC, MC and two bars
7. Richard Lehniger, with his wife Lilly and daughter Irene, 1940
9. Allan Williams with his mother, circa 1940
10. Major John Gwynne, planning officer
11. Major General Sir Colin Gubbins DSO, MC, 'M'
12. Brian Reynolds/Bingham
13. Lieutenant Freddie Bourne, DSC, RNVR
14. M's memo regarding recruitment into the SSRF
15. M's memo regarding Operation Froudesley
16. SOE's *Descriptive Catalogue of Special Devices and Supplies* – thumb knife and itching powder
17. Colin Ogden Smith
18. Major Oswald 'Mickey' Rooney
19. Lieutenant Colonel Bill Stirling
20. Lieutenant Henk Brinkgreve
21. The SSRF in the Lake District
22. Practising dory landings
23. Plan of the *Admiral von Tirpitz*
24. A Welman miniature submarine, 1942
25. Map of the English Channel, marking raids by MTB 344 in August and September
26. Operation Barricade: the intended targets

27. Operation Dryad: Casquets Rock
28. Wartime map of Sark
29. Intelligence photo of the Hog's Back, Sark
30. Aerial photo of Baleine Bay, Sark
31. La Jespellaire, 1979
32. The annexe to the Dixcart Hotel, 1979
33. Operation Fahrenheit: aerial photograph of the Pointe de Plouzac
34. Operation Witticism: aerial photograph of St Peter Port, Guernsey
35. Operation Huckaback: intelligence photos of Herm
36. Intelligence photo of the main house for Operation Huckaback
37. Intelligence photo of Belvoir beach and Shell beach, Herm, for Operation Huckaback

Introduction

This book is the second in a two-part study of Major Gus March-Phillipps DSO, MBE, and the extraordinary bands of seaborne commandos and secret agents that he led during the first half of World War Two. In *Ian Fleming and SOE's Operation Postmaster*, I described that operation and set out the facts that led me to an inescapable conclusion: that Ian Fleming had based his fictional secret agent James Bond on the characters of Gus March-Phillipps and three of his comrades, Geoffrey Appleyard, Graham Hayes and Anders Lassen. However, the 'James Bond connection' was not the point of that book. The story of Operation Postmaster is a remarkable one, and in many ways, the links with Fleming and James Bond were an unwelcome intrusion. However, so much has been written about Ian Fleming and the possible inspirations behind his creations, Bond and 'M', that when I discovered the evidence, I felt it should be put on record. Of course, most of us enjoy a good Bond film or book without worrying about the history that lies behind it. For those who do want to know, this book and its predecessor tell the story.

'James Bond' was an agent of the Special Operations Executive (SOE), which was run by a man who really did use the code name 'M', Major General Sir Colin McVean Gubbins DSO, MC. Ian Fleming worked with SOE very closely in the early years of the war, and knew the characters involved well. Indeed, Gus March-Phillipps was Ian Fleming's exact contemporary, and was everything that Fleming was not – a successful commando secret agent and a genuine hero, and at the same time a successful novelist with three published novels already to his name. Had Gus March-Phillipps survived the war there is little doubt that he would have written the 'James Bond' series.

My own father, Major Gordon Lett DSO, was a member of SOE, and remained in the intelligence community after the war. It always interested me that he had such a low opinion of Fleming, and was rather dismissive of the exploits of his James Bond. I know now that this was because Fleming was in fact writing of SOE, and deliberately came very close to giving away significant secrets. My father knew M (Sir Colin Gubbins) well, but whether he ever met Fleming I do not know.

Although Fleming was closely involved in Operation Postmaster, and met the personnel engaged on it, I have found no direct evidence to suggest that he had anything to do with the activities of the Small Scale Raiding Force. However, it was a quasi naval unit (a part of M's secret navy), and there is no doubt that Fleming would have been aware of its activities in 1942 and 1943. Indeed, he was involved in the setting up of a not dissimilar unit to the SSRF within the Royal Navy – 30 Assault Unit. Thus Ian Fleming plays no direct part in this book, although he would no doubt have followed the remarkable careers of March-Phillipps, Appleyard, Hayes and Lassen to their conclusions.

Accordingly, this book makes only minimal reference to Ian Fleming and his fictional agent, Bond. Indeed, when with the SSRF, March-Phillipps and his men were working as commandos rather than secret agents, albeit that they remained on the roll of M's Secret Service and under his operational command. The reader is left to judge whether the continued true life exploits of March-Phillipps, Appleyard, Hayes and Lassen, after they had completed Operation Postmaster and parted company with Ian Fleming, also provided inspiration for Fleming's eventual Bond character. The members of the Small Scale Raiding Force described in this book were all courageous men who command my deep respect. I only hope that I have done them justice.

Chapter 1

Return to England

To any casual observer who might have been watching, the arrival of Gus March-Phillipps and Geoffrey Appleyard in Baker Street on a cold winter's morning in February 1942 would have seemed unremarkable. They were two ordinary-looking men, one in his thirties with a moustache and receding hairline, the other in his mid-twenties and rather handsome, amongst the many thousands who thronged war-damaged London that winter. The premises that they entered, 64 Baker Street, was to the outside world the headquarters of the Inter Services Research Bureau (ISRB), which regularly received men from all branches of the military through its doors, some in uniform, some not. What an observer could not have known was that March-Phillipps and Appleyard were actually secret agents, reporting back to their boss at his Secret Service headquarters, after completing one of the war's most remarkable commando operations.

Their boss was Brigadier Colin McVean Gubbins DSO, MC, code name 'M' – the name that Commander Ian Fleming would later borrow for the controller of his fictional secret agent, James Bond. Fleming, who knew the workings of M's Secret Service intimately at this stage, described 64 Baker Street in his books as 'a large grey building near Regent's Park'. March-Phillipps and Appleyard were two of the real 'licensed to kill' secret agents upon whom the character of Bond was to be based.

The 'Inter Services Research Bureau' was itself a code name. M's Secret Service was the most secret of all the British wartime services. Officially, it did not exist, nor did its agents. Their activities were deniable. The real name of the ISRB was the Special Operations Executive (SOE), and M was its Operations and Training Director. Even after the Second World War had come to an end, and SOE had been officially disbanded, the fact that it had existed remained a secret, and not until the eventual collapse of the Soviet Union did the whole truth about its activities begin to be told.

Those who have read *Ian Fleming and SOE'S Operation Postmaster*, or others of the increasing number of books available on the history of SOE, will be familiar with the varied and extensive role that SOE played in the Second World War. However, for those who are new to the complexities of SOE, a summary of its history and activities is appropriate here. SOE was not bound by the Army's rules and red tape, it was a covert organization of irregulars, supported by a sophisticated gadgets and 'dirty tricks' department. Since officially SOE did not exist, it operated on a strict 'need to know' basis, both in its relations with the three regular Armed Services, and within its own ranks. Its operatives were, in the early years, often paid in cash, to avoid the necessity of banking entries and wage records. SOE had been born in July 1940, in the desperate days after the great British defeat at Dunkirk. A secret high-level meeting took place at the Foreign Office, which resulted in the setting up of a new and very secret Secret Service. Dr Hugh Dalton, the Minister for Economic Warfare, described the purpose of SOE in a lettter to Lord Halifax:

> We have got to organize movements in enemy-occupied territory comparable to the Sinn Fein movement in Ireland, to the Chinese Guerrillas now operating against Japan, to the Spanish irregulars who played a notable part in Wellington's campaign or – and one might as well admit it – to the organizations which the Nazis themselves have developed so remarkably in almost every country in the world. This 'democratic international' must use many different methods, including industrial and military sabotage, labour agitation and strikes, continuous propaganda, terrorist acts against traitors and German leaders, boycotts and riots. It is quite clear to me that an organization on this scale and of this character is not something that can be handled by the ordinary departmental machinery of either the British Civil Service or the British military machine. What is needed is a new organization to co-ordinate, inspire, control and assist the nationals of the oppressed countries who must themselves be the direct participants. We need absolute secrecy, a certain fanatical enthusiasm, willingness to work with people of different nationalities, complete political reliability. Certain of these qualities are certain to be found in some military officers and, if such men are available, they should undoubtedly be used. But the organization should, in my view, be entirely independent of the War Office machine.

The War Cabinet was looking for any and every way in which it could fight back in what was now regarded as a 'no holds barred' war, and on 16 July 1940 Churchill sent for Dalton, who was a left-wing Labour old Etonian, and invited him to take ministerial charge of the new organization (SOE) that was to progress and control the subversive warfare that had been proposed. Dalton accepted. Churchill did not like Dalton, but felt that he was well suited to the job. Dalton appointed Sir Frank Nelson, an industrialist, to be the first head of the new service. Nelson was appointed initially to the rank of Wing Commander, and not long after to Air Commodore. Colin Gubbins was recruited as the Director of Operations and Training, and adopted the code name M, the initial of his middle name, McVean.

The ordinary rules of warfare and military life were never intended to apply to SOE. It was created at a time of desperation and all-out war, and grew up in a climate of indiscriminate bombing by the Germans of British cities and civilians. The secret activities of SOE inevitably involved normally unethical and illegal methods. As secret agents in the field, SOE operatives would be expected to lie, deceive, bribe, blackmail, and, where it furthered their objective, to kill. It is interesting to note that both March-Phillipps and Appleyard were devout Christians who found no difficulty in reconciling their religious beliefs with a fierce patriotism in their country's hour of need. An SOE agent's conscience would, where necessary, be subjugated to that sense of duty to country. Further, the agent would know that his activities could never be publicly acknowledged, and that if he was captured, quite possibly he would be disowned by the British Government, probably he would be tortured and shot. Every agent sent into the field was given, before his mission, what was nicknamed 'communion'. This was a suicide pill that the agent could take if he or she feared that they would break under torture. Fleming was later to supply his James Bond with a similar pill, which Bond was in the habit of throwing away.

SOE's role in placing agents behind the lines in enemy-occupied countries is now well known, but the true ambit of their activities was far wider than that. SOE established a presence in virtually every neutral country, and conducted a huge number of campaigns against enemy interests. They employed anyone who could prove themselves to be useful, and their recruits came from many different backgrounds. Ewan Butler, a German expert within SOE, listed the occupations of a number he knew personally: an eminent young actor, a professional burglar, a man who sold rubber goods in Bucharest, two peers of the realm, a sprinkling of baronets, a pimp, two or three prostitutes, a jockey, an art expert, a publisher and several journalists. Many women joined SOE, and proved to be extremely successful agents in the field. All recruitment was by personal contact and recommendation (as one ex-agent later said, you could hardly advertise for employees for a Secret Service that was not meant to exist).

The very nature of SOE was bound to make the hackles of 'old school' military officers rise. Another of its own men, Professor G. H. N. Seton-

Watson, a Balkans expert, described SOE as, 'an upstart organization, inevitably viewed with suspicion and jealousy by all existing departments ... the first recruits were a mixture of widely different types from different places, bankers, business men, mining engineers and journalists ... Nearly all the earlier recruits lacked the habit of subordination to a regular hierarchy, were disciplined by no mandarin ethos and were impatient or even contemptuous of the bureaucratic conventions of the diplomatic service and its auxiliaries.' The same ethos became an essential part of the mindset of Fleming's James Bond, who whilst admiring his own boss M, had little time or respect for bureaucracy or 'mandarins'.

As the war progressed, SOE grew in numbers and diversity. They utilized many methods of deception, and invented a whole variety of covert devices and gadgets that would have delighted the 'Q' of the James Bond books. Some of the schemes they developed were ambitious and almost grandiose (like Operation Postmaster itself), others had the simplicity of schoolboy pranks. All were designed, however, to disrupt enemy activity and to damage enemy morale. In occupied countries, they also had the objective of boosting the morale of the oppressed local population.

Ewan Butler gives examples of minor operations mounted whilst he was the Head of Mission in neutral Sweden. Neighbouring Norway was in enemy hands. In the cold northern European winter, greatcoats were essential for the comfort of German officers and soldiers. Butler supplied his agents amongst the local population in Norway with capsules of extremely evil smelling fluid, the equivalent of a schoolboy's stink bomb. An agent would then slip into the cloakroom of a restaurant or bar frequented by Germans, and with two or three capsules, he or she could impregnate every coat in the room. The smell was so terrible that no one could bear to wear the overcoat until it had been thoroughly cleaned, which would take a matter of weeks. A shortage of wearable coats resulted, and in the depth of winter this obviously caused the Germans appreciable discomfort. An added advantage was that for the agents carrying the capsules the risk was relatively low.

Another ruse was to use catapults to break the windows of buildings occupied or used by German troops. There was a shortage of glass to repair windows in Norway, and in the bitter winter this caused considerable discomfort to the enemy troops. SOE also despatched from Sweden a large number of dummy packets of German foodstuffs covertly to German bases in Denmark and Norway. These in fact contained no food, but detailed instructions to ordinary, discontented German soldiers on how to 'pull a sickie', and get themselves into the comfort of a military hospital. The instructions came with little phials of chemicals which, when properly used, could produce false symptoms for a variety of medical complaints varying from a swollen knee to jaundice or tuberculosis.

Peter Kemp, who became another of the licensed to kill secret agents, commented that SOE utilized almost the whole range of children's joke toys for destructive purposes – there were imitation turds of horse or camel dung (depending upon the theatre of war), which contained explosive charges that would destroy the tyres of any vehicle that drove over them, and sickeningly realistic dead rats intended to be smuggled into German offices or barrack rooms – when picked up by the tail for disposal, they would explode with a small but lethal charge, usually killing the unfortunate handler.

SOE's 'special gadgets' department was formally known as the Scientific Research Department, and came under the overall command of SOE's director of scientific research, Dr (later Professor) Dudley M. Newitt. In the Bond stories, Newitt became 'Q'. The headquarters of the Scientific Research Department was Station IX at The Frythe, Welwyn in Hertfordshire, and many of their wartime inventions were given the prefix 'Wel', as with the Welpen and Welpipe, both disguised single-shot pistols, which are described later. Dudley Newitt was 46 years of age when recruited into SOE. He had fought in the First World War, on the North West Frontier of India, and in Mesopotamia and Palestine, and had won the Military Cross. After the war, he took a degree in chemistry at the Royal College of Science (later Imperial College, London), became a chemical engineer and later an academic. He controlled a large and enormously inventive department in SOE. Newitt understood military matters, and was an energetic and inspiring leader of his department. However, his appearance was deceptive, and he was described by some of those he came into contact with as 'a typical absent-minded professor' or 'absent-minded boffin' (in the style of Fleming's Q).

The *Maid Honor*, March-Phillipps' previous command, in which he had sailed to West Africa, had been a Q Ship. The letter 'Q' epitomized disguise and deceit, often in breach of the rules of war. The *Maid Honor* had masqueraded as a Swedish civilian ship, flying, when necessary, the Swedish flag. To outward appearance she was a fishing vessel, but within minutes she could collapse her innocent-looking deckhouse and bring her armaments to bear on any target. Her plain-clothed crew were in fact all trained commandos who carried military rank.

Newitt's department within SOE even produced a catalogue of special devices from which agents could choose their equipment for a mission, called the 'Descriptive Catalogue of Special Devices and Supplies'. This included a frogman's outfit (described as Amphibian Breathing Apparatus), an incendiary attaché case, briefcase and suitcase, and a variety of unpleasant covert knives and guns, including a Thumb Knife and a Sleeve Gun. The latter was described in the catalogue as: 'A short length, silent, murder weapon, firing 0.32 ammunition. It is a single shot weapon designed for carriage in the sleeve with the trigger near the muzzle to aid unobtrusive firing when the gun is slid from the sleeve into the hand. The gun is intended for use in contact with the target, but may be used at ranges of up to about three yards.' The catalogue included other deadly weapons, but also items such as tyre busters (concealed explosive charges like the horse and camel turds described by Peter Kemp, designed to explode when driven over) and secret ink. It was exactly the sort of catalogue that James Bond would browse through when visiting Q's laboratory.

Other weapons invented by Newitt's department over the years included the Welpen, Welpipe, Welwoodbine and Welcheroot. These were all disguised, close-range, single-shot .22 pistols, designed to be used either as a last resort weapon by SOE agents, or for the purposes of assasination. As the names suggest, the Welpen was a pistol disguised as a pen, the Welwoodbine was a pistol disguised as a Woodbine cigarette (although the agent could change the paper around the gun to suit the local brand of cigarette to the area in which he was operating) and so on. Newitt's team also designed incendiary cigarettes, thousands of which were supplied to the agents. The emphasis was always on the disguise. Like Fleming's Q Branch, Newitt and his research department were endlessly striving to create devices that would make a Secret Agent's life easier.

Chapter 2

Gubbins, March-Phillipps and Appleyard

Although many of the agents and administrators of SOE were recruited from civilian life, Colin McVean Gubbins, initially Director of Operations and Training and later head of the entire organization, was a battle-hardened and very experienced soldier. In February 1942, he had been running SOE operations for about fifteen months.

Colin Gubbins was born in Japan in 1896, the son of a diplomat and expert linguist, John Harrington Gubbins. John Gubbins was in fact an Englishman of Irish extraction, but his wife, Colin's mother, was a Highland Scot and to all intents and purposes Gubbins grew up as a Scot. He spent much of his early life with his grandparents on the Isle of Mull, whilst his father and mother were still serving in Japan. He was schooled at Cheltenham College, which he did not particularly enjoy, and attended the Royal Military Academy, Woolwich. He was commissioned into the Royal Artillery at the start of the First World War. Gubbins saw active service throughout that war in the mud of France and Flanders, and took part in the Battle of the Somme. He was awarded a Military Cross for conspicuous gallantry: 'When one of his guns and its detachment were blown up by a heavy shell, he organized a rescue party and personally helped to dig out the wounded while shells were falling all round.' On 7 October 1916, Gubbins suffered a gunshot wound to the neck, and was hospitalized for eleven days. In November 1917, he was gassed by mustard gas near Arras, but happily recovered. In April 1918, he was shipped home, sick with trench fever, but somehow survived. He remained a regular soldier after the war, saw service in Northern Russia in 1919, and was serving in Ireland during the insurrection of 1921–22.

Later, Gubbins served on the General Staff at British Army HQ in India, during a time of riots and civil disobedience. He was then sent to the Staff College at Camberley, and from there to a military intelligence role at the War

Office, where he spent a number of years. Between the wars he became an excellent linguist, passing interpreters' exams in French, Russian and Urdu.

In January 1939, with war looming, Gubbins was recruited into a small section of the War Office known as General Staff (Research). His brief there was to study the concept of guerrilla warfare, and he drafted three secret pamphlets designed for fighting a guerrilla war. They were entitled: 'The Art of Guerilla Warfare', 'The Partisan Leader's Handbook' and 'How to Use High Explosives'.

When war finally broke out, Gubbins was posted to Warsaw as Head of Intelligence with General de Wiart, but within days of his arrival the Germans reduced that city to ashes and Gubbins was forced to make a daring escape through Hungary and the Balkans. In 1940, he was sent to the defence of Norway, again under General de Wiart's command. Gubbins was tasked to set up and command the 'Striking Companies', an early version of the Commandos. With them, he fought a guerrilla war delaying the advance of German forces towards Narvik. He blew bridges, mined roads and set fire to forests, often working with local Norwegian civilians, before eventually exfiltrating, as Norway inevitably fell to the might of Nazi Germany. Thus, he too had suffered the ignominy of defeat.

When the Special Operations Executive was set up in July 1940, as part of Churchill and the British War Cabinet's response to Dunkirk, Hugh Dalton, the Minister for Economic Warfare, was given control over it. In November 1940, after something of a battle with the War Office, who did not want to let Gubbins go, Dalton secured his services for SOE. Initially Gubbins was appointed SOE Director of Operations and Training (becoming 'M', the initial taken from his middle name). Later, in the early autumn of 1943, he became the executive head of the whole of SOE, known as CD. Gubbins was still serving as CD when the war came to an end, and remained with SOE until it was dissolved in January 1946. Both of his predecessors as CD had written to him after they left the job, Sir Frank Nelson in May 1942 saying: 'Thank you for your ever genial, calm and brilliant help and support which you have so freely given me over the last 18 months,' and Sir Charles Hambro saying in September 1943 (when Gubbins was appointed as his successor): 'There is no one who has so much right to be where you are today, and if anyone can ensure dividends and success it is you ... what a wonderful support you have always been to me ... how much I admired your work. You provided all those qualities that I lacked ... I would happily come and work under you.'

It is obvious that Gubbins was much loved and admired by his superiors and subordinates alike. He was a man James Bond would have enjoyed working for, as the men of Maid Honor Force had and the men of the Small Scale Raiding

Force would. A typical accolade came from a young and beautiful actress recruited into SOE as a secretary in August 1941, Marjorie Stewart, who described him later as bursting with energy, vitality and strength. Talking of the hard work and achievements of SOE, she said: 'Every time you come back to M as the most fantastic activating and motivating spirit, with a fantastic capacity for work, great at galvanising everyone who worked for him.'

After his experiences in Norway, where he had seen the might of Hitler's invading armies too often at close quarters, Gubbins was the ideal man to take charge of the operations and training of Britain's new secret service. He joined them in Baker Street in mid-November 1940. The real M was 45 years of age when he arrived at SOE.

SOE had to work closely with the three established services, the Royal Navy, the Royal Air Force and the Army. It was their work with the Navy that brought M and the Secret Service into contact with Ian Fleming. From early 1941 through into 1942, Fleming was working as assistant to the head of Naval Intelligence, Admiral John Godfrey, who gave him the job of liaising with SOE over all matters affecting the Royal Navy. Since Britain was an island, and the Navy had responsibility for the surrounding seas, if SOE needed to go anywhere by sea, the Navy's consent had to be obtained. Thus Fleming came to know SOE very well.[1]

As they walked down Baker Street on that February morning, Agent W.01, Captain (soon to be Major) Gus March-Phillipps, MBE, and Agent W.02, Lieutenant (soon to be Captain) Geoffrey Appleyard, MC, were triumphant. They had planned, and only weeks before carried out, Operation Postmaster, a raid on the little port of Santa Isabel on the island of Fernando Po, in Spanish Guinea, West Africa. The raid had been a complete success, probably SOE's greatest success of the war so far. Having completed Postmaster on 22 January 1942, March-Phillipps and Appleyard had been called back to London immediately to report in person to M. Travelling by ship, they arrived back in London by 12 February. Now that they had returned to England they would soon lose the W tag to their code names (W.01 and W.02), which represented the West Africa section to which they had been attached for the purposes of Operation Postmaster. The 00 prefix later used by Ian Fleming for his licensed to kill secret agents was a thinly disguised version of the real-life code names of March-Phillipps, Appleyard and the men of Maid Honor Force.

Gustavus March-Phillips, Agent W.01, was, at 33 years of age, nearly nine years older than Appleyard, a significant gap. He was a romantic and in many ways a very old-fashioned soldier, but an inspirational leader. He looked to heroes of old, like Drake, Raleigh and Robert the Bruce, to provide the British Army with the spirit to defend itself against the German onslaught. As a practising Roman Catholic, schooled at Ampleforth College in Yorkshire, he believed fervently in God, followed closely by King and Country. He had been commissioned into the Royal Artillery at the age of 20, and had served for a number of years in India, rising to the rank of Lieutenant. He saw action on the North West Frontier, but by January of 1932 found himself stuck with 23 Field Battery in the garrison town of Meerut, involved in an endless round of ceremonial and social duties.

March-Phillipps had no time for pomp, circumstance and red tape. He became disillusioned with army life and by October 1932, at the age of 24, had resigned his commission and returned to England. For some years March-Phillipps led the life of a country gentleman. He wrote and had published three novels: *Storm in a Teacup*, *Sporting Print*, and *Ace High*. March-Phillipps demonstrated a clear understanding of human nature, and his novels were all well received. He was also a published poet.

In person, March-Phillips was slender and lightly framed, of medium height with dark, slightly receding hair and piercing eyes. He was obsessed by physical fitness, and every ounce of his fighting weight was tight as whipcord. He resembled a greyhound rather than a bulldog. He was described by the ladies as handsome, but had been bitten in the mouth by a horse when young, which had left him with a slight deformation and scarring of his top lip. He covered this with a moustache. He was an accomplished horseman, and had at one time been on the staff of the Dorset Hunt. He was also an enthusiastic amateur yachtsman. He had a love of the English countryside, its birds and wildlife. He suffered from a slight stammer, but never allowed it to impede him in anything that he wished to do – indeed, his friends suggested that he turned the stammer into an offensive weapon. He had a fiery but short-lived temper and in battle he was always calm and in control. He had the inspiration to conceive great enterprises, as well as the skill and daring to carry them out. He was a natural leader of men, had a great sense of fairness towards his subordinates, and inspired great loyalty.

March-Phillipps and Appleyard had met in a sandhole on the beach at Dunkirk, sheltering from enemy attack at what was one of their country's darkest moments, as the British Expeditionary Force was flung from mainland Europe by the military might of Adolf Hitler's Nazi Germany. Their friendship, born in adversity, became a strong and enduring one, as they worked together first as ordinary commandos, and then from January 1941 as Commnando Secret Agents under the control of M and SOE. When each signed up for SOE, they were given consecutive serial numbers, Appleyard's being 1441, March-Phillipps' 1442.

When they first met, Geoffrey Appleyard, Agent W.02, had been a Second Lieutenant of the Royal Army Service Corps (RASC). Appleyard was a handsome fair-haired young man, then 23, a Yorkshireman born in Leeds. He was known throughout his army career simply as 'Apple'. His family lived in the Manor House at Linton-on-Wharfe near Wetherby, where he had spent most of his life. They were well off, and his father ran what eventually became the largest motor business in Leeds. Geoffrey himself was educated at a Quaker school, Bootham in York, and later gained first class honours in engineering at Caius College, Cambridge. He too was a committed Christian. He was what can best be described as a 'muscular ornithologist', having won the Natural History Exhibition at Bootham School, and later pursued this interest at Cambridge, where he once hunted for the nesting place of a rare black redstart by climbing across the slippery rooftops of the city houses in pouring rain. He was not averse to swinging at the end of a rope on the cliffs of Bempton to recover gulls' eggs from their nests. Appleyard's good looks, athletic physique, and deep-set blue eyes made him always popular with the opposite sex. He was an accomplished oarsman and an expert skier, having represented Cambridge in international competition with considerable success, and having captained English ski teams against Norway in 1938 and 1939. He was also skilled at ice hockey and water-skiing.

March-Phillipps had been appointed after Dunkirk to command B Troop of the newly formed 7 Commando, and he chose Appleyard to be one of his troop officers. The activities of March-Phillipps and Appleyard thereafter came to the notice of M, and when they joined SOE, M had at first employed them separately, sending off Appleyard on an operation to collect agents from the coast of France as a part of Operation Savannah, whilst March-Phillipps was to become a training officer. However, March-Phillipps' concept for the small unit that became Maid Honor Force brought the two men back together again, and it was not long before M regarded them as an indivisible military unit – March-Phillipps the inspirational leader and ideas man, Appleyard the practical organizer and restraining influence. By February 1942, they had been close friends and fighting comrades for more than eighteen months.

After the triumph of Operation Postmaster, March-Phillipps, Appleyard and their specially trained Maid Honor Force were the toast of M's Secret Service. What they had achieved was truly remarkable, and had done much to boost the reputation of SOE with Britain's three established armed services. M had been fighting for SOE's continued existence in the face of fierce Regular Service rivalry and disapproval – what M himself referred to as 'The War Within'. This came not only from the Royal Navy, Army and Royal Air Force, but also from the Secret Intelligence Service (SIS), aka MI6, which was Britain's established international intelligence service.

On Operation Postmaster, Gus March-Phillipps and his men had pulled off the near impossible. In breach of international law, they had raided the neutral port of Santa Isabel, in Spanish Guinea and, scarcely having fired a shot, had stolen away three enemy vessels – two German ships and a massive Italian liner – from under the noses of the Spanish garrison. Furthermore, they had done so in such a way that the Spanish did not know who had carried out the operation. The market value of the Italian liner and her cargo was somewhere in the region of £300,000, a substantial sum in war-torn Britain.[2] More importantly, the threat that the ships might become a supply fleet for the German submarines that were the scourge of the West African convoys had at a stroke been removed.

The success of Operation Postmaster brought about, at least temporarily, a truce between SOE and the Regular Services. The Royal Navy (who, by accident, had nearly brought disaster upon the operation) and the Army (who had done absolutely nothing to help it), were keen to claim a share of the credit for its success. The Prime Minister, Winston Churchill, and the War Cabinet were delighted with the outcome of what had been a very daring and high risk operation. Because it had been unlawful, however, all those involved were sworn to secrecy about Postmaster, the truth of which had already been publicly denied by the British Foreign Secretary, Anthony Eden. Maid Honor Force in West Africa was quickly dispersed. Gus March-Phillipps and his second-in-command Geoffrey Appleyard had been ordered to return immediately to England, after the captured ships had been sailed into Lagos Harbour in British Nigeria. They had left at once by commercial liner, travelling in plain clothes, and using SOE's customary false passports. The use to which the remainder of the Maid Honor Force, March-Phillipps' team of licensed to kill secret commando agents, would be put would be decided later. As soon as March-Phillipps and Appleyard were back in England, not only M but many others in the know were keen to meet them, and to learn everything they could about the operation, including of course Commander Ian Fleming, the personal assistant to the Director of Naval Intelligence, Admiral Godfrey, who had been intimately involved in the operation from its London end. Written reports had already reached London, but M and the Admiralty wanted the full story from March-Phillipps and Appleyard.

Gus March-Phillipps himself could now have looked forward to a comfortable future within the planning and training sections of SOE, particularly since M had first recruited him into SOE with the intention that he should fulfil a training role. At the same time, had he wished, March-Phillipps could have settled down to write his fourth novel (to add to the three published before the war), featuring his own hero John Sprake, who had appeared in his book *Ace High*. But Gus March-Phillipps was not that kind of man. He was in many ways the opposite of his contemporary, Ian Fleming, in that he was not only a planner, but also a true man of action, an ardent patriot who both conceived the most daring plans, and longed personally to put them into effect. In West Africa, and on the voyage home, March-Phillipps and Appleyard were already planning their next projects. The secret agents' Q ship *Maid Honor*, in which March-Phillipps had sailed with his force to West Africa, had had to be left behind there, so they needed a new vessel to carry out any future raids. However, March-Phillipps had not given up hope of returning to West Africa. Eleven of his men were still there, either in West Africa or on leave in South Africa.

Operation Postmaster was one of two 'cutting out' operations that had been authorized in late December 1941 – there was a second called Operation Ramification, a planned raid on neutral Liberia to seize two German ships that were known to be sheltering there. Ramification was yet to be carried out, and M and March-Phillipps hoped that it might still be possible. However, now that March-Phillipps and Appleyard were back in England, they were very much in demand, and there were other calls on their services.

Notes
1. For a detailed account of Fleming's involvement with SOE and Maid Honor Force, see *Ian Fleming and SOE's Operation Postmaster* Pen & Sword, 2012.
2. The full story of Operation Postmaster is told in *Ian Fleming and SOE's Operation Postmaster*, by Brian Lett.

Chapter 3

The Future

One of March-Phillipps' new projects was the creation of a British-based Small Scale Raiding Force (SSRF). He intended to use the SSRF to strike across the Channel at selected enemy positions, with the aim of gathering intelligence and capturing German prisoners. The raids would also no doubt result in enemy casualties, creating fear in the ranks of ordinary German soldiers as they went about their routine duties along the coastlines of the occupied countries. Fast and silent Motor Torpedo Boats or Motor Gun Boats (MTBs and MGBs) would strike out of the darkness at a chosen point on the coast, and a small band of SOE commando agents would land to carry out the raid, returning the same night to England with the enemy prisoners and seized documents for immediate examination by the British Intelligence services, and probably leaving a number of enemy dead behind them. The enemy would not know how the attack had been carried out, or who was responsible. The morale of their troops would be undermined, and they would worry about where the next attack might come. They would use up valuable manpower in reinforcing their coastal garrisons. In the brief time that they were on enemy territory, the agents would also be able to survey the enemy defences, and carry out all sorts of menial but vital tasks, such as gathering soil samples to see whether, come the day when Britain would strike back and mount an invasion of the mainland, an area was suitable to land tanks or other heavy vehicles.

This project coincided with Lord Louis Mountbatten's desire to increase the number of commando raids across the Channel. Mountbatten was in command of Combined Operations, a body intended to bring together Commandos and the Royal Navy in joint attacks. It was agreed that SOE would provide support for Mountbatten's efforts, and that March-Phillipps's SSRF would operate under a joint command with Mountbatten. This would hopefully solve SOE's problems of getting naval permission for their operations. March-Phillipps' plan was to start with a single base for his Small Scale Raiding Force, but then, once a core of men had been trained in the special needs of such raids, to expand the Force so that there were numerous bases all along the British coastline, capable of attacking a whole variety of targets across the Channel and the North Sea. Maid Honor Force's problem the previous year, before their transfer to West Africa, had been that the Royal Navy, whose approval it needed for any seaborne operation, would not trust it, and rejected out of hand any plan that Gus March-Phillipps (an Army officer) had put forward. Now with the triumph of Operation Postmaster behind him, and with Mountbatten's support, March-Phillipps hoped that the Navy would feel obliged to approve his new plan, and remove all the obstructions it had placed in his way previously.

Gus March-Phillipps knew Poole Harbour and its bay well. He had sailed there before the war, and had based and trained his Maid Honor Force there in the spring and summer of 1941. Now, he hoped to base the SSRF in the same area. He intended to bring into the SSRF all the men of his Maid Honor Force, but since they numbered only 13 in total, he needed to recruit more. As the SOE was a totally secret organization that officially did not exist, he would either have to recruit from within its ranks or seek out new men from elsewhere by word of mouth and personal recommendation. However, by early March 1942, the SSRF was not the only project March-Phillipps was working on. He and Appleyard were also developing a plan to attack Germany's one remaining 'super battleship', the *Tirpitz*, of which more later.

Thus, when March-Phillipps met with M at Baker Street on 12 February 1942, following his arrival back in London, he did not simply debrief on Operation Postmaster, he also sought M's immediate permission for his other schemes. The meeting was undoubtedly a warm and happy one. M was a great leader of men, who knew how much he was asking of his agents, and would give them all the support he possibly could in return. M himself (known within SOE's headquarters by his code name or simply as 'the Brig'), had fought a guerrilla war against the Germans and knew the difficulties experienced by 'secret armies' and agents operating behind the lines. Understandably, the offices of SOE had been abuzz with the exploits of the Maid Honor Force for some months before March-Phillipps' return, though the code of secrecy meant that those in the know talked amongst themselves – others did not ask questions. One of the secretaries in the Polish and Czechoslovakian section at this time was Marjorie Stewart, who had been recruited partly because as an actress it was thought that she must have a good memory. Stewart believed that she heard regular mention of a lady called May Donna. She was too junior to ask questions, and it was only after March-Phillipps and Appleyard had returned to London that she realized 'May Donna' was in fact the Q ship, *Maid Honor*!

March-Phillipps and Appleyard were undoubtedly feted by SOE upon their return. A party was held in their honour, and to celebrate Operation Postmaster, to which only guests in the know were invited. Although no guest list now exists, Ian Fleming would undoubtedly have been invited. He had been deeply involved with the Maid Honor Force and with Postmaster, liaising regularly with M, and helping to persuade the Admiralty to grant the necessary authorities. It was also Fleming who had been assigned the task of perfecting the cover story for the operation – most fairly described as a set of lies – that would be (and were) publicly told, after Postmaster had taken place. Ian Fleming had visited Maid Honor Force at their training base in Poole in early June 1942, before they set off for West Africa, and he knew its officers and men.

The question remained how best to use March-Phillipps' talents next. M was clearly attracted to his plan for the SSRF, which undoubtedly would get Mountbatten's support. He approved it on SOE's behalf, but warned March-Phillipps that approval would also be necessary from Combined Operations HQ. This inevitably would involve the Admiralty, and their friend Commander Ian Fleming. As before, March-Phillipps was proposing seaborne operations for M's 'Secret Navy', and the Royal Navy's consent would be required. However, it seems that March-Phillips also harboured a desire to return to West Africa, to gather together his existing Maid Honor Force, and to carry out Operation Ramification, the twin operation to Postmaster.

According to M's desk diary, Gus March-Phillipps had a second meeting with M a few days later on 16 February. No doubt he and Appleyard also visited the SOE HQ in Baker Street on many other occasions in the first few weeks after their return. M and his deputy (Julius Hannau, code named Caesar), tried to balance the possibilities. A memo dated 7 March 1942 records that three projects were under consideration at that time: Operation Ramification, the SSRF, and an operation against the German battleship *Tirpitz*. The memo comments on all these three projects, saying of the SSRF:

> It had been intended by M that ... W.01's role ... would be as recruiting officer, leader and organizer of this special sea commando consisting of 50 to 60 volunteers, our job being to provide, train and equip personnel to be used. [The *Tirpitz* was to become an SSRF operation] Considering the nebulous chance of getting the Foreign Office to agree to Ramification, we should give up any idea of W.01 or his assistant returning to West Africa, and he should be instructed to commence forthwith with the 'sea

commando'. With regard to the eleven still out in West Africa ... M to consult with W.01 in order to try and get the best of both worlds, that is to leave an Officer and two or three other ranks in West Africa as a cadre to organize the Operation Ramification teams recruited on the spot, the remainder to be sent home to form the nucleus of the new commando. Now that so many individuals in West Africa have tasted blood, it should be possible for a small nucleus of old pirates to work up teams good enough to deal with Ramification ... local volunteers will be able to do the trick, provided they are led by a small nucleus of W.01's people.

In fact, Ramification never happened. With Mountbatten's enthusiasm for the new Small Scale Raiding Force, and the Foreign Office's reluctance to give the go-ahead for another raid against a neutral country in West Africa, all of Maid Honor Force were recalled from Africa to rejoin March-Phillipps and Appleyard.

On one of his visits to Baker Street, March-Phillipps met Marjorie Stewart, who initially tried to persuade him that she was only the lift attendant. In truth, she was a forceful young woman who was to rise quite quickly through the ranks of SOE during the short time she was with them. Initially a secretary, she was soon appointed as what was known as a 'conducting officer', with the responsibility of escorting the female field agents of SOE around the various training schools that they had to attend. At the parachute school at Ringway (now Manchester International Airport), Miss Stewart was to insist that she too undertook the parachute course, thereby becoming one of the first women to qualify. Gus March-Phillipps and Marjorie Stewart quickly fell in love, and after a whirlwind romance were married at the Church of Assumption in Warwick Street, London W1, on 18 April 1942. M was one of their guests, and many other colleagues from 64 Baker Street attended. The wedding also provided an opportunity to gather together some members of March-Phillipps' intended new force. Appleyard, Hayes and Lassen were there, back from Africa, together with new recruits Peter Kemp, John Burton and Major John Gwynne, who was to be in charge of operational planning.

Even the delights of love and marriage failed to distract Gus March-Phillipps from his work to establish the SSRF. Having had the go-ahead from M, and pending the expected Combined Operations and Admiralty approval for his plans, March-Phillipps began to recruit essential members for his SSRF team. When March-Phillipps met M again on 10 March, he was with Major John Gwynne, who was now officially named his Planning Officer for Operations. The following day, M met with Admiral Godfrey, the Director of Naval Intelligence (and Ian Fleming's boss). On 17 March 1942, a meeting took place at the Combined Operations HQ during which the principles for the SSRF were discussed and agreed. It was decided that SOE would be responsible for selecting the necessary men, and that Gus March-Phillipps would be the Force commander. SOE would provide the base from which they would operate, and would train them and equip them with all necessary armaments. The Royal Navy/Combined Operations would provide two motor launches, their crews and armaments. They would be responsible for fuelling and repairing them. Each motor launch would have its own naval commander, but they would be under the overall command of March-Phillipps. M aimed to raise a force of about 50 men, of whom between 15 and 20 were to be foreign nationals – members of the armed forces of the various occupied countries or the Pioneer Corps. Such men would have obvious value when the SSRF carried out raids on foreign soil, and could be used on occasion as guides, as pilots for the motor launches when they were close to shore, and for liaison with local people. M was keen that Dutch, French, Belgians and Poles of suitable quality and experience should be recruited. He requested on 28 March that SOE's foreign sections arrange for the relevant foreign governments to give their permission for the release of their personnel to the SSRF, and sent March-Phillipps round the sections to hunt for suitable candidates.

On 21 March 1942, authority for the establishment of the SSRF was formally given by the Chiefs of Staff, and on 27 March, March-Phillipps received the formal charter under which he was to operate his force. The final plan was that there should be 30 British members of the Force, divided equally between officers and other ranks; the foreign contingent was to comprise 3 officers and 17 other ranks. There was to be a British support staff at the SSRF base of 14 additional men. March-Phillipps for a time retained his code name W.01, or MH, the initials of the Maid Honor Force that he had led so successfully in West Africa. In true Secret Service style, the activities and personnel of the SSRF were allotted an all-embracing code name 'Fyfield'. Each member of Fyfield was given a cover story: they were to say that they were engaged at a training school as a preliminary to acceptance for commando training. The true objectives of the SSRF were to remain top secret.

Chapter 4

Anderson Manor

March-Phillipps did not allow the grass to grow under his feet. With M's blessing, towards the end of March, he and Appleyard journeyed down to Poole to begin their search for a training base. They stayed at the Antelope Hotel, the old on-shore base of the Maid Honor Force, and began to scour the countryside for a suitable property. March-Phillipps knew Dorset well. It did not take him long to find the house he wanted.

Anderson Manor is a Grade 1 fine old Jacobean country house, set in large grounds on the edge of Anderson Village, and surrounded by countryside. The Manor House had its own chapel. The house had fallen into disrepair until it was restored before the First World War, and in early 1942 the building remained sound, but not modernized – it had no electricity, no mains water, and drainage was to a cess pit. However, the fabric of the building was in fine condition and the formal gardens were beautifully maintained. When March-Phillipps found it, he fell in love with it. It was ideally placed for the SSRF, being about seven miles from Wareham and twelve from Poole. It was sufficiently remote to provide the secrecy that March-Phillipps and Appleyard needed.

The quartermaster of Maid Honor Force, Lieutenant Leslie Prout, was sent down to inspect the Manor House on 13 April 1942. The efficient and thorough Prout visited, and then prepared his report, which still exists amongst his papers at the Imperial War Museum in London. It is headed: 'Anderson Manor – Report on visit 13th April 1942', and reads:

The first reference to the Manor at Winterbourne Anderson dates from 1237 when William de Stokes held the Manor. The next family to own it were the Turbevilles of Bere, who are stated to have acquired it in 1366, and held it until about 1450, when it passed to the Mortons of Milbourne. It was acquired by John Tregonwell who bought the Manor in 1620, and commenced building the house two years later. Mrs Gordon Gratix purchased house from Tregonwell family. Purchased in disrepair by Mrs Gordon Gratix in 1910. She removed later additions and restored it to good condition. Gardens reformed, based on traces of the original. Foundations of the old terrace forecourt and the garden house and sluices of the moat found by excavation.

It was sold to Mr John Tabor in 1915, he sold it on to present owner, Mr Hugh Cholmondeley. At date of visit, it was occupied by a tenant, Mr Young. The Manor is quadrangular brick built house with stone dressings and quoins. On the south side (the entrance front) there are gables on the south-east and south-west corners and in its centre is a semi octagonal entrance porch. The design of the manor is attributed to Inigo Jones, but there is no confirmation.

References: Country Life April 3rd 1915, Country Houses of Dorset by Arthur Oswald, Garner and Stratton Domestic Architecture.

Although March-Phillipps discovered that the Ministry of Health were also after Anderson Manor, it happened that he, through his Dorset connections, knew the Cholmondeley family who owned it. He contacted Hugh Cholmondeley, warned him of the possible fate of the house and its beautiful gardens if requisitioned and handed over to a disrespectful tenant, and promised that he and his men would look after it properly. Having obtained Cholmondeley's consent to his tenancy of Anderson Manor, March-Phillipps duly won the battle for its use. He was not a man who accepted the answer no and, once he had squared the owner, the Ministry of Health really stood no chance.

A generator was rapidly acquired for the SSRF, and once it had arrived at Anderson, the manor could be supplied with electricity, and water pumped from the well. The head gardener, Reginald Mullins, was retained by March-Phillipps, to ensure that the grounds remained in perfect condition, even though the walled garden, an acre in size and once a tennis court, had already been dug up for vegetables as a part of the Dig For Victory campaign. No doubt, if the lawn had remained March-Phillipps would have preserved it for such English pastimes as tennis and croquet. With the Maid Honor Force, March-Phillipps had been billeted on two houseboats at Poole – now he could finally take control of what was fairly to be described later as a Commando Camelot. March-Phillipps was a romantic soldier and an accomplished poet, he believed in the standards and ethos of the likes of the Elizabethan Francis

Drake. For him, the ancient manor house of Anderson represented everything he loved about the England that he was fighting to preserve. There would be an intensely practical side to everything that went on with the SSRF at Anderson Manor, but March-Phillipps was not the only one to be inspired by the history of the place, and comforted by its beauty and the peace of its chapel.

One of the significant features of the SSRF was that it included a number of non-British commandos, who had either fled from Nazi oppression in their homelands, or whose countries had been occupied by Nazi Germany. These were men whose background and outlook on life were very different from those of March-Phillipps, and they obviously did not share his love of English history. Nonetheless, the peace and tranquillity of Anderson Manor appealed to them all. One was Richard Lehniger, a Communist Sudeten German. As all soldiers were advised to do before going into battle, Lehniger wrote a 'final letter' to his wife on 6 June 1942, against the event of his death or capture. He began: 'I am in a beautiful garden, the sun is shining, there are flowers and bird-song all around – I wish you and our little child were with me.' He sent the letter to his cousin Leo who was also in England, to hold for him and to deliver only if Lehniger was declared dead or missing. Even to his cousin he wrote: 'We have cows and goats in a beautiful garden, but all I can do is to think and daydream.'

Before the SSRF moved in at the end of April 1942, Anderson Manor was cleared of most of its fine furniture, and the majority of its panelling was covered over with beaver-boarding. March-Phillipps issued the strictest of instructions to his high-spirited team that not only was the house to be preserved from damage, but also the handsome gardens were not to be despoiled. In discreet areas of the extensive grounds an assault course and a pistol range were built, the ditches and the moat were filled with barbed wire, and a ropeway was slung across the drive between two tall oaks. The old butler's pantry became the armoury, an air raid shelter became the explosives store, and a Nissan hut was erected for close combat training. In the way of all secret organizations, M's Secret Service used code names – Anderson Manor became Station 62, and the SSRF itself became 62 Commando. It was difficult to pretend that a fine manor such as Anderson did not exist (as SOE officially didn't), and therefore its cover was that it was 'just another commando training centre'. Thus did the Special Operations Executive, alias the Inter Services Research Bureau, spawn an officially totally unrelated unit called 62 Commando – in truth staffed exclusively by secret agents of SOE, albeit now under the joint command of SOE and Lord Mountbatten's Combined Operations.

March-Phillipps, having fallen for Anderson Manor, wrote later to his new bride: 'It is a really marvellous place ... I think when the war is over we must settle down here, perhaps in this house if we're very great people then, and spend a lot of time in the garden. It is one of the most perfect gardens I've ever seen.' Marjorie visited Anderson Manor two or three times, and found it 'a beautiful house'.

Some months later, in October 1942, after the Small Scale Raiding Force had been in action a number of times, Appleyard wrote to Hugh Chomondeley, the owner of Anderson Manor, saying: 'I have been wanting to tell you how much we appreciate the Manor – it has proved an ideal house in every way, and to this unit a real home. There is such a quiet and peaceful atmosphere about the house and gardens and often, after a night raid, coming back in the first light next morning tired and often rather strung-up and on edge, it has been a real relief and relaxation to get back to such a lovely place ... I think the atmosphere of this house has, in an appreciable way, contributed to the making of what has been regarded in the high places up to date as a very successful little show. We have a grand crowd of men here and they have universally respected the privilege of living in this house.' Perhaps most importantly, Anderson Manor was a very British haven, and acted as a constant reminder to the British members of the SSRF of the country and way of life they were fighting for. Tony Hall, one of the recruits to the SSRF, certainly felt that way, and added: 'Gus at Anderson created a world of people who loved doing things honourably. With him as leader, you knew that nothing would ever be done with evil intent.'

Having secured their base, Major March-Phillipps and Captain Appleyard began to gather together the men. Those who had served in West Africa with Maid Honor Force were automatic choices upon return to England. Operation Postmaster had led to a number of promotions for those involved, and when they were reunited there were almost as many officers as other ranks. Indeed Appleyard wrote home to say that initially about thirty men of the Small Scale Raiding Force moved into Anderson Manor – nearly all of them officers.

Chapter 5

The Old and the New

Initially, M assigned the whole of the existing Maid Honor Force to the Small Scale Raiding Force. The idea of leaving one or two of them in West Africa to organize and carry out Operation Ramification was abandoned, and they all returned home. In order to understand the character of the SSRF, and to fully understand its achievements, it is necessary to consider the character of some of the men who carried out its objectives. No nominal roll for the SSRF appears to still exist, but at the heart of the unit were the comrades of the original Maid Honor Force. The list below includes them, together with a selection of some of the new recruits to the SSRF.

Graham Hayes
Third in command of Maid Honor Force, and known as W.03 whilst in West Africa, had been Lieutenant (soon to be Captain) Graham Hayes MC. Hayes was born on 9 July 1915, and therefore some seventeen months older than Geoffrey Appleyard, his childhood friend. The boys had grown up together in the then small village of Linton-on-Wharfe, Yorkshire. Hayes had trained as a wood sculptor in London, and in 1938 set up a studio in Temple Sowerby in Cumberland. He was described by military colleagues as a quiet, serious-minded man, of great personal charm, and with an enormous capacity for work. He had the ability to mix with and understand people from all walks of life. Graham Hayes had always had a love for the sea, perhaps because of a seafaring ancestor who was often mentioned in the Hayes family – a Captain Hayes who had been a West Indies trader in the late eighteenth and early nineteenth centuries, regularly fighting off the attentions of pirates. Before the war, Graham had taken part in the famous Grain Race from Australia to England, and after his return from that adventure, when he discovered that his

open Austin Seven motor car had a rather flexible chassis, Hayes apparently strengthened it by fitting it with a small mast, blocks, tackle and stays. He was an experienced sailor who had proved himself time and again with Maid Honor Force. He was also an excellent swimmer and 'underwater man', a skill that Ian Fleming found useful for his own fictional secret agent.

Anders Lassen
Newly commissioned Second Lieutenant Anders Lassen, twenty-one years of age, was a Dane. He would be the fourth component for the character of Fleming's James Bond. Anders Frederick Emil Victor Schau Lassen was born on 22 September 1920, into a wealthy and well-connected Danish family. As a boy he learned to be a skilled hunter with bow, knife and gun, and an expert in silent killing. He became very accurate with a throwing knife, and adapted this skill to hand grenades with great effect. One of Lassen's greatest gifts was an ability to move speedily without sound towards his quarry. He was one of those men who, though they do not hesitate to hunt and kill animals, also love to keep pets, and become very fond of them. He had first cousins, through marriage, who were German, and with whom he was friendly when a boy, but once the Germans had invaded his country, Lassen was determined to avenge himself and his country upon them, and wished only to kill as many Germans as possible.

Lassen was tall, slim and broad-shouldered, with the palest of light blue eyes. When fully mature he weighed about 12 stone. Lassen's quest for adventure had led him to leave home as a teenager, to go to sea. In January 1939, at the age of eighteen, he signed on as cabin boy and general dogsbody on the Danish ship *Fionia*. In June the following year, Lassen was taken on as a cadet on a Danish tanker, the *Eleonora Maersk*, which took him to Bahrain, and he was at sea in the Persian Gulf on 9 April 1940 when Germany invaded and took possession of his home country. As soon as he was able, Lassen made his way to Britain and signed up with M's Secret Service, SOE.

Like many of those recruited into SOE, Lassen never did any basic army training – the customary course of nine weeks' square bashing – nor was he assigned to a regiment. He was entered on the 'General List', and the only training he had was with SOE. M had visited Scotland between 14 and 18 April 1941, a time at which March-Phillipps was setting up the Maid Honor Force. He dropped into the SOE training school at Arisaig, hoping to find a suitable recruit – Lassen was recommended and M accepted him. Lassen was ideal commando material. He had absolutely no hesitation about killing a man with a knife (unlike many Englishmen), and his hunting skills have already been described. During his time with Maid Honor Force, under March-Phillipps' careful tutelage, he matured from being an angry young man into a commando of great potential and effectiveness.

Anders Lassen was also a very successful ladies' man. One of his colleagues, Ian 'Bunny' Warren commented that, at the local dances that they might attend, his chance of winning the affections of the 'belle of the ball' on the night in question would go straight out of the window once Appleyard and Lassen arrived. Lassen's ruthless streak in relation to women led him into scrapes, and he sometimes had to rely on his athleticism to get him out of an embarrassing situation. The fact that a girl was married was no bar to him – like James Bond, it sufficed that she was desirable. Yet he retained his detachment, and did not become emotionally involved, as illustrated by a remark he made whilst at Anderson Manor. Lassen was having an affair with a woman who had twice been widowed. He spoke humorously of her to his male friends as his 'widow and Bar', in the fashion of a soldier who wins the same medal twice, and therefore adds a 'Bar' to it. In the first James Bond story, *Casino Royale* (1953), Bond's attitude is summed up: 'Women were for recreation. On a job, they got in the way and fogged things up with sex and hurt feelings and all the emotional baggage they carried around.' No doubt Anders Lassen would have agreed. Lassen had joined Maid Honor Force as a raw and rebellious youngster of twenty, but with March-Phillipps as his mentor, he became an effective leader. Hence, after Operation Postmaster, March-Phillipps had secured Lassen's promotion from private to second lieutenant.

March-Phillipps, Appleyard, Hayes and Lassen had been the outstanding figures of Maid Honor Force, and continued in similar vein with the SSRF. For that reason, this book will follow each of them to the end of their military careers.

Leslie Prout

Leslie Ewart Prout was born on 23 May 1912, and was schooled at King's College School, Wimbledon, where he excelled at cricket, rugby and boxing. After school he trained as a motor engineer and set up a business as motor agents and engineers. He joined up at the outbreak of war and had as a corporal been with Geoffrey Appleyard in France before Dunkirk. Following their return to England, Appleyard had selected him for No. 7 Commando, and then for Maid Honor Force, where he was commissioned and had become the Force's quartermaster. He was an experienced and reliable commando. Prout's job on Operation Postmaster had been the vital but unglamorous one of ensuring that the black African stokers deep in the bowels of the steam-driven tug *Vulcan* kept piling coal into her furnaces, despite the violent explosions going on in the world above them. As it turned out, Prout was to suffer from a serious bout of amoebic hepatitis in 1942, quite possibly acquired in the unhealthy climate of West Africa, which substantially reduced his involvement in events at Anderson Manor.

Thomas Winter

Company Sergeant Major Thomas William Winter RASC, was about 37 years of age and had initially proved the hardest man for March-Phillipps to obtain for the Maid Honor Force. Now he ensured that he held on to Winter for the SSRF. Winter, as his rank suggests, was a very experienced soldier. He was parachute trained (as was Graham Hayes), having won his wings in October 1940, and had been a member of the newly formed 11 SAS Battalion. They had not wanted to part with him. However, Graham Hayes had strongly recommended him early in 1941 when the Maid Honor Force was formed, and March-Phillipps had been determined. Eventually, after what Winter later described as a 'hell of a battle', March-Phillipps' had prevailed with the War Office, and Winter had been transferred to Maid Honor Force. Now he joined March-Phillipps at Anderson Manor.

André Desgranges

Maître Quartier André Jules Marcel Desgranges was a Free Frenchman who had seen service in SOE with Geoffrey Appleyard on Operation Savannah the previous year. When Maid Honor Force was set up, Appleyard called for him. Desgranges was a chief petty officer in the French Navy, and a trained diver. He was officially on loan to SOE from the Free French. After a year with Maid Honor Force, Desgranges still spoke little English, but he was always very popular with his comrades. He was immensely strong and always cheerful. He had proved himself with Maid Honor Force, and upon his return to England was given the honorary rank of second lieutenant (since officially he remained in the Free French Forces) and, more importantly perhaps, a second lieutenant's pay. As a Frenchman, he was obviously of considerable value to the SSRF, much of whose raiding was intended to be on French soil.

Frank Perkins

Frank 'Buzz' Perkins was a youngster of eighteen, born on 15 December 1923. When first recruited into Maid Honor Force, he had seemed even younger than his then age of seventeen. His uncle apparently was a major known to March-Phillipps, who had been prepared to take Perkins on as by far the youngest member of Maid Honor Force. Perkins had proved himself an excellent seaman and a good commando, though he still looked far too young to be a secret commando agent licensed to kill.

Denis Tottenham

Private Denis Frederick Gwynne Tottenham was 22, and had previously been a lieutenant in the RNVR. He was a well-educated young man, who had been sailing since the age of eight. He abandoned his rank in order to join the Maid Honor Force as an ordinary private. He later described himself (accurately) as the only 'proper Navy' member of the *Maid Honor* crew. At 6ft 3ins, he had been the tallest man in the Maid Honor Force – ironically, he was later to be assigned to SOE's midget submarines.

Ernest Evison

Londoner Ernest Evison, of the East Surrey Regiment, was another Maid Honor Force veteran. He was the unit's cook, a very important role for any effective fighting force. Hotel trained, Evison had worked before the war in Germany and France, and spoke both languages. At Anderson Manor, he was working in far easier circumstances than he had experienced in West Africa.

Jock Taylor

'Jock' or 'Haggis' Taylor (of course, a Scotsman) was March-Phillipps' batman, but as much a commando as any of the Maid Honor Force. He had boarded the *Duchessa d'Aosta* right behind March-Phillipps in the Operation Postmaster attack, and had been in the thick of the action.

These eleven agents all knew each other very well indeed, worked comfortably together as a fighting unit, and trusted each other with their lives. However, eleven men were clearly not enough for the project that March-Phillipps and Appleyard now had planned. They needed to find many more suitable candidates in order to set up a credible SSRF. Details of some of the more interesting recruits are set out below.

Peter Kemp

Captain Peter Kemp was a man with considerable, but unusual, military experience. When he came down from Cambridge in 1936, at the age of 21, he began studying for the Bar, but interrupted his studies in October when, seeking adventure, he travelled to Spain to join the Nationalist/Carlist forces and fight in the Spanish Civil War. A strong anti-communist, Kemp felt that this was the proper cause to serve. He fought for the better part of three years in the Carlist militia, enlisting as a cavalry trooper and ending up in the Spanish Foreign Legion. He was wounded three times, eventually suffering severe injuries from a mortar bomb in 1938 which shattered his jaw and severely damaged both hands. He was awarded the Cruz de Guerra twice. In due course he returned to

England to recover, and the outbreak of war found him in London. Kemp applied for a commission in the British Army, but the medical board turned him down, telling him to come back in another six months. For a time he worked in postal censorship, but once restored to full health Kemp was quietly recruited into Special Operations, then known as MI(R), the organization in which Brigadier Colin Gubbins, the future M, was then working. In April 1940, Kemp was sent on a mission by the submarine HMS *Truant* to blow up the Bergen–Oslo railway line in Norway. He was promoted to the rank of captain for this mission, and one of his fellow officers was Captain Bill Stirling, elder brother of the later famous David Stirling, founder of 1 SAS Regiment. Unfortunately for them, HMS *Truant* was attacked and damaged on its way to Norway, and the mission was aborted. The ship limped home to Rosyth.

Following this, Stirling, Kemp and four others had been sent to Lochailort, north of Fort William in Scotland, to set up the first of what became a series of special training schools. Bill Stirling's brother David was amongst the first batch of students who arrived in June 1940. The new training school became part of M's SOE. In early 1941, Kemp was transferred to the Spanish Section of SOE, and was duly despatched with others, including his future comrade in the SSRF, John Burton, to Gibraltar. The refusal of the British Ambassador to Spain, Sir Samuel Hoare, to allow SOE to operate in any way at all on mainland Spain led to a frustrating time for Kemp and Burton, and eventually they returned to London in late August. In fairness to Hoare, his specific brief was to ensure that Franco's Spain did not join the war on Hitler's side.

Further training courses followed, between which Kemp found time to get married, but his craving for real action increased, until finally, in late February 1942, when he and Burton were informed that March-Phillipps was back in London and recruiting for the Small Scale Raiding Force, both applied. Kemp and Burton were interviewed by March-Phillipps and Appleyard, and both were accepted at once.

Kemp later described his new bosses as follows: 'March-Phillipps combined the idealism of a Crusader with the severity of a professional soldier ... in battle he was invariably calm. Appleyard combined a flair for organization and planning with superb skill in action, and a unique ability to instil confidence in time of danger.'

One of the difficulties for the Army in Britain after the defeat at Dunkirk in June 1940 was that so few of their regular troops had battle experience. The war was raging in North Africa, but Britain's European forces now spent the vast majority of their time on defensive duties on the British side of the Channel. Thankfully, Hitler's invasion never came, so the fighting abilities of most UK-based troops were not tested. March-Phillipps and Appleyard worried that, unlike the First World War, when troops had the chance to get 'acclimatized' before going into battle, for the men of the SSRF, action came in very short, very violent bursts. Thus war experience of the sort that Peter Kemp had was of great value, and it really didn't matter who he had been fighting for when he gained it. Marjorie March-Phillipps described Kemp as 'so incredibly gallant'.

John Burton

Captain John Langthorne Burton-Burton, usually known simply as John Burton, had become a good friend of Peter Kemp, whose partner he had been from early in their respective careers in SOE. Burton was a tall, burly, ginger-haired officer of the Lincolnshire Regiment. According to Peter Kemp, he had a quiet, almost gentle manner which concealed strong determination, courage, and considerable powers of endurance. Despite an austere appearance, he combined a sense of humour with genuine humility, common sense and efficiency. Kemp found him to be a good antidote to his own exuberance and volatility, and the two men complemented each other well, in much the same way as March-Phillipps and Appleyard.

Colin Ogden Smith

Captain Colin Malcolm Ogden Smith was born on 30 August 1910. He was two years younger than Gus March-Phillipps, but already a married man with one child. Ogden Smith had been a manager in the family business of fishing tackle manufacturers before the outbreak of war, and had first joined the Royal Artillery, transferring to No. 7 Commando as soon as it was set up. With the rank of lieutenant, he had served as one of March-Phillipps' troop officers in No. 7 Commando before March-Phillipps left to join SOE. Whilst March-Phillipps was serving with Maid Honor Force, Colin Ogden-Smith had been sent with No. 7 Commando to Egypt, and saw action at Bardia and Crete. Few of 7 Commando had escaped from Crete, but Ogden Smith was one of them, and he returned to the UK at the end of 1942. When March-Phillipps heard he was available, he was keen to have him. He duly recruited Ogden Smith into SOE early in the life of the SSRF, on 30 March 1942. Ogden Smith was immediately promoted to the rank of captain, and soon persuaded his brother Bruce, eight years his junior and still a private, to join the SSRF too.

Hamish Torrance

Captain Hamish Torrance MBE , of the Highland Light Infantry, was another experienced SOE officer who, like M, had seen service in Norway.

Patrick Dudgeon

Lieutenant Patrick Dudgeon was 21, born on 10 July 1920, a mere two months older than Anders Lassen. He was described by Peter Kemp as 'young and earnest'. His parent regiment was the Royal Signals, and he was a big man, 6ft 1½ ins tall, weighing a little short of 15 stone. His nickname amongst his comrades was 'Toomai', after the elephant boy in Rudyard Kipling's story. His father, Christopher, held the rank of lieutenant colonel in the Royal Army Medical Corps, and had won a DSO in the First World War. Patrick had been schooled at Oundle, and he spoke passable German, albeit with a Swiss accent, and reasonable French. Both languages were of obvious value to the SSRF. Like Lassen, Dudgeon would grow into an effective and charismatic leader.[1] He later joined Bill Stirling's 2 Special Air Service (2SAS).

Francis Howard

Captain Lord Francis Philip Howard of Penrith, described by Peter Kemp as quiet, intellectual and conscientious, was an older man, unmarried, and now aged 36, born on 5 October 1905. Like March-Phillipps, he was a Roman Catholic, schooled at Downside. He had read law at Cambridge and at Harvard, and before the outbreak of war had practised as a barrister in Lincoln's Inn. His mother, Isabella Guistiani-Bandini, was an Italian aristocrat who had assumed British citizenship upon her marriage, long before the advent of Benito Mussolini, and Howard grew up fluent in Italian and French. His parent regiment was the Royal Artillery, but he had joined SOE in January 1942. He was initially posted to SOE's Belgian Section, but found himself with not very much to do there. He applied to the SSRF, was interviewed by Appleyard, and accepted. A tall man, his nickname within the SSRF became 'Long John'.

Thomas Hall

Thomas Anthony Inglis Hall was born on 12 August 1912 at Windermere. He was a single man 5ft 8ins in hight, and was schooled at Sedbergh. Before the war, after a year spent working in forestry in Sweden, he had built a career for himself as a scriptwriter and radio producer, specializing in variety, as well as writing occasionally for *Punch* magazine. He as a cheerful, witty man, who became something of a *bon viveur*. He spoke some French and Swedish, and was known to love French cuisine. Following the outbreak of war, Hall joined up, was commissioned onto the General List in March 1940, and saw service in Norway as part of an Intelligence Corps Unit. He was later attached to the London Scottish Regiment (Royal Artillery), and joined SOE in April 1942.

Ian Warren

Lieutenant Ian 'Bunny' Warren, Royal Artillery, was a Yorkshireman like Appleyard and Hayes. Early in the war, he had been posted to West Africa with what had once been the Leeds Territorial Army Battery, and by chance had been a member of the Royal Artillery mess that had played host to Maid Honor Force during their stay at Lumley Beach, Freetown, in Sierra Leone between September and December 1941. Life in an artillery battery on the coast of West Africa was extremely dull, and when Warren met the Maid Honor Force, and observed something of what they were doing, he immediately became obsessed with the idea of joining them, and exchanging his boring existence for their glamorous and exciting one. As Leslie Prout later put it: 'Ian immediately fell for the *Maid* and lost no opportunity of entreating Gus to let him join. These entreaties gave birth to his nickname – "The Man". Gus remarked to Ian's commanding officer that that "bloody little man" had been pestering him again, and from that moment on he was known to all as "that bloody little man", which in course of time became just "The Man".'

According to Leslie Prout, Warren had had a favourite piece of music called 'Stardust', which he would always play if he was in the mess. Gus March-Phillipps hated it, and when his temper snapped one night he smashed the gramophone record over Warren's head. 'Stardust' seemed to be equally disliked by others of the Maid Honor Force, since Prout comments that by breaking the record, 'the state of purgatory was relieved.' However, Warren's enthusiasm to join the Force remained undimmed, and eventually Gus March-Phillipps promised that when Warren was eventually posted back to Britain, if he applied to join Maid Honor Force and SOE, March-Phillipps would accept him. Whatever the banter within the Maid Honor Force and the Royal Artillery Mess at Lumley Beach, March-Phillipps appreciated Warren's obviously genuine desire to join the sort of body of men that Maid Honor Force was.

Because of the unhealthy climate in West Africa (it was famously known as the 'white man's grave'), all troops and public servants stationed there were sent home on leave every fifteen months. Warren's turn came, and back in England he immediately made his application to SOE, notifying March-Phillipps that he had returned. The *Maid Honor* had long since been left behind in Lagos, so it was the SSRF that Warren now applied to join. However, moving unit was never straightforward, particularly not from a regular unit into SOE, and in any event the army in West Africa (under overall control of General Giffard) remained implacably hostile to SOE despite the recent triumph of Operation Postmaster. Warren actually had his bags packed, ready to return to West Africa, before the call came. He was ordered to report to Room 98, Horse Guards (where interviews of prospective SOE recruits always took place), and as Warren himself put it many years later: 'I was off like a shot'. Once Warren was within the machinery of SOE, March-Phillipps was able to ensure his speedy despatch to Anderson Manor.

John Gwynne

Major John Gwynne, of the Sussex Yeomanry, was aged 37, had served with the British Expeditionary Force (BEF), and like so many had been evacuated, wounded, from Dunkirk. He had later joined the auxiliary units run by Gubbins, and then SOE. Gwynne was an old Etonian, and an Oxford graduate in English and French. He was married, and before the war had worked as a solicitor and company director, as well as being a parliamentary candidate. He was appointed to the SSRF as officer in charge of planning. He was a vegetarian, a teetotaller, and was said always to shave in cold water. Marjorie March-Phillipps remembered him as 'a scholarly-looking man, but with a fanatical gleam in his eye.'

Brian Reynolds

Second Lieutenant Sylvanus Brian John Reynolds, alias Bingham, of the Welsh Guards, was 34, just a couple of months older than March-Phillipps. Educated at Felsted School, and briefly at Pembroke College, Oxford (he did not take his degree), he had been something of a playboy before the war, with a reputation for high living. Indeed, when asked by SOE for his home address, he gave Bucks Club, Clifford Street, London W1. He gave his pre-war occupation as 'accountancy', and had spent three years working on a sugar plantation in South Africa, as a result of which he had learnt the Zulu language. He had seen action in the Russo-Finnish war, fighting for fourteen months as a volunteer with the Finns, and consequently also spoke Finnish and Swedish.

In late March and early April 1942, under the auspices of SOE, Reynolds took part in a quasi-smuggling operation out of Sweden called Operation Performance. Sweden was a neutral country and Britain was trying to buy vital war supplies from them, to ship home. The supplies were of perfectly innocent materials such as wire rods, steel, pig-iron, and most importantly machines for the manufacture of ball bearings (the latter were in very short supply). The Germans took action through the Swedish courts to try to prevent these deals, but failed. They were therefore determined to attack and sink the British ships carrying the goods from Sweden to Britain, once they were at sea in international waters. The British plan was to smuggle the materials out of Sweden by means of bluff and decoy. One of the largest ships to carry the genuine cargo was the *Newton*, a vessel of 10,324 tons and Brian Reynolds volunteered to command the Lewis gun contingent that comprised the

Newton's defences. In due course, having sailed from Sweden, the *Newton* was identified by the enemy, and at 1610hrs on 1 April 1942, it was attacked by three enemy aircraft. Reynolds and his Lewis gunners successfully shot down one of the enemy planes and fought off the attack. The *Newton* survived virtually unscathed and was able to complete its journey. A report on Operation Performance commented, 'but for the dogged handling of her Lewis guns, of which Mr Brian Reynolds was in charge, it is unlikely that the *Newton* would have reached her destination. Special credit is due to him.'

March-Phillipps began the process of recruiting Reynolds after his safe return in April 1942, and on 12 June 1942 Reynolds was assigned as a second lieutenant to SOE, and thence to the SSRF. Because of the danger of capture on foreign soil, being already a wanted man in occupied Europe under his own name, Reynolds now adopted the *nom de guerre* Bingham (which will be how he is referred to hereafter).

Henk Brinkgreve and Jan Eire Hellings

Lieutenant Henk Brinkgreve, of the Royal Netherlands Army, was born on 6 June 1915 in Utrecht. Before the war and the subsequent invasion of his country, Brinkgreve had been a law student at Leiden University. He had been a Reserve Officer, mobilized in June 1939. He spoke Dutch and English fluently, French and German moderately, and a little Russian. He was attached to SOE, and sent to the SSRF at Anderson Manor on 20 May 1942. He was joined there by a second Dutchman, Jan Eire Hellings, a soldier who had also served with the Royal Netherlands Army before the Germans overran his country.

Graham Young

Sergeant Major Graham Salter Young was an older man, born in London on 17 June 1900. He was a doctor's son, who had gone straight from Mill Hill School into the RAF in September 1917, to serve in the First World War. Between the wars, he had run a market garden, trading in fruit and vegetables at Spitalfields Market in London. Young had been a member of No. 7 Commando, and like Colin Ogden Smith had been posted to Egypt and had experience on Crete. March-Phillipps recruited Young as soon as he had the go-ahead from M to form the Small Scale Raiding Force, and even before official approval had come from Combined Operations Headquarters. Young signed up with SOE on 4 March 1942, and was commissioned as a second lieutenant on 1 May. Peter Kemp was later to describe Graham Young in an official report as 'probably one of the best small boat men in the country'.

Allan Williams

Sergeant Allan Marcus Williams (known within his family as 'Nick') was born in Maidstone, Kent, in 1920. The family later moved to the village of Sedlescombe in East Sussex, 7 miles north of Hastings, where he grew to adulthood. He was the third of seven children, having one elder brother, Frederick, and five sisters. He was a big fine looking man of about 6ft, and was the 'live wire' of the family. His elder brother Fred was badly injured at Dunkirk, losing an eye and a hand, and suffering from severe shell shock. He was invalided out of the army as a result. Allan became the sole member of the immediate family in the Armed Forces, and proved himself to be a good young soldier, rapidly rising to the rank of sergeant. He was very fit, and, growing up in the Sussex countryside, had always been an outdoors boy. He was well suited to the work of the SSRF. By the mid-summer of 1942, still just 22, he was engaged to be married to a Canadian girl.

Herbert Rowe

Rifleman Herbert Maurice Rowe was 25. He was a Londoner, schooled in Ealing, who had decided at the age of sixteen to become a missionary. Choosing a French Roman Catholic Order, Rowe trained first in Belgium, before becoming a novice in Algiers. Understandably, his French became very fluent, but he decided missionary life was not for him and returned to London, taking an office job in Acton. In 1938, he joined the Territorials, and was duly called up when war broke out. Later he joined No. 2 Commando and from there volunteered for Special Forces. As it happened, Rowe had missed the St Nazaire raid in March 1942 because he had been in London waiting for an interview with SOE when his commando had been called out on the raid. He commented later that as the whole of his section was wiped out at St Nazaire, he too would have died had it not been for the interview. As a French-speaking commando, he duly found himself selected by SOE, and posted to Anderson Manor.

Jack Nicholson

Sergeant Jack Nicholson DCM, was grey-haired, and was the oldest in the Force. He was a veteran of No. 7 Commando, March-Phillipps' and Appleyard's original unit, and he too had served with them in Crete before being evacuated in the British withdrawal the previous year.

Abram Opoczynski (alias Orr)

Abram Opoczynski, alias Adam Orr, was a Polish Jew, though he did not practise his religion. He was born and brought up in Lodz, and had worked there as a journalist before coming to England in 1938 to work as the foreign correspondent of a Polish newspaper.

Richard Lehniger (alias Leonard)

Private Richard Lehniger was 41 years of age, born on 9 June 1900 at Petschau (now Becov Nad Teplou), which was then a part of the Austro-Hungarian empire but is now in the Czech Republic. He grew up on the Sudeten border between Karlsbad and Beyreuth. His father was a Lutheran, but his mother was a member of a German Jewish family from Berlin, though she was content to marry in a Lutheran church. Richard Lehniger left school at 14 to go to work. In 1916, his father died of wounds suffered when fighting for Austria in the First World War and in 1917, Richard himself joined up, to fight for Austria against the Italians, Britain's allies in that war.

After the war, Lehniger had worked as a slater and tiler, and as a steeplejack. When he lost his job in the economic depression of the early 1930s, he went to study for a time at Prague University, becoming a dedicated communist and an activist. Lehniger, as befitted a steeplejack, was an outdoors man. He kept himself very fit, and was a keen mountain climber and skier. However, with Hitler in power, life for Lehniger became increasingly difficult – he was both half-Jewish and a communist. Eventually, in March 1939, he fled to Norway, and from there travelled to England where he met up with his fiancée Lilly (Julia) Dorfler, a Czech, who had also fled from the Nazis. They were married in November 1939.

Following the outbreak of the Second World War, Lehniger, like many other foreign nationals, joined the Pioneer Corps – during the early days, the only unit that admitted foreigners. Lehniger duly signed the declaration required of all 'aliens' entering the Corps: 'I hereby certify that I understand the risks ... to which I and my relatives may be exposed by my employment in the British Army outside the United Kingdom. Notwithstanding this, I certify that I am willing to be employed in any theatre of war.' He was sent to France with the British Expeditionary Force, and when they were overwhelmed in the early summer of 1940, he was evacuated back to England from St Malo. Not long after his return, his wife gave birth to their daughter, Irene. Richard Lehniger was recruited into SOE in 1941. The reports on him from training camp were mixed – he was said to be too ready with his fists, regularly getting into fights, but was described as being a pleasant tough man, quite without fear of any kind. Now in his early forties, Lehniger remained very fit, and of course spoke fluent German. He was signed up for the SSRF in May 1942. Because of his German Jewish background, for operational purposes he was given the name of Richard Leonard, and a fresh army number.

The new recruits to the SSRF were a mixed bag, the majority of them officers. They were all, in their different ways, strong characters. March-Phillipps and Appleyard's first task was to mould them into an effective fighting unit, bonding together such apparent opposites as Peter Kemp, who had fought against the communist forces in Spain, and Richard Lehniger, the dedicated communist. The SSRF operated in small units – there was no room for personal differences or ideological conflict.

Note
1. See *SAS in Tuscany* Pen and Sword, 2011

Chapter 6

Training

Whilst preserving the formal gardens at Anderson Manor, March-Phillipps set out to build as complete a commando training centre in the grounds as possible. Lord Howard remembered building an assault course which involved many of the standard obstacles – crawling under wire, climbing walls, crossing ropes slung between trees. They trained with plastic explosive, essential for demolition work, and with grenades and various firearms. Howard remembered there were live detonators stuck in potatoes, which they threw at one another – if you did not duck out of the way you got hurt. Also, the men of the SSRF had to practise swimming with helmets, rifles and equipment through deep water, jumping the moat filled with barbed wire, and practising manoeuvres in all craft, preferably in stormy weather, in the wider reaches of Poole Harbour. For those recently returned from the warm African climate, it was a painful contrast, but the rougher and wetter the weather, the better the training was thought to be. There were long and often hungry route marches across empty countryside – usually the commandos would be dropped off in the dark at an unidentified point and left to navigate their own way back to Anderson Manor. Andy Lassen, in particular, distinguished himself in this kind of training – he appeared tireless, with a perfect sense of balance and coordination on ropeways and rockfaces alike. Rock climbing was an essential skill that they all had to learn, and an expedition was duly arranged to the Lake District, where the SSRF recruits climbed a number of internationally rated rockfaces. March-Phillipps and Appleyard believed that on their raids the SSRF should choose the least expected landing point, and this would often include a climb up a sheer cliff face, to take the enemy by surprise at the top.

Sometimes, the super-fit men of the SSRF would be used as training 'guinea pigs' to try out new survival techniques and ideas. On 21 June 1942, Richard

Lehniger wrote to his wife Lilly: 'Today, two officers – curse them – arrived to try out some tests on us. From tomorrow until Saturday we are going on a march. We shall only get concentrated food, have to sleep in the open – only if it rains can we find some straw – we have to drink spring water. We are to get extra pills [presumably Benzedrine], and from all this they will deduce how many miles one can do in one day, and whether one's stomach can survive this food.'

A later recruit at Anderson Manor, Lieutenant John Cochrane, a Canadian from the Toronto Scottish Regiment, wrote home to his family: 'The day is pretty well taken up with shooting, cross-country marches, rope climbing and a nice little pastime called "unarmed combat" which is a combination of murder and the Spanish inquisition. I have never been twisted into so many different shapes in my life. The bane of my existence is a little game called night compass marching. You are given a squad of men, two or more compass bearings and told to "get on with it". If you are unlucky enough to find the odd stream (usually in flood) in your path, in you go, a most unpleasant experience on a pitch black night. So far I've managed to get back home only a couple of hours behind time – did I mention barbed wire and brambles?'

Lassen was also the most expert in silent killing. He had been a hunter of all types of game since boyhood, and amongst the weapons with which he had achieved expertise was the longbow. Lassen wrote to the War Office, seeking approval for the use of bows and arrows on operations – they were, he said, the perfect weapon for silent killing from a distance. They had apparently been used for the killing of sentries in the Spanish Civil War. Lassen claimed that he could fire up to 15 arrows a minute, which could kill 'without shock or pain'. In response, the War Office apparently supplied him with two longbows and arrows, but declined to give him permission to use them on a raid. The bow and arrow was classified 'an inhuman weapon'. Lassen was no doubt disgusted, and Appleyard was later to pour scorn on the decision, pointing out that the bow and arrow had been perfectly acceptable since the days of Crécy and Agincourt, and compared well with the horrors of bombing and other modern armaments. Nonetheless, Lassen enjoyed practising with his bow. Ian Warren, who shared a small dormitory with him at Anderson Manor, told of occasions when he would be greeted as he entered the dormitory by an arrow thudding into the door by his ear. Lassen would hunt rabbits with his bow with great success.

Most importantly, the men at Anderson Manor, both the veterans of Maid Honor Force and the new recruits, bonded into a happy band. When at home at their base, the SSRF adopted complete informality amongst themselves, and all were known by their first names or nicknames, from Gus (March-Phillipps) and Apple (Appleyard) down to the private soldiers. Discipline was unaffected.

March-Phillipps' commands were law, to be obeyed instantly, but rank and dress code were considered unimportant.

As preparation and training for the SSRF's intended raids progressed, March-Phillipps also needed to find a new craft in which to carry out the night-time raids on the enemy coast. His old Q ship, the *Maid Honor*, had been left in West Africa, and besides, although in many ways she had been an ideal covert vessel and SOE had done a good job of providing her with hidden armaments, she was a sailing ship and what was needed now was something fast, powerful and as silent as possible. The Small Scale Raiding Force was therefore initially allocated two MTBs (motor torpedo boats), one of them particularly well suited to the work they planned. That was the brand new MTB 344, and with her came one of the most significant individuals to feature in March-Phillipps' campaign with the SSRF, her skipper Lieutenant Freddie Bourne (although he was in fact never actually a member of the Force).

Lieutenant Freddie Bourne, DSC, RNVR, was born in Hammersmith, London, on 1 October 1919. He was educated at Guildford, and trained as a chartered surveyor. Bourne joined the Royal Navy in 1939, and served first in the Fleet Air Arm. After apparently crashing a plane in training, he transferred to ships, and served as an able seaman on a destroyer. He was commissioned in 1941, and was sent on a motor torpedo boat course at Fort William in Scotland. It is said that here Bourne ran into Lieutenant Roger Thorneycroft, of the ship-building family, who asked him if he was interested in commanding a new and somewhat experimental MTB built by Thorneycroft at Hampton. Bourne said he was, and was duly appointed to command MTB 344, and to take charge of its crew of eight other men. The new boat was launched in February 1942.

MTB 344 was indeed an experimental craft. It was designed to travel low in the water, presenting a negligible profile to enemy detection equipment. It was potentially very fast – fitted with port and starboard Thorneycroft engines, which were capable of propelling it over calm water at up to 42 knots per hour. However, facing a wind of more than Force 4, because it ran so low in the water, its speed was restricted to little more than 20 knots, and it was in danger of shipping considerable quantities of water. In addition, it had a virtually silent auxiliary Ford V8 engine, which together with its low visibility, enabled it to creep close to the enemy coast without detection. Its range was about 420 miles (780km). Tom Winter recalled that the exhaust was in fact below the water, and because of the constant stream of water from the exhaust when it was running on its main engines, it was irreverently christened 'the Little Pisser' by the SSRF. The boat was too low-slung to be used safely in extremely rough weather, and even in reasonable weather everyone on board got a good soaking when travelling at speed. MTB 344 was an uncomfortable ride. One of its regular passengers later on, Bombadier Redbourn, formerly of No. 12 Commando, complained that, 'an MTB is unlike other boats. It doesn't bob up and down: it ploughs steadily until it hits a wave – then it shakes, seems to stop and then surges forward again.' Nonetheless, its low profile and silent auxiliary engine guaranteed that MTB 344 became the preferred vessel on which to approach the hostile enemy coast.

MTB 344 had been stripped of her torpedo tubes, and was now armed with two Vickers machine guns. Some believe that she also carried two Lewis guns. Two guns or four, it meant that in a firefight with an enemy gunboat she packed only a very light punch, and would by preference always cut and run. However, because the torpedo tubes had been stripped out there was space to carry a light landing craft, in addition to the dinghy that MTB 344 routinely carried, provided that it was lashed to the aft deck. The landing crafts favoured by the Small Scale Raiding Force were the Goatley, a flat-bottomed boat with canvas sides capable of carrying upwards of a dozen people, or the 18ft Dory.

In most ways, MTB 344 was ideal for the work the SSRF were going to do. Her only real disadvantage was that because she ran so low on the water (essential for camouflage purposes), she was more easily defeated by bad weather. Lieutenant Freddie Bourne commanded MTB 344 throughout the lifetime of the SSRF, and he later calculated that he and his crew carried them on seventeen raids and attempted raids against enemy positions. Bourne came to know March-Phillipps and Appleyard very well indeed and referred to both as very brave men. March-Phillipps, said Bourne, was slightly more aloof, very well connected, and had all the dash and flair. Appleyard was much more the thinker, giving every detail consideration. Bourne would attend at Anderson Manor for every briefing session, and would then go and prepare the boat for the night's raid. The men of the SSRF would join him on board at dusk.

Returning from West Africa to the waters of the English Channel in February, March and April was as stark a change as can be imagined – March-Phillipps, Appleyard and the Maid Honor Force had spent the last months of 1941 in oppressive heat, creeping up and down the African coast disguised as fishermen. Happily, many of them had had ample experience of commando training in the worst of British weather. During the winter of 1940/1, before Maid Honor Force was set up, they had worked together training as members of 7 Commando on the Isle of Arran. Conditions in the unheated hotel used as their base camp had been basic and bitter, and they had trained for long hours on the icy waters of the Atlantic. Now they faced the grey, cold sea of the English Channel.

Chapter 7

Sink the *Tirpitz*: Operation Frodesley

In the early months of 1942, the Admiralty were very much concerned to put out of action the mighty German battleship *Tirpitz*. This was the sister ship of the *Bismark*, which had been sunk at considerable cost to the British Navy in May 1941. The *Admiral von Tirpitz*, to use her full name, was a 35,000 ton battleship, the most powerful vessel in the German navy. Her firepower was devastating, and it was feared that if let loose on Allied shipping in the North Atlantic, the *Tirpitz* would wreak destruction wherever she sailed. However, since the sinking of the *Bismark*, the Germans no longer considered the *Tirpitz* invincible, and Adolf Hitler was eager that she should not be exposed to unnecessary danger. In early 1942, she was sheltering in the Norwegian fjords. The Admiralty feared that soon she would soon be deployed in the battle for the North Atlantic, and the Royal Air Force mounted a number of bombing raids against her, but without success. The German air defences were very effective, and the RAF lost an unacceptable number of planes.

On 1 March 1942, only a couple of weeks after March-Phillipps and Appleyard had returned from West Africa, Admiral John Godfrey, head of the Naval Intelligence Division and Ian Fleming's boss, circulated a memo to all his staff, and copied it to Sir Frank Nelson, the head of SOE. The subject was finding a way to destroy the *Tirpitz*, and the memo encouraged 'any member of staff (male or female) to pass on their ideas as a matter of urgency, however fantastic or unattainable they might seem at first sight.'

Perhaps not surprisingly, SOE responded immediately to the invitation. Fantastic and apparently impossible tasks were meat and drink to them, as they had recently demonstrated in Operation Postmaster. It seems most likely that when M received Admiral Godfrey's appeal for suggestions on how to sink the *Tirpitz*, he consulted the recently returned March-Phillipps and Appleyard. The two commandos were men of ideas, and SOE speedily came up with a plan that would make use of its sophisticated special gadgets department, Station IX at the Frythe under Dudley Newitt. That department was already experimenting with miniature submarines. The proposal was that March-Phillipps and Appleyard should attack and sink the world's largest battleship using one-man pedal-powered miniature submarines, in effect silent submersible pedallos. This was typical of SOE – their activities were always covert and wherever possible a silent approach to any target or rendezvous was of paramount importance. One of the many virtues of the *Maid Honor* had been that as a sailing ship she was so much quieter than any vessel with an engine.

Thus within forty-eight hours of Godfrey's circular, SOE had hatched a suitably fantastic plan, replying to Godfrey's invitation on 3 March 1942:

> SOE is in fact at present working on the construction of a one-man submarine to be propelled like a bicycle by pedalling. The submarine would tow a special delayed-action explosive charge of, say, 600 pounds of suitable explosive, using the magnetic principle to make this charge adhere to the bottom of the ship. Such a submarine should be able to dive below the booms which protect the *Tirpitz* and the charge should be sufficient to sink her. It might be necessary to fasten the submarine beneath an ordinary Norwegian fishing boat, which would proceed up the fjord until near the *Tirpitz*, when the submarine would be released and would proceed independently on its task.

SOE followed this up almost immediately with a detailed operational plan, dated 4 March 1942. This made clear that after the charge had been placed on the hull of the ship, beside the keel, the agent would then land, scuttle the submarine, and make for safety with the help of the local Norwegian Resistance. The submarine would need to suit the particular needs of the operation, and its construction and sea trials were therefore expected to take about six weeks. M's team proposed to employ extra staff at SOE's Station IX, where the submarine would be built and the explosive device designed, and asked for sanction to spend £2,000 on labour and materials for the project.

M himself in fact had considerable reservations as to whether the technical work could be completed in the time available. SOE's operational plan suggested that the attack on the *Tirpitz* might take place as early as mid-April, at which time March-Phillipps and Appleyard would still be available, but M suggested that his technical team should approach the Admiralty to request information on midget submarines – he suspected they were far more knowledgeable than SOE. Nonetheless, the operational plan was approved by the Admiralty for further consideration, and M was informed on 7 March 1942 that it had received approval in principal, and had been given the official name Operation Frodesley.

Geoffrey Appleyard's father confirmed after the war that the idea for the use of the pedallo submarine against the *Tirpitz*, and the operational plan itself, had come from March-Phillipps and Appleyard. He described their intended craft as a two-man miniature submarine (this must be wrong, since the official project specified one-man craft), with both men sitting astride and pedalling away to power the paddles. Each man was to wear a specially designed diving suit. The submarine would be propelled for the first part of its journey with the heads of the two crew above the water and then, when close to the *Tirpitz*, it would submerge fully, pass under the boom that protected the battleship, and thus reach the hull and keel of its target. Station IX created a pedal-powered prototype, and Appleyard spoke to his family of his practice sessions using it.

In the event, M's prediction that the equipment would not be ready for a raid in mid-April proved accurate. A memo dated 10 April describes how the project was progressing. Rather than the operator wearing breathing apparatus, it had now been decided that the whole of his compartment in the submarine would be oxygenated, which would enable him to put in a greater sustained physical effort. The operator was still to pedal the submarine, carrying its explosive charge, to the *Tirpitz*, but the designers had now decided to provide auxiliary power to enable the submarine to make a speedier escape after the charge had been attached to its target. The power would come from batteries, which could propel the submarine for at least five miles. However, much work still had to be done and, as of 10 April, the auxiliary power units had not yet arrived. March-Phillipps and Appleyard were invited to spend several days at Station IX to test the controls, and to consult with the technicians over the final dimensions of the operator's compartment.

Progress remained slow. By early May, the design of the submarine had altered again. It was now to be fully powered by the batteries, would have a maximum speed of 5 knots, and could submerge to a maximum depth of 75 feet. A technical report dated 7 May 1942 made clear that the project was still months from completion: 'It is hoped that the submarine will be ready for depth and trimming tests in about six weeks time. If these prove satisfactory, fitting out will be completed during August.' The report also suggested that four agents should be sent on a course of submarine training. This would take seven to ten days, and the next available course started on 17 May.

March-Phillipps and Appleyard were by now fully occupied in building and training the Small Scale Raiding Force, and did not feel that they or any of their men could take that much time out for the submarine training course. M agreed, and on 12 May he formally vetoed their assignment to Operation Frodesley, on the grounds that they were actively engaged in preparing for other operations, and that since Frodesley was clearly not now going to take place for some months, the benefits of such training would be diminished by the passage of time and other work. However, the idea of SOE's miniature submarine lived on, and development of what became known the Welman submarine progressed. A number had been built and were undergoing trials at Helford in Cornwall by the end of 1942. The pedal-powered design was abandoned in favour of a submarine powered entirely by electric batteries, with oxygen sufficient for 10–14 hours supplied to the one-man crew. The overall length of the Welman, including the explosive charge that it would carry, was 20 feet. The charge itself, to be attached to the hull of a target ship, was a little over 3 feet in length and capable of causing serious damage to a capital ship. The submarine was 'capable of being driven by anybody with reasonable intelligence after the briefest possible period of training', which made it eminently suitable for use by SOE agents at short notice. Dennis Tottenham, late of Maid Honor Force, was in due course to be assigned to work with miniature submarines. The operational uses of the Welman submarine were described as:

1. For attack on capital ships by placing a large charge
2. As a means of transporting stores by means of the charge container
3. For reconnaissance
4. As a submersible canoe

The Welman was eventually perfected, and underwent her sea trials, but did not prove to be a long-term success. SOE eventually made the comment that 'the Welman is too large for conventional transport, too small to attack from a distance.' March-Phillipps and Appleyard's original idea for a pedallo miniature submarine had envisaged a vessel that would have been far easier to carry covertly close to its target.

The Operation Frodesley project was later handed to the Navy, although SOE remained very much involved in the necessary intelligence work. They controlled the network of agents in Norway who would facilitate the operation against the *Tirpitz*, and would help those who carried out the attack to escape to neutral Sweden. An operation was mounted by Navy personnel in late October 1942, using two battery-powered 'Chariots' – or two-man 'human torpedos' copied from the successful Italian midget submarines. However, the Chariots were lost to bad weather before the target was reached, and the *Tirpitz* remained unscathed. Eventually, in September 1943, a successful raid was carried out by a new generation of 'X craft' midget submarines, and the *Tirpitz* was badly damaged. She was repaired, but further air attacks against her were mounted, and a strike by Lancaster bombers on 12 November 1944 finally sank her.

Chapter 8

Operation Barricade

Having established his base at Anderson Manor and recruited his team, March-Phillipps was keen to put the Small Scale Raiding Force in action. He had been assigned two MTBs, and initially used them both. It was only later that the SSRF came to favour the low-slung MTB 344. March-Phillipps knew the abilities of his old Maid Honor Force, but there were many new faces amongst those now assembled at Anderson Manor, and they needed to be tested and to prove themselves. On the wider stage, the same was true, of course, of the Small Scale Raiding Force as a whole. The Maid Honor Force had proved its worth, now the SSRF must do the same.

March-Phillipps had planned to carry out his first operation in the middle of June, but just as during the previous summer he had been obliged to lurk with Maid Honor Force in Poole Harbour, waiting for clearance, now he found himself facing the frustrations of traffic jams in the Channel and a run of bad weather. Even though the SSRF was operating under the umbrella of Combined Operations, there was a lot of competition for clearance to cross the Channel, and SOE, though its reputation was improving, had to fight for the right to carry out its raids. During June and July, things were not helped by regular doses of bad weather and bad luck. There were plenty of potential targets for small-scale raids, and March-Phillipps had a number of operations ready to go, but initially his efforts were met only by frustration.

One of the planned operations was a raid on a lighthouse at Casquets, in the Channel Islands. Prisoners were to be taken and code books seized. March-Phillipps had obtained outline approval, and a codename of Operation Dryad had been assigned to the raid. However, whenever Dryad was given a set date, at an appropriately dark phase of the moon, bad weather or other problems intervened. Three times in June and July, March-Phillipps set out for the Casquets lighthouse, and three times he had to turn back – the first time because of fog, the second because of engine trouble on the supporting MTB, and the third because of bad weather. Within the SSRF, bad weather became known as 'Dryad weather'. It was enormously frustrating for the men involved – they had to endure the nervous tension of the hours preceding an operation, only to find that the operation itself was cancelled or that they had to turn back before reaching the target. In such circumstances, the leadership qualities of March-Phillipps and Appleyard were of the greatest importance.

A second operation that had gained approval was a raid on the Channel coast a few miles south of Barfleur, on the east coast of the Cherbourg peninsula. This was given the codename Operation Barricade. German Direction Finding Stations (DFS) were proving to be a considerable problem for Allied shipping in the Channel, particularly for covert missions on the French coast. Operation Barricade was originally intended to destroy a DFS and its detection apparatus – which was of two types, the Freya Apparatus and the Wuerzburg Apparatus. Originally, Barricade had been planned for a far larger force than the SSRF. The objective had been to destroy both the DFS and the nearby anti-aircraft gunsites on the coast between Barfleur and St Vaast, to kill Germans, and if possible to bring back prisoners. Enemy prisoners were always useful for intelligence purposes and, since the retreat from Dunkirk, the only way that the British forces could take prisoners was to cross the Channel. The original plan had called for the use of 120 men of the East Yorkshire Regiment under the command of Major A. A. Benn, and a flotilla of ships – a parent ship, 8 landing craft and 4 gunboats. Fighter aircraft from No.11 Group were to provide air cover. There had been detailed reconnaissance, and a number of aerial photographs had been taken of the target area.

However, Combined Operations eventually decided against a major assault and chose instead to use the SSRF to carry out a much smaller raid. Partly because of the numerous false starts they had already experienced, there was considerable tension at Anderson Manor as March-Phillipps formulated his final plan and chose his team for the operation. Peter Kemp later described how the waiting period over the previous weeks had proved to be a heavy strain on the nerves. In fact, Kemp was not to be chosen for this raid – March-Phillipps anticipated a difficult climb over the rocks upon landing, and felt Kemp was not up to it, partly no doubt because of his injuries in Spain (that at least was the reason that he gave Kemp). John Burton was also ruled out because of a damaged calf muscle.

No complete list appears to exist of those whom March-Phillipps decided to take with him on Operation Barricade. However, of the final force of eleven, at least half were *Maid Honor* veterans. Probably, March-Phillipps wanted to take a good number of his most tried and tested men with him, because if this were to be the first raid to actually come off, it would be of considerable importance for the SSRF's morale and reputation. He chose to use MTB 344, under the command of Lieutenant Freddie Bourne, to carry his force. Appleyard was to be the navigator – a difficult role once they were close to the French coast. The MTB could only safely approach to within about a mile of land, and the remaining part of the journey would have to be made by paddling a Goatley, one of their favoured landing craft.

Obviously, with only eleven men, the plan was now much more modest. The DFS had been discarded as the primary objective and the plan was now 'to carry out a reconnaissance raid on French coast NW of Pointe de Saire and to capture or kill enemy in A.A. gun-site.' As always, the men of the SSRF would be heavily armed, each carrying a Tommy gun (the machine gun favoured by American gangsters), a Colt .45 automatic and hand grenades, as well as knives, and any extra weapons that they chose to take with them.

On the morning of 14 August 1942, March-Phillipps delivered a careful and detailed briefing as to the plan of action, and what they might expect on landing in France, aided by the earlier reconnaissance and aerial photographs. They would leave that evening. The chosen men settled down to rest and to wait. When the transport, an army lorry, left at dusk to carry them to the shore base of HMS *Hornet* in Gosport, from where they would embark on MTB 344, Kemp, Burton and the others watched them go with a mixture of envy and anxiety.

During the ride on the lorry their spirits lifted, as always happened once the waiting was over, and the men of the SSRF were in good heart when they arrived at HMS *Hornet*. The cheerful and competent Freddie Bourne greeted them as they embarked on MTB 344. Together with the MTB's own crew, the arrival of the eleven SSRF made the Little Pisser quite crowded, although there would always be room for any prisoners they might bring back with them. They cast off at 2045 hrs, and set a course for Pointe de Barfleur.

Whatever else could be said about March-Phillipps, Appleyard and the force they led, they could rarely be described as lucky. During Operation Postmaster, Maid Honor Force's great success in West Africa, they had had to overcome numerous problems and mechanical failures. Now, once again, mechanical failure made life difficult. Just a few miles out from Gosport the port engine of the Little Pisser began to give trouble, and three times Bourne had to stop the boat whilst attempts were made to correct it. Finally, the port engine cut out altogether, and the MTB had to approach the French coast on the starboard engine, while work continued on the other. As they approached the coast a radio message from Portsmouth enabled them to correct their position, which was too far to the east of the target area. At about 2300 hrs, having been at sea for two and a half hours, it was with great relief that they sighted the Cape Barfleur light flashing in the distance. They calculated that they were now 15 miles off the French coast.

The initial approach was made at a reduced speed of 18 knots per hour, but once they arrived within 3 miles of the shore the main engines were shut down (the port engine was still out of action anyway), in case their approach was heard. The Little Pisser proceeded on its silent auxiliary engine alone. Against a strong tide, their progress was now slow. They prayed that the German DFS would not be able to pick up their low profile, and that the intelligence on coastal defences was acccurate.

March-Phillipps, Appleyard and Bourne scanned the dark coastline for a landmark. They had been briefed that a good landmark would be some high ground at La Pernelle, but either it never appeared or they missed it. They navigated as best they could by the position of the Barfleur light, but due to the way the MTB's compass was positioned it was impossible to take a bearing without pointing the ship's head at the lighthouse. Appleyard had to navigate by dead reckoning. It was very dark, and the coastline looked very unfamiliar. Every so often, they stopped to measure the depth of the sea with a plumb line. All the time they had to observe total silence on board, since noise carries surprisingly far across the sea and they had no wish to alert the enemy's defences. Eventually, having crawled to within about a mile of the coast, the MTB dropped anchor at a point about three-quarters of a mile east of what was in fact the Pointe de Fouli. It was now 0130 hrs, and the raid was already one and a half hours behind schedule.

The raiding party now launched the Goatley, and silently began the final stage of their journey to the shore, four men paddling on each side of the boat. They navigated their way through great outcrops of rock to land eventually on a shelving sandy beach. What they did not realize in the dark was that a strong inshore current had carried them about three-quarters of a mile north of where they needed to be. This added to the problem of their late arrival – they had only 50 minutes left in which to carry out their raid on land. Nevertheless, the SSRF had at last arrived on enemy territory.

The Goatley was pulled up above the waterline and one man was left to guard it – it was their only means of escape after the raid, and they expected to have to leave fast. The Little Pisser could be of no help to them until they had put a good distance between themselves and the shore. March-Phillipps led his men forward in single file. It remained a very dark night (Germans in the vicinity later described visibility as no more than 10 metres) but much time had been spent at Anderson Manor on night exercises, and they were able to move at a reasonable pace off the beach and over the rough ground of the neighbouring fields. March-Phillipps still thought they had landed in the right place and were therefore close to the targets. When he made out what he thought was a house across the darkened fields, he believed it must be one they had had pointed out to them on the aerial photographs, close to the DFS and anti-aircraft position. He led his men towards it. They crossed a low stone wall, and came upon a fence made of galvanised wire, easy to cut. March-Phillipps made certain that they created a decent sized gap in the wire, to ensure they could retreat at speed if necessary. Once through, they continued to advance silently until they came to a second wire fence, by which time the 'house' had come into better focus and could be identified as a large vehicle or instrument covered in camouflage netting. Whatever it was, it had to be some sort of enemy target.

The second fence was a far more formidable obstacle than the first. It was a mesh of barbed wire 15ft wide and about 3ft 6ins high. The wire itself was thick and difficult to cut with the pocket-sized wirecutters that the men of the SSRF carried. Within the fence, the head of a sentry could be seen, beside what looked very much like a guard hut. In truth, the SSRF had arrived not at the anti-aircraft battery or the DFS, but at German Defence Post No. 4, an enemy position manned by 16 enemy soldiers, and defended with a heavy machine gun and two light machine guns. It was one of a series of interconnecting defence posts along the enemy coastline. March-Phillipps, however, still hoping that this was one of the official targets, perhaps the anti-aircraft position, gave orders that the fence be cut so that they might attack. Whilst a very careful watch was kept on the sentry, laborious attempts were made to cut a way silently through the wire, but it soon became obvious that the task would be slow and probably impossible with the cutters they carried.

March-Phillipps sent a section of men to scout their way along the wire to the right, where he could just about make out another building. Their orders were to attack that if it proved possible. The section returned after a few minutes to tell March-Phillipps that the building was of substantial size and appeared to be a hangar. The size of the encampment was now becoming obvious. Either they were in the wrong place, or the intelligence they had been given was wildly inaccurate. The men of the SSRF doubled their efforts to cut through the wire, hoping to discover what the encampment was, but progress remained limited. Inevitably, they made more noise as they tried to hurry things along. Time was now running very short, and they had so far achieved nothing except for the most basic form of reconnaissance.

Then fate took a hand. The sentry finally seemed to notice that something was going on outside the fence. He went into the guard hut, and emerged with three comrades. All four German soldiers then began to make their way along the inside of the fence, towards the point where the SSRF were still trying to cut through. March-Phillipps reacted immediately, deciding that the SSRF should do what damage they could, and get the hell out of there. He quietly ordered his party to advance on hands and knees towards the guards, then await his order to fire. The attack was to be with Tommy guns, and three 'plastic bombs' – the equivalent of hand grenades made of plastic explosives.

The four enemy soldiers were advancing slowly, rifles at the ready, towards the spot where the SSRF men were crouching. As they approached, one of the Germans called out a challenge in a low voice. The words could not be distinguished. When there was no reply, the challenge was repeated, but was met with silence. The Germans were then heard to draw back the bolts of their rifles and prepare to fire. March-Phillipps now gave the order and instantly the quiet of the night was shattered by Tommy-gun fire. A second or two later, the three plastic bombs arced over the wire fence and exploded within a few feet of the four Germans. The effect on the soldiers was devastating. The SSRF then opened fire on any target they could see within the wire, as more enemy soldiers came into view. In the brief firefight that followed, March-Phillipps later estimated that his force had definitely killed three of the enemy, probably another three, and had wounded three or four others. The SSRF suffered no casualties.

After no more than a minute or two, March-Phillipps ordered his men to cease firing and withdraw, and they disappeared as silently as they had come into the darkness, heading for the beach and the waiting Goatley, whilst chaos and confusion reigned within German Defence Post No. 4. The Germans clearly did not know where the attack had come from, or how many men there were. Happily, they showed no sign of realizing that their attackers were now escaping via the beach. A few Verey lights went up, and desultory firing continued for about an hour, but March-Phillipps and his men were able to find the Goatley and head out to sea without interference. Again they experienced considerable difficulty with the current, and did not finally reach the waiting MTB 344 until 0345 hrs. Lieutenant Freddie Bourne, who had been waiting anxiously, welcomed them back on board, hauled up the anchor and made full speed for home.

However, the effect of delay was now felt. As the Little Pisser sped across the Channel, daylight approached. About 10 miles out from the French coast, a plane was heard approaching. At this stage it was still dark, but the very real fear was that the plane was searching to attack them. The two gas-cooled Vickers machine guns were capable of defending the MTB against air attack, but their effectiveness would inevitably depend on the type of aircraft that had been sent after them. Many pairs of eyes scanned the sky anxiously as the plane drew near – happily, its crew apparently did not spot them. The sound of its engines passed overhead and droned away into the distance. All March-Phillipps could report afterwards was that it was a twin-engined craft and flew over them very low, but did not open fire. No one was able to identify what type it was.

As daylight broke, in mid-channel the SSRF had a second scare. What they believed to be a German Dornier DO 17 flew close by along their port side, and this time the Little Pisser opened fire with everything she had. Some of the tracer from the Vickers guns appeared to hit the Dornier, but it flew on and did not return fire. Nonetheless, the danger to any Allied vessel crossing the Channel was that, once spotted, a report of its presence would be radioed in by the enemy and attack planes might be despatched to sink it. There was no doubt at all that the Dornier had seen the Little Pisser and felt the impact of its bullets. As they headed as fast as they could for the relative safety of the English coast, Freddie Bourne, Gus March-Phillipps and the SSRF remained on full alert. They survived without attack, however – the Dornier did not return and no other enemy planes appeared. At 0700 hrs on 15 August, MTB 344 reached the safety of its harbour. A lorry was waiting to take the men of the SSRF back to the tranquillity of Anderson Manor for breakfast. They were strained and exhausted, but content with their night's work. The only injury March-Phillipps had to report was an officer who had badly bruised himself by falling on an iron stake.

Without doubt, Operation Barricade had not been perfect, but March-Phillipps had proved that his concept of a small scale raiding force could work. In their single MTB they had been able to approach the coast, and to land without detection by the enemy's Direction Finding Stations. They were able to get within striking distance of the enemy without interference. In contrast, a flotilla of five or six ships and a raiding force of 120 men, as first planned, would have undoubtedly been detected early and would have faced organized resistance. Small parties, argued March-Phillipps, were better than large ones – a party of 10 or 12 men was ideal, and could produce an effect out of all proportion to its size.

In his operational report he commented: 'The effect of such raids, though small in itself, can be cumulative if they are continuous. If carried out frequently and over a wide area they would have a most demoralising effect on the enemy and corresponding heartening effect on our troops. They present the best form of training both for commandos and home forces.'

Since this was the first time that the SSRF had landed on enemy soil, March-Phillipps was eager to justify the concept of small raids. Even though they had arrived late and in the wrong place, they had carried out a difficult and dangerous raid without loss, had killed a number of enemy troops, and had caused local havoc in France. A report later captured from the German 320 Infantry Division HQ, under whose command Defence Post No. 4 had been, made clear that the Germans never knew what really happened. They did in due course work out that the attack had come by sea, but concluded there had been only four men involved, that they had arrived in a pneumatic boat, and had intended to land at dawn. The report was, not surprisingly, something of a whitewash for the German garrison, and its author commented: 'The occupants of Post No. 4 on the whole behaved correctly. Owing to the alertness of the sentries, the enemy was detected as he was about to cut through the wire obstacle, and the garrison were soon ready for action.' No mention was made in the report of the fact that the unit sustained significant casualties, while the attackers sustained none.

Even though the SSRF had not found its intended target and had not returned with any prisoners, nonetheless the operation was considered a success by High Command. Already, with the United States of America having joined the Allies in the prosecution of the war, an invasion of France was under consideration. Therefore all intelligence about the French coast was of value, and March-Phillipps was able to report in detail as to conditions on the beach where they landed, and the state of the German defence forces that he encountered. First-hand knowledge was priceless and difficult for the Allies to obtain. Further, the Germans had been taken by surprise, casualties had been inflicted on them, and their morale had no doubt been damaged. Finally, the SSRF team had seen action on French soil, and now all on the raid had experience of cross-Channel raiding that they could pass on to others.

Most important to the SSRF was the fact that after all their training, and after numerous frustrated attempts to go into action, they had finally opened their score.

Chapter 9

Operation Dryad

Operation Dryad, the planned attack on the Casquets Lighthouse in the Channel Islands, had been attempted a number of times before Operation Barricade, but without success. Various problems had beset the SSRF, most often with the weather, but also mechanical difficulties similar to what happened on Operation Barricade on 14 August, when one of the Little Pisser's engines broke down. Casquets was an extremely difficult target, with a long and frightening history of shipwrecks. As long ago as 1744, despite the presence of a recently built lighthouse, the British man o'war HMS *Victory* (a predecessor of Nelson's famed flagship) sank with the loss of 1,100 lives. In more recent times, the SS *Stella* went down in 1899 with the loss of 112. Casquets is set in a remote area of rocky islets and outcrops about 6 miles west of Alderney, where even a landing in peacetime conditions is difficult. The largest and highest islet rises 90ft above sea level, and on it stands the lighthouse and two other stone towers.

March-Phillipps and Appleyard were provided with an intelligence docket that left them in no doubt about the difficulty of the operation. The main island is surrounded by smaller rocky outcrops, and the tidal streams and eddies rush through the gullies between these rocks with great velocity. There were offically only three possible landing points, and customarily a signal flag would be flown from a flagstaff on the main island to indicate which of the landing points, if any, might be safely used at any particular time. No flag would mean that no safe landing was possible.

The object of the raid was to take prisoners, and to seize codebooks and any other useful documents. It was believed that there was a garrison of about six Germans on the island for the purpose of operating the light, and that they had a small radio transmitting set. They were expected to be adequately armed, but nothing was known about any defences that there might be. There was a proviso in the briefing docket – it was not 100 per cent certain that the garrison was German. It was known that some of the lighthouses in the Channel Islands had Vichy French, not German crews. The SSRF were ordered that they should take the garrison prisoner irrespective of whether they were German or French. Even if French, prisoners and their radio codebooks would be of value. In truth, there was very little hard intelligence about what was happening on Casquets Rock, and the job of the SSRF was to find out as much as possible.

The original outline plan had provided for a raiding force of 22 officers and men of the SRRF, using 2 MTBs. The operation was ordered to take place as soon as possible after 10 June 1942. The MTBs would stand off half a mile from the Casquets rock, and the raiders would land by means of landing craft such as the Goatley. The raiders were to have a maximum time on shore of 90 minutes in which to carry out the raid and to seize prisoners and documents, and were to leave the rock not less than an hour before the beginning of dawn. The MTBs would leave no later than dawn itself. They could not afford to be exposed in enemy waters in daylight.

To help, the SSRF were lent the services of a seaman who knew Casquets well. William George Barker was 32 years of age and had been born and bred on the nearby island of Alderney. Barker had already been on two missions for SOE, and was prepared to offer what help he could to March-Phillips and the Force in their raid on the Casquets Lighthouse. Apart from the particular information he was able to pass on, Barker agreed to accompany the raid and to act as guide. Three times, in June and July, Barker set out with the SSRF on Operation Dryad, only to be frustrated. Each time, the raiding party was assembled and briefed at Anderson Manor. Each time there were tense hours of waiting before the road transport ferried the raiding party to the docks. March-Phillipps knew that on this raid into the unknown, the SSRF faced two separate enemies – the Germans, and the treacherous seas around the Casquets rock. The party were to use two MTBs, one to carry the raiding party and one to provide cover and support if necessary. On the first occasion, the attempt was foiled by fog, which meant that a successful landing on Casquets Island was impossible. The second time, the supporting MTB suffered engine trouble, so the raiding party again had to turn back. On the third occasion, in July, again bad weather defeated them. After the third failure the SSRF lost the services of Barker, who was required on another operation on a fishing boat bound for Brittany from Dartmouth.

However, by the time Barker left them, March-Phillipps, Appleyard and the others had acquired a thorough picture of the Casquets Lighthouse and the rock on which it stood. They had maps and charts obtained from the Admiralty and Trinity House, aerial photographs taken for them by reconnaissance planes, and most important of all a detailed scale model of the Casquets rock, the lighthouse, and the adjoining buildings, which had been created from the photographs and from Barker's personal knowledge.

After the successful completion of Operation Barricade, March-Phillipps looked for a window in the weather that would enable him to have another go at Operation Dryad and the Casquets Lighthouse. All night-time operations were governed by the phases of the moon, and March-Phillipps wanted a suitably dark period. This time they would use only MTB 344, and a much smaller raiding party than the 22 men originally assembled. March-Phillipps decided to take just 12 men, including himself, Appleyard, Hayes and Winter from the old Maid Honor Force, together with some newer recruits: Kemp, Burton, Dudgeon, Warren, Howard, Orr, Brinkgreve and Reynolds. The fact that the party comprised 10 officers and only 2 other ranks didn't trouble March-Phillipps at all. To him, it was the quality of the men that counted, not their rank. In any event, March-Phillipps' long term plan was to train enough officers and senior NCOs to set up a whole series of small scale raiding forces up and down the coast, each unit training their own men in the art of cross Channel raiding, based on what they had learned at Anderson Manor. Although the initial plan had been that the SSRF would be handed over by SOE to the joint control of Lord Mountbatten, Chief of Combined Operations (CCO), on 1 September 1942, by the third week of August there was no sign of that happening, and SOE continued to administer and supply the SSRF, subject only to obtaining final approval for any operation from CCO.

Briefings at Anderson Manor took place in a specially appointed conference room and, shortly after Operation Barricade, March-Phillipps set up a briefing centre in the conference room for Operation Dryad, complete with charts of the immediate area around the island, the aerial photographs, and the scale model. He briefed his men intensively, and allowed them all the time they wished to spend with the maps and other materials. What March-Phillipps, Appleyard and Gwynne (the Operational Planner) did not tell their men, however, was the location or name of their target. For security purposes, a raiding party was never given this information until after the operation had been completed. Thus even though the SSRF had attempted the raid on Casquets before, none of the men except March-Phillipps, Appleyard and Gwynne knew where they were going.

The raiding party was to be divided into five sections: Graham Hayes would act as coxswain of the Goatley that they would use for landing, and he and Bunny Warren would remain in it whilst the rest of the party were on the rock. The other ten would climb up to the lighthouse enclosure in single file, and would then split up to carry out their specific tasks. March-Phillipps, Dudgeon, Howard and Orr (A party) would tackle the main building, which contained the living and sleeping quarters. Orr and Dudgeon both spoke German, and were to shout confusing orders to distract the enemy garrison, while Kemp and Burton (B party) attacked the wireless tower, with the object of killing or capturing any Germans there before they could use a radio transmitter to call for help. Appleyard and Winter (C party) would take possession of the lighthouse tower, and quell any resistance therein, while Brinkgreve and Bingham (D party) were to occupy the engine room. All members of the party would be heavily armed.

The first proposed date for the redesigned Operation Dryad was within a week of Operation Barricade, but the problems of 'Dryad weather' persisted and, as Peter Kemp was later to describe, there were again a number of false starts. On one occasion, the Little Pisser got them to within about a mile of Casquets island before fog forced them to turn back. It was not until the night of 2/3 September that the SSRF finally reached the Casquets rock.

In between the abortive attempts on Dryad, normal training at Anderson Manor continued. Thus, Kemp recalls that much of the night of 1/2 September was spent crawling on their stomachs in the rain, practising silent movement. When he finally got to bed he slept badly, but a run before breakfast the next day with Appleyard and Burton restored him to good spirits. After breakfast came the news that they would attempt the raid on Casquets again that evening. The morning was spent in the conference room, going over the now familiar details once more. This time, the landing point chosen was not one of the three recognized ones. The plan was to go for the most difficult option, and to land on the face of the rock immediately under the engine-house tower, thus avoiding any possible sentries or booby traps at the usual landing points. During the afternoon, the selected party rested. Some took time to visit the small chapel attached to Anderson Manor and seek some comfort there.

Between tea and supper, each man checked and prepared his equipment. Kemp later listed the items he had to carry: a tommy-gun and seven magazines, a pair of wirecutters, two Mills grenades, a Fairbairn and Sykes fighting knife, a torch, emergency rations, and two half-pound explosive charges with which to blow up the German radio set. He wore battledress, a balaclava and felt-soled boots, and was under orders also to wear a cumbersome naval lifebelt which, he commented, might save his life in the water but would very probably lose it for him in action.

After a nervous afternoon, and a somewhat hurried supper, the raiding party climbed into its lorry in the stableyard of Anderson Manor. All those remaining behind turned out to cheer them on their way. Once the lorry moved off, spirits rose amongst the raiding party and they began to sing as the tension relaxed. It was always so – the nervous last few hours before departure was followed by a release of tension and a sense of real comradeship and adventure. They headed towards the dockyard at Portland, where Freddie Bourne and the crew of MTB 344 were waiting. As they approached the docks, the singing stopped. Now they had to be as discreet as possible. The last thing the SSRF wanted was to broadcast the fact that their commando force was heading out for a raid against the Germans. Arriving on the dock alongside the Little Pisser, ten of the dozen commandos scurried below decks. Only March-Phillipps and Appleyard joined Bourne on the bridge. Appleyard was entrusted with navigating the MTB close enough to the Casquets rock for the Goatley to be launched. With inter-service rivalry remaining strong despite the war, he took it as a great personal compliment that the Navy were prepared to entrust the navigation of one of their MTBs to him, an Army man.

Five of the raiding force, Kemp, Dudgeon, Bingham, Warren and Orr, found themselves confined to the forecastle. With the forecastle hatch battened down to avoid any light showing, conditions for the five men were not only cramped but hot. Once they had set off, around 2100 hrs, the wind got up from a Force 3 to a Force 4, and occasionally Force 5. Conditions in the forecastle became decidedly unpleasant. All except Kemp stretched out as best they could to try to get some sleep, but he felt that the effort was pointless, and sat up attempting to read a novel by the cabin light.

MTB 344 was capable of a good turn of speed, and would normally cruise at 33 knots per hour. Unhappily, despite a very careful overhaul, the port engine again began to play up. Whatever the real problem was, it had not been solved. For the first 25 miles of the journey, the MTB was forced to travel at a reduced speed of 25 knots; only then was Bourne able to increase the engines' revolutions to the normal cruising speed. At 2245 hrs, the Casquets rock was sighted, and a course was set to approach it from the north against the tide. The main engines of the MTB were switched off, and it crept forward on its silent auxiliary engine. Appleyard warned the men waiting below to get ready. After a final equipment check, those below switched off the cabin lights to accustom their eyes to darkness.

As predicted the approach was difficult, made worse by the fact that they arrived later than intended and the north-east flood tide was running hard. The many conflicting eddies made it even harder and the crew found it easy to see why the waters around the Casquets rock were a graveyard for shipping. The MTB finally dropped anchor about 800 yards offshore, in 50 fathoms of water. It was now up to the raiding party in the Goatley to negotiate the treacherous final stage of the journey and to secure a landing point. Appleyard opened the hatches and called the men up on deck shortly before the MTB dropped anchor. It was a clear starry night, and those who had been stuck below in the oppressive heat now shivered at the change in temperature. They could make out their target across the water – the tall column of the lighthouse, and the whitewashed wall that surrounded the compound. The men gathered at the stern of the MTB beside the Goatley, which was dropped into the sea just after midnight and was followed rapidly and silently by its crew. March-Phillipps was last aboard and softly gave the order to push off and start paddling. The Goatley set out on its journey.

Four men paddled on each side, pushing the boat silently over the swells and eddies, still battling the fast-running north-east tide. Appleyard was crouched in the bow, navigating the small craft, Hayes was at the stern with the tiller. After twenty minutes of hard paddling, the Goatley forced its way into the small, rocky bay that Appleyard had been aiming for. A moon had now appeared, casting light across the water, but the Goatley was lowslung and hopefully still impossible to spot from shore. Appleyard picked out a sloping slab of rock at the base of the cliff and ordered Hayes to steer for it. Despite a heavy swell, Hayes brought the Goatley to within a short distance of the rock, then dropped the kedge anchor to prevent the Goatley from being smashed against it by the rough sea. Appleyard, in the bow, rose to his feet with the bowline and readied himself to jump for the flat rock. Judging the swell to perfection as it lifted the Goatley he cleared the gap between boat and rock, but slipped as he landed and only just prevented the sea from reclaiming him. He scrambled up the rock to the base of the cliff and made the line fast. As Hayes held the Goatley off the rocks with the stern line to the kedge anchor, one by one the remainder of the raiding party jumped for land. With the kit they were carrying the slippery rock proved quite a challenge, but with the help of the bowline all ten men eventually made their way safely to the shore. March-Phillipps timed the landing at 0025 hrs. The booming of the sea covered any noise that they made. As planned, Hayes and Warren remained on the Goatley to ensure its safety both from the enemy and the waves. Hayes manned the stern line, Warren the bowline, as they stood off some 20 feet from the rock. As always for the SSRF, the Goatley was their only way home.

Fortune sometimes favours the brave. March-Phillipps and Appleyard had chosen to land below what looked to be a very difficult cliff to climb. In the event, the men of the SSRF found no great difficulty in scaling the 80ft cliff. They moved in single file and the only hazard encountered on the ascent was a coil of wire, which they cut through without difficulty. They arrived at the top, to be confronted by the wall of the compound. It was now that the fitness upon which March-Phillipps always insisted became so important. The trip from the

Little Pisser to dry land had been physically draining, as had the climb up the cliff. Now, without pause or respite, they had to go on the attack.

The party caught its breath, while March-Phillipps scanned the wall of the compound. There was an entrance, but that was blocked with a heavy and daunting barbed wire entanglement. March-Phillipps decided that they would go straight over the wall. He leapt for it, hauled himself up and dropped down the other side, quickly followed by the rest of his men. Now there was no time to be wasted. It could only be moments before the alarm was given. The men split into their assigned parties and raced towards their individual targets: March-Phillipps, Dudgeon, Howard and Orr to the main building; Kemp and Burton to the wireless tower; Appleyard and Winter to the lighthouse tower; Brinkgreve and Reynolds to the engine room. It was shortly before 0100 hrs on 3 September 1942.

Unknown to the men of the SSRF, there were seven Germans on the rock, rather than the six anticipated. Four were specialists, members of the German Navy under the command of a Chief Petty Officer Mundt. The other three were German Army soldiers, there to guard the outpost. At the time of the attack, all seven were in the main building. The garrison was well-armed – an Oerlikon cannon was loaded and leaning against the wall of the living room, and two boxes of stick grenades were also in the building, one of them open. Each German also had his personal weapons, including a Steyr rifle. Had they seen or heard the approach of March-Phillipps' force, the garrison would have had little difficulty in defending the rock. Happily, that was not the case.

As March-Phillipps and his three companions burst into the living room of the main building they took the two Germans who were supposedly on watch totally by surprise. Both Orr and Dudgeon spoke German, but the guns wielded by the commandos spoke for themselves. The watchmen surrendered without further ado. Orr was left to guard them, while the others moved on through the building. In the sleeping quarters the other five Germans were found, and they too demonstrated no will to resist. Two telegraphers were preparing for bed, their three comrades were already fast asleep. Dudgeon took two men prisoner in one room, immediately beginning to interrogate them in German as to the number and whereabouts of the rest of the garrison and the disposition of their weapons. As March-Phillipps and Howard stormed guns in hand into another of the bedrooms, March-Phillipps noticed that one of the sleeping forms was wearing a hairnet over a luxuriant head of hair. He called out to Howard: 'Francis, you can't take that one, it's a woman!' But when the sleeping form stirred and sat up, it became clear that Howard could and should take him – it was after all a man.

All seven Germans were captured without a shot being fired. In truth, the delayed arrival of the SSRF had worked in their favour. Had they arrived as intended they might have had an easier landing, but would almost certainly have encountered the garrison rather more alert than they were at 0100 hrs.

Appleyard and Winter, Brinkgreve and Reynolds found their targets deserted. Burton and Kemp found the door of the wireless tower open, with a light burning inside. They stormed in, but there was nobody there. The transmitting room was a treasure trove – signal pads and notebooks were strewn across the table in front of radio sets, and codebooks lined the walls. Burton and Kemp stood guard over it all until Appleyard informed them that the whole area was secure. Then Burton destroyed the radios with an axe, collected up the codebooks and message pads, and made for the Goatley. Kemp went with Appleyard to help control the prisoners.

With the rock made safe and with the prisoners under control, the men of the SSRF searched for anything else that might be of intelligence value. In addition to the radio logs and codebooks, they seized ration cards, identity books and passes, personal letters and photographs, the station log, ration log and light log, and a gas mask and gas cape. They initially took an assortment of the Germans' weaponry with them, but eventually dumped these in the sea, because they were too heavy to risk in the Goatley. Tom Winter took a fancy to a German helmet, which he appropriated and wore on the return journey, attracting adverse comments from his comrades such as 'Tom, you look like a bloody hun.' Nonetheless, Winter kept the helmet as a souvenir. Without any doubt the most valuable assets were the prisoners themselves. They included three radio men, two of them Leading Telegraphers. The problem was how to get all seven prisoners safely back to the MTB.

The rock close to which the Goatley waited was wet and slippery, and sloped at an angle of 45 degrees into the sea – and before they reached it they had to descend the 80ft rockface. The prisoners were understandably in very different physical condition to March-Phillipps' super-fit commandos, so although the Germans were apparently totally unresisting and demoralized, it is greatly to the credit of the SSRF that all seven were successfully brought down the cliff and embarked on the Goatley, under the supervision of Burton and Hayes. Including the 12 SSRF, the total number of men on the Goatley was now 19. There was an emergency Dory on board the Little Pisser, but she was some distance out to sea, it would take time for the Dory to reach them and the seas were difficult. The decision was taken to attempt a single trip out to the Little Pisser in the Goatley.

Not a shot had been fired on the Casquets rock and no violence had been needed. However, at the point of embarkation, the SSRF suffered two casualties. Peter Kemp had been ordered by March-Phillipps to stand in the bow of the Goatley, to steady those coming aboard. Adam Orr still had his fighting knife in his hand as he jumped aboard, and as the boat lurched he fell against Kemp. His knife entered Kemp's right thigh, causing a wound that was to put Kemp out of action for some weeks.

Appleyard was the last man to come aboard, and he therefore had the task of detaching the bowline that held the Goatley to the shore. This done, there was no longer a fixed line to help Appleyard board the Goatley, and nothing to steady the boat while he did so. As he slid down the slippery rock towards it, Appleyard's leg somehow got doubled up beneath him and he broke the tarsal bone in his ankle. He fell into the sea just as the swell took the Goatley away from the rock, and had to swim back 20 feet through the icy water in his full kit. Hauled into the Goatley by his comrades, Appleyard did not yet realize how severe the damage was. He believed that his 'crocked ankle' was merely sprained.

The Goatley cast off at 0110 hrs. The SSRF had been on the Casquets rock a mere 45 minutes. In that time, the prisoners had been taken, the premises searched, and the radio smashed into silence – it took 24 hours for the Germans to discover why the Casquets radio had gone off air. Now the Goatley was undoubtedly grossly overloaded and low in the water, in dangerous seas. The journey to the MTB was difficult, but thanks to the skill and strength of the crew they arrived safely at the Little Pisser, waiting about 500 yards offshore. March-Phillipps was later to praise the Goatley's remarkable ability to withstand such a difficult sea and coastline.

The seven prisoners were herded into the forecastle of MTB 344 under the watchful eye of Patrick Dudgeon and two others, where they remained throughout the voyage, cowed and giving no trouble. During the course of just 45 minutes their lives had fundamentally changed. MTB 344 had a bumpy, wet, but uneventful trip back to Portland, docking there before 0400 hrs. The prisoners were immediately handed over to Intelligence (MI9) for interrogation, together with the documents and other items that the SSRF had brought back.

The prisoners proved of considerable value. All were cooperative, and prepared to talk about their military careers and experiences. The three soldiers, named Abel, Kepp and Klatwitter, were found to be of 'low mental and medical category ... drafted into the German Army for fatigues and guard duty'. Nonetheless, they were able to talk about the places where they had been stationed before Casquets, and of conditions generally in the German army. The three skilled men, wireless telegraphers Dembowy, Kraemer and Reineck, and also Chief Petty Officer Mundt, were of greater value. Together, the seven prisoners supplied detailed information about the German staffing and defences on various parts of the Cherbourg Peninsula, the Channel Islands, Calais and Heligoland.

Thus taken together, Operation Barricade (which killed Germans but took no prisoners) and Operation Dryad (which took prisoners but killed no Germans) had been a great success. With British forces in Europe still effectively confined to the British mainland, these raids were exactly what Prime Minister Churchill was calling for. They carried an obvious intelligence value, a propaganda value for the beleaguered British people, and they damaged enemy morale. The garrison at the Casquets had disappeared to a man and no one on the German side knew what had happened. Indeed, for some hours the Germans did not know that anything had happened.

The Casquets garrison had been supplied with everything that it needed (apparently including fresh water) from the nearby island of Alderney, with whom they were in regular radio contact. However, as it happened a routine message had been sent from Casquets just a few minutes before the raid, so it was quite some time before their radio silence was noticed, the alarm raised, and a party sent to investigate. When eventually that German party arrived at the Casquets lighthouse compound, they found a scene reminiscent of the 'ghost ship' *Mary Celeste*. All the inhabitants had disappeared, leaving no bloodstains or bullet holes behind them, only smashed radio sets and an absence of radio logs or codebooks. Some of the prisoners were taken off the rock still wearing pyjamas, so presumably their clothes lay by their beds. When Adolf Hitler learned of the raid three days after it had taken place, his initial reaction was to declare that the Casquets rock was indefensible, and should be abandoned. However, the garrison had in fact already been replaced, and the German Navy (the Kriegsmarine) eventually persuaded Hitler that the rock was too tactically important to abandon. The garrison was substantially increased to a total of 33 men (25 soldiers and 8 Kriegsmarine), and its defences and armaments were strengthened. Thus, the Small Scale Raiding Force scored another tactical victory. Those extra German troops could no longer be deployed against Allied forces – they were tied up on a remote island far from any future front line.

It was hoped that the effect on enemy morale would also be significant. As with Operation Barricade, the Germans knew little about the raid and how it had been carried out. The Dryad and Barricade attacks were geographically far apart, and apparently random. As was demonstrated at Casquets, many of the guards employed by the Germans in the Channel Islands and on the Channel Coast were far from being battle-hardened frontline troops. When word spread of what had happened to their comrades, low-quality troops were likely to lose courage and become unsettled. The more the Germans felt the need to strengthen their coastal and Channel Island defences, and to tie up troops there, the better the result for the SSRF. Gus March-Phillipps' theory was that a very small band of men, with proper training and the right equipment, could inflict disproportionately high damage on the enemy of the various kinds set out above. Barricade and Dryad had proved him right. The SSRF had suffered no serious casualties. Peter Kemp would be out of action for a while, and Appleyard's activities would be restricted in the immediate future – but through 'accidents' that could easily have happened in training.

Anderson Manor had been a happy training base from the outset, and morale was certainly very high when the raiding party returned from Operation Dryad. Their persistence had paid off. Several times they had been defeated by the weather in their endeavours to raid the Casquets lighthouse, but now finally they had pulled it off and it had been a great success. The only man who did not return to Anderson Manor was Peter Kemp, who was taken straight from MTB 344 to the Naval Hospital in Portland, but it was known that his wound was not serious. For Gus March-Phillipps, however, as always, the only question was 'what next?' Ever since Dunkirk, he had been driven by the desire to even the score, in the knowledge that there was a war to be won. The SSRF would not pause now. Having finally pulled off Operation Dryad, March-Phillipps would make sure that it was only a few days before his Small Scale Raiding Force put to sea again.

Chapter 10

Operation Branford

The interest of the SSRF in the Channel Islands was growing, and a few nights after the successful Dryad raid, March-Phillipps decided to go there again – this time to take a close look at the tiny island of Burhou, which lies 1.4 miles (2.25km) north-west of Alderney. Following the defeat at Dunkirk, the British Government had taken the view that the Channel Islands were indefensible, and had withdrawn all troops to the mainland. Now, March-Phillipps hoped that the Germans might, with his help, experience the same problem. He believed that the Channel Islands could prove a fruitful hunting ground for the SSRF and MTB 344.

The night of Monday 7 September was chosen for the next operation, which this time was to be purely a reconnaissance raid (unless of course some enemy troops were found on the island). It would also serve as good training for all those involved. March-Phillipps and Appleyard's plan for Burhou was daring, ingenious and almost romantic warfare. It was in some ways reminiscent of their brilliant raid on Fernando Po the previous January.

Burhou Island was within clear view and close range of the larger island of Alderney (which had a German garrison), and it was believed to be uninhabited. It was a mere 700 yards long and no more than 300 yards wide at any point. The long-term plan was to land a party of the SSRF armed with light artillery on Burhou, and to open fire on German targets on Alderney. Such action would certainly come as a total and very unwelcome surprise to the enemy. The SSRF would approach silently at night in the Little Pisser (and if necessary other transports), land their force and their guns, lay down sustained fire on the island of Alderney for a short period of time, and then retreat as rapidly and as silently as they had come. With the power of the Little Pisser's engines, and its low profile on the sea, they would hopefully get clean away before the Germans fully woke up to what was going on. No written record of the plan now appears to exist, but it can be inferred that discussions with William Barker, the seaman from Alderney, had revealed to March-Phillipps and Appleyard the possibilities of Burhou, and their fertile imaginations had done the rest.

However, before such an operation could be carried out, a careful reconnaissance was necessary. March-Phillipps chose a different team for this – it was important that all his men gained as much experience as possible, and of course he needed a gunner's opinion of the terrain. He and Appleyard would go, as always, even though Appleyard was hardly able to walk, but they would stay on board MTB 344. Appleyard's value would be as navigator – he now had very considerable experience of the often perilous shores that they visited. Further, he, March-Phillipps and Freddie Bourne wanted to take a closer look at the waters around Burhou in the hope that they would be returning there to carry out the main operation. March-Phillipps decided to take Lassen with them, another expert seaman. His job would be to steer the landing craft. Colin Ogden Smith, one of his original platoon officers in 7 Commando, was to command the landing party. Ogden Smith was an ex-gunner, having served in the Honorable Artillery Company and the Royal Artillery. He was therefore well suited to carry out the type of reconnaissance required.

The official description of the objective of Operation Branford on 7 September was, 'to carry out a reconnaissance on Ile Burhou to see whether Burhou is occupied, and whether the landing of light pack artillery would be possible.' Pack artillery often meant the American 75mm Pack Howitzer M1. Supplied by the United States to British Forces, the Howitzer M1 was designed to be carried by pack animals over difficult terrain unsuited to wheeled or tracked guns. It could be broken down and carried if necessary, in parts, by a number of fit men. The range of the Howitzer M1 was over 8,000 metres, and thus the whole of the island of Alderney (3 miles/4.8km long and 1.5 miles/2.4km) wide) would be an easy target from Burhou. It should be possible to drop shells on any German position on Alderney.

On the night of 7 September the party totalled 11 men in all and, unusually, the other ranks outnumbered the officers 6:5. A lorry carried them as normal from Anderson Manor to Portland, where they embarked on the Little Pisser, with Freddie Bourne and his crew. The weather was appreciably better than on the Dryad raid five days earlier, with only a light wind and a gentle swell of the sea. However, intelligence warned that there was considerable movement of enemy shipping in the Channel that night, and there was a fear that they might be spotted by enemy E boats – fast surface craft capable of doing fatal damage to MTB 344 (which was only lightly armed) if they caught her.

MTB 344 departed from Portland a little after 2100 hrs, and the course was set. All went well for about an hour, until the port engine yet again cut out. The old problem was still unresolved. Despite an enormous sense of frustration, March-Phillipps and Appleyard decided that they had no option but to cancel the operation, and to turn for home. With both engines working they would have had a chance to outrun any E boats they might have encountered. With only one engine, escape would be impossible. The return course was laid, and for fifteen minutes the SSRF headed back the way they had come. Bourne's engineer kept working on the port engine. The problem seemed to be that the fuel pressure to that engine had dramatically fallen, causing the engine to cut out. The engineer eventually found a way to solve this and to re-establish the correct fuel pressure to the engine, and at about 2215 hrs the port engine started up again. March-Phillipps and Appleyard now had to decide whether to continue home, or to turn round and give the operation another try. Not surprisingly, they decided on another go. Fortunately, that proved the right decision, since the port engine behaved itself for the rest of the night.

As always in those waters, the approach to Burhou was far from easy. *The Channel Pilot* of 1906 described the area thus: 'Between Ortac, Verte Tete and Burhou Island are scattered many dangerous rocks and ledges, among which the streams run with great velocity.' With considerable skill, the MTB was manoeuvred inside the Burhou reef, and dropped anchor about 600 yards off Burhou island itself. At 0020 hrs on 8 September, Ogden Smith, Lassen and six other ranks including a Corporal Edgar, set out in the Goatley to paddle to the shore. Lassen, acting as cox, brought the flat-bottomed craft close to the rocky beach and dropped the kedge anchor. Ogden Smith, Edgar, and four others of the SSRF, clambered out and made their way 60 yards across the slippery, seaweed-clad rocks to above the high-water mark. As at Casquets, two men remained to guard the Goatley – Lassen and another.

Ogden Smith moved forward cautiously. Intelligence had suggested that the island was uninhabited (it had always been), but nothing was certain, and apart from enemy personnel there might be mines or booby traps. Ogden Smith led his men towards the single building on the island, which for years had been used as a refuge for stranded sailors or fishermen. Encountering no opposition, the men reached the building to find that it had been partly demolished by artillery fire – the roof and first floor had collapsed inwards, filling the ground floor with rubble. German gunners on Alderney had apparently been using it for target practice, thereby demonstrating the viability of March-Phillipps and Appleyard's plan. Ogden Smith then divided his party in two: Corporal Edgar took two men with him to examine the westward end of the island; and Ogden Smith took the others to cover the central and eastern parts. It soon became clear that no one else was on the island and they discovered no defensive works of any kind. The greatest danger could be unexploded shells.

Casting his trained eye over the terrain, Ogden Smith concluded that there were a number of places where high-angle guns could be sited, but that because of the lack of sandy beaches (the island was surrounded by rocks) it would be impractical to use wheeled or tracked guns. Only pack artillery and mortars, and any loads which could be carried by two or three men, would be suitable both to the landing point and the island's terrain. In short, Ogden Smith concluded that March-Phillipps and Appleyard's plan could work. Having completed their reconnaissance, the SSRF returned to where Lassen was waiting with their boat. Since the weather remained benign, and the sea calm, the return journey in the Goatley to MTB 344 was straightforward. By 0205 hrs on 8 September, the SSRF were on their way home and at 0430 hrs, they docked at Portland.

March-Phillipps reported back to HQ that all had gone well, and that it was possible to land pack artillery and mortars on Burhou, but nothing heavier than that. He commented:

> The landing was carried out within a mile of Alderney on a clear night (no moon) and no interest was excited on the mainland. The landing party reported the MTB to be just invisible at 600 yards. The Goatley is just visible at 100 yards ... these islands would appear to present innumerable targets, with obvious advantages over mainland targets in that they are so much more easily recognised. An MTB once within the wilderness of rocks and tide is safe from hostile surface craft and indistinguishable from the rocks themselves, and the landing craft is in a similar position.

Geoffrey Appleyard was in the habit of writing home to his family, sometimes in a rather indiscreet way. He wrote to his father following the visit to Burhou:

> We were out again the other night (Monday) but it was a small and very unobtrusive party whose mission was purely a reconnaissance with a very particular end in view. No one was met, and I am quite sure that no one on the other side ever knew we had been. It was in the same district as the previous one in which we robbed the nest and removed the seven eggs! [A reference to the Casquets raid.] By the way, these 'eggs' have hatched very nicely and produced a great deal of extremely interesting information. The other night's party was completely successful and we got all the information we wanted. I was unable to go ashore, of course, because of my ankle, but I navigated the party, and, from that point of view, it was by far the most interesting of anything we have yet done. It was great fun, as there was quite an element of cheek involved!

Thank you for your prayers, Dad. And Mummy's too. I know they are a great help, and many of us pray very earnestly for the success of these parties and for the whole future of this type of operation, which I am convinced can play a real part in winning the war if taken up on an effective scale. When you pray, don't just pray for our safety, but also pray for our success and our cause, and for one of the greatest things our little unit may help to achieve – the building up of morale in our own forces. When you pray for me, pray for courage and steadfastness, and for my team spirit and loyalty to the other chaps on the job ...

The 'battle of Whitehall' is, of course, now going a lot better. Never was the old adage 'Nothing succeeds like success' more apparent, and our few small successes have helped enormously in London. In fact people are only too willing to give us what we ask. Gus has had several interviews with Mountbatten, and he has written us a personal letter of congratulation and encouragement.

In early September 1942, the SSRF were riding the crest of a wave of success. March-Phillipps and Appleyard had followed up their brilliant success in West Africa by creating an innovative and very effective commando force operating from Anderson Manor (or Station 62 as it was officially known). Their morale was extremely high, and all seemed set fair for the future.

On the night of 12/13 September 1942, all that was to change.

Chapter 11

Operation Aquatint

The SSRF's next operation was planned for the night of Friday/Saturday, 11/12 September, as always weather permitting. It was given the codename Aquatint. This time the target was an enemy post and small group of houses on the French coast at Sainte Honorine des Pertes, to the west of Port-en-Bessin and east of Cape Barfleur, in the Calvados region. The plan was to land under the cliffs, climb up, and then circle round behind the houses to attack the enemy from a direction that they would not expect. The objectives were to capture prisoners and obtain intelligence, causing enemy casualties and creating havoc. Aerial reconnaissance was carried out, and a likely looking gully that it was believed would give climbable access to the top of the cliff was chosen as the landing point. The SSRF preferred to land beneath cliffs and then scale them, in the hope that they would find the coastland above less well defended. By this time, Hitler had decided that there was to be no immediate invasion of the British mainland and that therefore the Channel coast should be fortified. The fortifications were stronger where there was a beach that might look attractive to a seaborne landing force.

March-Phillipps selected a mixed force of 11 men to be the landing party. Kemp was injured, and Appleyard was still suffering from his damaged ankle so would act as navigator but remain on board the Little Pisser. Lassen was to be rested, as was Colin Ogden-Smith. March-Phillipps' landing party thus comprised Graham Hayes, André Desgranges, Francis Howard, John Burton, Tony Hall, CSM Tom Winter, Sergeant Williams and Privates Lehniger (Sudeten German), Orr (Polish) and Hellings (Dutch). It was a good mixture of the more and less experienced of the SSRF, and was in line with March-Phillipps' policy of training up enough men to set up a series of raiding forces around the coast.

Morale was high amongst the men of the SSRF as they prepared for this next operation. Since mid-August they had enjoyed considerable success and suffered only minor casualties, none of which had been inflicted by the enemy. In March-Phillipps they had an inspirational leader, and in Appleyard and Gwynne meticulous planners. They looked forward to a continued run of success, with exciting projects such as an artillery attack on Alderney in the offing.

Shortly before 11 September, March-Phillipps had managed to take a night off, which he spent in the company of his beautiful young bride before she went off to Manchester to start her parachuting course. Marjorie was always a popular figure at Anderson Manor, but when he could Gus would go up to London, to spend a night at the borrowed house that was their marital home.

There was always tension and suppressed fears before an operation, and the daytime of 11 September was no different. March-Phillipps' presence on any raid, however, calmed the nerves. He was an iconic figure to his men. He had taken the Maid Honor Force to West Africa and back, and had pulled off the most extraordinary coup there without losing a man. He had led the SSRF on three cross-Channel operations with conspicuous success, and again without significant casualties. With Geoffrey Appleyard at his side, March-Phillipps seemed invincible.

However, the night of 11/12 September turned out to be a non-event. The SSRF team boarded MTB 344 at Portland and set off, passing the Needles off the Isle of Wight at 2030 hrs. It was soon clear that the weather was against them (as so often) and bad visibility forced March-Phillipps to cancel the operation shortly before midnight. Freddie Bourne took them back to Portland, and they returned to Anderson Manor. It was decided to try again the following night. Hard though it was, the SSRF had experienced the frustrations of bad weather many times, and understood that it was a part of their job. It would not have been a great surprise to their comrades at Anderson Manor when the lorry from Portland returned early, and they learned that Operation Aquatint had been aborted. Hopefully, the following night would bring better weather.

The day of 12 September was a beautiful one. Richard Lehniger took the opportunity to write to his wife Lilly, starting: 'It is very sad that I cannot be with you and our little child on this glorious day…' and concluding, 'I always think of you. A thousand kisses – your Richard.' His cousin Leo Felix still held the 'final letter' to Lilly written three months earlier. Not surprisingly, this is a very personal and moving letter, which his daughter Irene still possesses today. It includes: 'I shall take the pictures of you and of our little child with me and you may be quite sure, my darlings, that I will be thinking of you if anything were to happen to me … If I should live, I shall continue to look after you as before, and if not, I want you both to know that I died in a just cause for both of you. In any case, after the war, I would ask you to go to my mother and kiss her for me. Time and again I think of you all.'

That evening, March-Phillipps set off again from Anderson Manor with the same squad of men, including Lehniger. Freddie Bourne and his crew of eight were waiting for them at Portland, and they duly embarked on the far from comfortable MTB 344. It was an unusually dark night, with patches of fog in the coastal regions. They passed the Needles at 2012 hrs. MTB 344 took a substantial detour on their route across the Channel to avoid a significant enemy minefield that had been laid across the Seine estuary and on to the west some three miles beyond Cape Barfleur. Appleyard and Bourne took the MTB west of the minefield, and then approached eastwards along the French coast, on the inside of the minefield, along the inshore shipping route used by enemy vessels. They travelled slowly, since they had to pass within four miles of Cape Barfleur, and did not want the enemy to hear the noise of their engines.

There was no fog now, but the night was so dark that it was impossible to see the coastline from a distance of more than half a mile. Even though Appleyard estimated that the cliffs were 100 feet high, they were very difficult to see. Despite approaching as close as they possibly could in the MTB, the men of the SSRF were unable to make out the gully which they had decided would be the only climbing point of the cliffs.

Eventually, after a word with their men, March-Phillipps and Appleyard decided that rather than abandon the operation again, they would land on the Sainte Honorine beach, which was sandy and inviting, and would attack from there. As Tony Hall later put it: 'We were meant to climb up a little kink in a certain cliff, but we couldn't find the ruddy kink ... Gus said: "What do you think, chaps, shall we have a bash?"' Of course, all agreed to give it a go.

They hoped that the darkness that had caused them problems in finding their preferred landing point would now work to their advantage.

It was now very early on Sunday, 13 September. MTB 344 dropped anchor in 3 fathoms of water, between 300 and 400 yards from the beach, and the raiding party quietly launched their Goatley at 0020 hrs. Eleven men, led by March-Phillipps, paddled towards the beach, while Appleyard, with his injured ankle, remained aboard the MTB. It was the first time since Dunkirk that March-Phillipps had gone into action without Appleyard at his side.

The paddle to the beach was uneventful. As soon as the Goatley landed however, the raiding party realized that they had arrived very close to some houses. It would not have been safe to leave the Goatley there, so they hauled it 200 yards along the beach and up above the high-water mark, to the base of a low cliff. Along the cliff ran a track from east to west. Francis Howard was left to guard the Goatley, and March-Phillipps led the remainder of the party directly inland, crossing a track to the east of the houses they had seen. His intention was that they would reconnoitre the area thoroughly, choose a suitable target, and then regroup on the beach before carrying out their attack.

In the black of the night, moving silently as they were trained to do, the ten SSRF circled inland and carried out what Tom Winter was later to describe as a 'good recce'. It took them about half an hour and they then returned towards the beach and the Goatley, as planned. As they approached the track from inland, they heard the sound of an enemy patrol moving towards them from the east, and immediately went to ground. They were in a small depression and well under cover, invisible in the dark from the track along which the enemy patrol was moving. They crouched low and waited for the patrol to pass by. But at 0050 hrs on the morning of Sunday, 13 April 1942, such luck as March-Phillipps had enjoyed (and it had so often seemed to be against him) ran out.

The SSRF had unknowingly chosen a very dangerous section of the French coast. They had not landed anywhere near their intended target at St Honorine des Pertes, but had paddled into the middle of a hornet's nest on the beach of St Laurent sur Mer. (Although they could not know it, this stretch of sand would form a part of 'Omaha' beach in the 1944 D-Day landings.) Advancing towards them along the coastal track was the regular patrol between three fortified German positions on that stretch of coastline, the trio being collectively known as Stutzpunkt (Stronghold) 29. They were manned by more than 50 German troops, armed with a variety of heavy machine guns, flame throwers and lighter weapons. Stutzpunkt 29 was one of a series of such strongholds along that stretch of coast. Most significantly, the particular patrol now approaching the SSRF (Patrol No. 1 of the 3rd Reserve Company of the 726th Infantry Regiment) was accompanied by a guard dog. There were between five and eight men under the command of a Corporal Wichert. They were armed with a light machine gun, a submachine gun, rifles and grenades. Had it not been for the dog, Tom Winter believed that he and his comrades would have remained unnoticed as the patrol passed by. However, the dog picked up the scent of the commando agents and raised the alarm.

The men of the SSRF were better trained, more numerous than the German patrol, and had the element of surprise on their side. As soon as the dog raised the alarm, they opened fire, confident that they could shoot their way out. They burst from cover to make their way through the enemy to the beach, and Tony Hall, following the order to take prisoners, grabbed hold of the dog handler, Private Kowalski, and dragged him too towards the Goatley. Kowalski, obviously terrified, cried out that he was a Czech not a German, to which Hall replied in English, 'oh well, we'll sort that out on the boat'. Slowed down by his prisoner, Hall was the first to fall, his skull smashed from behind by a German wielding a stick grenade as a club. He fell senseless to the beach, sustaining also a shrapnel wound to his leg as the German guard posts opened up with everything they had got.

The tide had turned while the raiding party had been on land, and the sea had receded further from where the Goatley lay under the low cliff. Miraculously, despite the enemy fire March-Phillipps and his men cleared the enemy patrol out of their way and, rejoining Howard, managed to carry the Goatley to the water and launch it. All except Hall were able to clamber on board. Howard by now had been wounded in the leg, but his friends managed to pull him on board. Tony Hall, deeply unconscious, was left for dead on the beach. The Germans started to put up Verey lights and flares, and the darkness of the night, which had been such a great help to the SSRF on land, now dissolved.

Appleyard and Bourne were sitting in darkness aboard the MTB out at sea when the mayhem broke out on shore. At first they heard Tommy gun and pistol fire from the foot of the low cliff – no doubt the SSRF trying to fight their way out. They then heard the explosions of what they believed to be German stick grenades, and an increase in small arms fire, before the first of the Verey lights went up. Some of these were apparently signal lights, because a number of coastal guns then began firing out to sea, apparently not yet having picked up any targets. The only good news was that a German searchlight mounted on the clifftop appeared to malfunction, unable to cast its light on the action below.

MTB 344 was of course well within range of the shore. Lieutenant Freddie Bourne had a crew of eight for whom he was responsible. The accepted position was that if a situation like this arose, it would be entirely up to Lieutenant Bourne's discretion as to whether he felt it safe to stay, or whether, for the safety of his ship and crew, he would turn and head out to sea.

For the time being, MTB 344 stayed exactly where she was, hoping that the Goatley, which Bourne and Appleyard still could not see, would reach her. The MTB had a dinghy on board, but there was little point in launching that whilst the exact location of the raiding party was unknown.

According to Tom Winter, the Goatley with its load of 10 men got about a hundred yards out to sea before the Verey lights enabled the enemy to locate it and bring fire to bear. The SSRF were doing their best to paddle towards the as yet unspotted MTB 344, and were in no position to return any defensive fire. It was not long before the Goatley was raked by machine guns from the shore, badly holed and capsized. Its passengers were thrown into the water, some wounded by the same machine-gun fire that sank the Goatley. Winter describes swimming in what he believed to be the direction of the MTB, though he could see nothing in the dark. The Germans were still firing at anything in the water they could see, and Winter recalled that Gus March-Phillipps shouted out 'Go back' towards where they believed that the MTB was. He himself shouted the same thing. Appleyard and Bourne still could not see what was going on from where the Little Pisser was moored. They remained in position until about 0120 hrs, hoping against hope that the Goatley would reach them. Appleyard apparently thought at one point that Gus March-Phillipps and his men were still on the beach, under the cover of the small cliff.

Having seen and sunk the Goatley, it was obvious to the German forces on land that the British commandos had a ship waiting offshore to pick them up. Even without the searchlight, the MTB was eventually spotted, and coastal guns began to bring fire down upon it. Six or eight shells passed overhead, as the guns struggled to get their range, and Bourne and Appleyard now had no option but to retreat out to sea. Decision taken, they cut the anchor rope in order not to waste any time in departing, but on trying to start up the engines, they discovered that the starboard engine had already been hit and was virtually without power. Effectively reduced to one engine, MTB 344 made its way as speedily as it could away from the shore into the engulfing darkness of the sea. The Germans soon lost sight of her, and could only hear the waning sound of her engine. The Little Pisser's low profile had yet again proved invaluable.

However, Appleyard and Bourne had no intention of abandoning their comrades yet. Having steered directly out to sea for 2 miles, Bourne declutched the engine and gradually throttled down, trying to give the impression to the enemy behind them that the MTB was still heading away towards the English coast. He brought the Little Pisser to a halt, and let her drift – still just a couple of miles out, Appleyard and Bourne could now watch and hear the activity on the beach. Gradually everything died down, the firing eventually stopped, the Verey lights became sporadic and then they also ceased. Once all was quiet, Bourne brought the MTB about and, using only the silent engine, crept slowly back towards the beach. They got to within about 500 yards of it, then stopped, watching carefully for anything that might indicate what had happened to their friends and hoping that the Goatley might still appear. Both sensed it was highly probable that total disaster had befallen their comrades.

In fact, three of the raiding party were now dead, four more had been captured, and four were on the run. When the Goatley had capsized, all the men were thrown into the water. Tom Winter's attempt to swim out to the MTB failed because he couldn't see it. The tide was in full flow, Winter soon tired and realized that his only hope of survival was to make for the shore. He eventually arrived on the beach in a state of exhaustion, was challenged and fired upon from very short range, but miraculously uninjured. He was then taken prisoner and, too exhausted to walk, was dragged to German Headquarters, which turned out to be close by where the SSRF had landed.

Francis Howard, already wounded in the leg before he had been dragged into the Goatley, was lucky. Though badly holed and capsized the vessel continued to float upside down and provide support for any who managed to hang on to it. Howard recalled later how they had got a certain way out, when 'everything went up. Flares and more shooting. The Goatley sank. I don't know if it capsized or was hit by a shell. I could still swim despite my wounded leg, though not very much. Luckily, I bumped into the overturned boat which saved me. André Desgranges was on it too. I don't know what happened to the others.' Howard and Desgranges were able to hang on to what remained of the Goatley and make their way back to the shore, where both men were taken prisoner.

Tony Hall, left for dead on the beach, was grievously wounded but still alive. The Germans took him into custody, and provided him with excellent medical attention, which saved his life. Francis Howard's leg wound later turned to osteomyelitis, and he was eventually repatriated to England in 1943, where he remained in hospital for many months. John Burton, Adam Orr and Jan Hellings swam away from the wreck of the Goatley uninjured. All the hard training that they had undergone kept them alive. They stripped off their belts and heavy equipment, and were able to use the darkness at sea to swim away from the lights and the shooting. Eventually, they were able to creep up on to dry land some distance further down the coast. Allan Williams and Richard Lehniger were not so fortunate. No record that the author has found shows whether they were killed by gunfire when the Goatley was hit, or were killed or wounded by gunfire in the sea, or simply lost their battle with the sea and drowned. In both cases their dead bodies washed up on the beach.

Graham Hayes was always at home in the sea. His aquatic feats whilst with Maid Honor Force had been remarkable. He found himself in the water with little more than a scratch. As a very strong swimmer, he had every hope of making it to land somewhere further down the coast. However, Hayes saw that his commander, Gus March-Phillipps, was also in the water nearby and was in difficulty. Hayes went to his aid, and for a while was able to help March-Phillipps to swim for the shore. Again, no records that the author has found show what wounds March-Phillipps had sustained, but they were to prove fatal. Though super-fit, March-Phillipps was unable to keep swimming, and eventually he slipped away from Hayes' grasp and disappeared. His body was washed up on the beach with those of Allan Williams and Richard Lehniger.

Graham Hayes swam along the coast and, like Burton, Orr and Hellings, safely made it to dry land.

On board MTB 344, 500 yards off the beach, Bourne and Appleyard waited for as long as they possibly could. Finally, at 0225 hrs, their presence was again discovered and they were fired on by two German patrol boats. They had no option but to abandon their vigil and head out to sea. In fear of pursuit, and with no real speed due to the loss of one engine, they took a truly desperate decision and decided to run straight across the German minefield. Fortune, having done nothing else for the SSRF that night, finally smiled, and they passed through unscathed, docking back in Portsmouth at 1035 hrs. Of the landing party of eleven men, not a single one returned to Anderson Manor. That morning, nothing was known of their fate – who had lived and who had died.

Chapter 12

The Survivors

Tom Winter, once his surrender was accepted, was immediately dragged off to the German headquarters building nearby. There he found two other survivors of the raid – André Desgranges and Francis Howard, the latter lying injured on the floor. Any possessions the men had were taken from them. When morning arrived, Winter and Desgranges were taken out to the beach, where the retreating tide had left the bodies of March-Phillipps, Williams and Lehniger washed up below the high-water mark. The loss of March-Phillipps, with whom they had both served in Maid Honor Force, was a particularly bitter blow.

The Germans were alert to the propaganda value of having repulsed the raid, and of having killed and captured a number of British commandos. An army film unit had already arrived and was in place to film Winter and Desgranges when, following the orders of their captors, they carried the bodies of their dead comrades up above the line of high tide. The two prisoners were then marched back to the HQ building. The Germans now had film to prove that they had killed and captured at least five British commandos. The ruined Goatley was also found washed up, and a number of British weapons and items of kit were recovered. The German plan was obviously to make as much as they could of the incident. They arranged a formal funeral for the three dead commandos in the village cemetery and again filmed the ceremony. Thus they would be able to demonstrate the folly of British raids, and of resistance to the might of the Third Reich, whilst at the same time showing how honourably Germans behaved towards their fallen enemies. The film was made, but there is no evidence that it was ever shown publicly. Probably this was because of events which followed swiftly on the disaster at St Laurent sur Mer. On the night of 2/3 October, the SSRF attacked again, this time on the island of Sark, as a result of which German policy towards British commandos was to change dramatically.

Winter and Desgranges having carried out the unhappy task of moving the dead bodies of their comrades and friends, they were taken by lorry to Caen. For Tom Winter, two months of what he described as 'knocks and kicks' under interrogation now began. The two men were separated and Winter was placed in solitary confinement. He was taken in and out of his cell at all hours of the day and night over an initial period of eight days of interrogation. His uniform was removed and very carefully searched for any hidden aids to escape or evasion.

Each man in the Small Scale Raiding Force had been given training and equipment against the eventuality of capture, or separation from the rest of their unit in enemy territory. Desgranges later revealed that he had a compass concealed in the rear collar stud of his shirt (which the Germans did not find), and Winter's account describes a compass that was made out of two of his fly buttons when fitted together, which again the Germans did not find. Winter also says that each man had been supplied with a code which, should he become a prisoner of war, would enable him to communicate with the MI9 and SOE in England through apparently innocent letters. MI9 had been working on such codes since early in the war. Using the code, Winter later sent information home to his wife.

During the early part of his interrogation Winter stuck to name, rank, and number, but then deployed his prepared cover story, which was that his regiment was the Royal Army Service Corps (RASC), to which he had indeed once belonged, and that his job as an RASC sergeant with the commando forces had simply been that he was in charge of stores. Thus he was able to deflect questions about the objectives of the raid, and how many commandos had been involved. Winter protested that he was really only the storeman and knew nothing of the bigger picture. Although his interrogators repeatedly tried to catch him out, Winter stuck to his story throughout the eight days at Caen.

In an attempt, perhaps, to get Winter to let something slip, the Germans allowed him a visit to Lord Francis Howard in the hospital at Caen, and left them to talk alone. Winter suspected that their conversation was covertly recorded, and made sure that neither he nor Howard said anything of any value to the enemy. Winter also discovered the fact that Tony Hall was not dead, as they had believed, but was lying still unconscious in the hospital. After the hospital visit, the Germans kept Winter under interrogation in Caen for another two days, and then sent him to Rennes, where he spent between eight and ten days suffering similar treatment.

At Rennes, however, Winter was reunited with Burton, Hellings and Orr. For a while he shared a cell with John Burton, who told him that after the capsize of the Goatley, he and his two companions had dumped all their heavy kit and managed to swim west away from the beach at St Laurent sur Mer. They had met up ashore, further along the coast, and the three of them had planned to make their way on foot to the Spanish border. They stayed at liberty until 17 September, having changed into civilian clothes thanks to help given by local French people, but then had the misfortune to run into a German parachute company on exercise, and were captured. For Burton, capture meant the unhappy prospect of seeing out the war from behind the wire of a prisoner-of-war camp, Hellings was a Dutchman and likely to be treated in the same way, but Orr was in fact a Polish Jew, and if the Germans found that out, he would be treated very differently to his comrades. Once the Germans sorted out ranks, Burton was separated from Winter to be sent to an officers' camp. Winter, Orr and Hellings were put on a train to Germany, but ominously, Orr and Hellings were taken off the train at Frankfurt in order that they could be further interrogated at Gestapo Headquarters there. Winter was taken on to Stalag VIIIB (later renamed Stalag 344) at Lamsdorf in Poland, close to the Czech border, where happily he was eventually joined by both Hellings and Orr. Hellings had survived his interrogation and as a Dutchman who had been a part of the Dutch Armed Forces he was an ordinary prisoner of war. The story for Orr, the Polish Jew, was rather different. He too had satisfied his interrogators, at least for the time being, but his problems were far from over, as the next chapter tells. Stalag VIIIB became known as a reprisal camp. Conditions were very tough, and from mid-October 1942 the prisoners were manacled. The manacles remained on for eleven months.

Tom Winter got himself a job in the post office in Stalag VIIIB, and in due course became sufficiently trusted by his guards to be let out of the camp from time to time on post office duty. He was able to stay in touch with British Intelligence by using the MI9 code with which he had been supplied by SOE, in letters to and from his wife. Gradually, Winter managed to make some useful contacts outside the wire, and began to undertake some sabotage work. He liaised with Czech dissidents and partisans, and trained them in the use of weapons and explosives. Winter reported that he even bribed some Czechs to take part in disruptive activities. Eventually though, the Germans became suspicious of what Winter was up to and curtailed his trips out of camp. Winter was placed under special detention. Happily for him, because of the Russian advances, he and others were moved in early 1945 to a different camp, near to the Belsen concentration camp, from which he escaped and crossed the advancing Allied line. Winter was awarded the Distinguished Conduct Medal for his work whilst at Stalag VIIIB.

Chapter 13

Adam Orr

When Private Adam Orr fell into enemy hands on 17 September, he knew that he was up against a very different danger to that faced by his comrades. Adam Orr had been born Abram Opoczynski in Lodz, Poland on 2 August 1915. He was 27 years old, and although by the time he joined M's Secret Service in July 1942 he professed to be an atheist, he had been born a Jew. Hitler and Nazi Germany had long made obvious their hatred of the Jews, and although the full horrors of the concentration camps had yet to be discovered, it was well known to the British authorities that captured Jewish soldiers would receive inhumane treatment if their racial origin became known. Since Abram Opoczynski's job with the SSRF obviously carried a real danger of capture in enemy territory, Abram Opoczynski had become Adam Orr, in the same way as Richard Lehniger had become Richard Leonard.

M and SOE were always aware of the risks their agents took, particularly those of Jewish extraction, and such agents were given cover stories that might enable them to remain undetected and to be held in ordinary prisoner of war camps. Abram Opoczynski's real father, Hersz Opoczynski, lived in Lodz with Abram's mother, two brothers and a sister. Abram also had an uncle who lived in Forest Gate, East London, his mother's brother Leopold Spiro. Abram himself had worked as a journalist in Lodz for a number of years before arriving in England in 1938, where he became a foreign correspondent for a Polish newspaper. In March 1940, he had joined the Pioneer Corps, and from there found his way into SOE. He spoke good English.

As Adam Orr, he was given a new family history, which he had to memorize and which ran as follows. He had been born in London. His father, Charles, was British and a member of the Church of England. Charles Orr had married a Christian Polish lady, Jadwiga Swatko, in London. Adam's education had included six years' schooling in Poland, but he had returned to England at the age of sixteen, and had worked as a freelance journalist. His mother had died when he was sixteen, and his father was in poor health. He had an uncle in London, Leopold Spiro (which was true), who was estranged from his father (untrue). If and when it became known that Orr had been captured by the enemy, his affairs would be handled by a special department based at the Hotel Victoria in Northumberland Avenue, London SW1. 'Charles Orr' would be in touch with his 'son' for as long as was necessary to satisfy the Germans of Orr's origins.

Orr and Hellings both survived an unpleasant period at Gestapo Headquarters in Frankfurt, and in due course were transferred to Stalag VIIIB. Orr, in an attempt to strengthen his position and obtain better treatment, told the Germans during interrogation that he was in fact an acting sergeant. Back in England it was confirmed that Orr was missing in action – either captured or dead – and his case was taken over by Major Neville Murray, of Room 238 at the Hotel Victoria. Major Murray assumed the role of Opoczynski's fictional father, and all correspondence concerning Opoczynski/Orr now went through his hands. On 26 September, Murray wrote to Opoczynski's real next of kin in London, his uncle Leopold, informing him that his nephew was posted as missing, and asking him to come to Room 238 on 30 September. Leopold Spiro kept the appointment and Major Murray briefed him fully on the situation. He swore Spiro to secrecy for his nephew's sake, and asked him to sign a declaration that read: 'I, the under-signed, recognise that if I make any disclosure whatever concerning the aliais or real whereabouts of my nephew Abram Opoczynski, other than: "that he has been reported as missing whilst proceeding overseas", neither the War Office nor the witness to this document can be held responsible for the consequences of such disclosure.'

In mid-October, the first notification came through that Orr was a prisoner of war, and in mid-November an official message dated 5 October finally reached Major Murray, confirming that Orr was presently held at Stalag VIIIB. Postcards and letters began to arrive from Orr, all beginning 'Dear Father' and addressed to 'Charles Orr' in accordance with the cover story, at an address where they would be redirected to Major Murray. The contents of the letters are still available at the National Archives and clearly Orr, like Winter, was using code to send information to Murray and SOE. Murray would copy the letters on to Leopold Spiro, substituting the name Abram for Adam – Murray kept Spiro informed at all stages of Abram's welfare.

Throughout the autumn of 1942, all seemed to be going well, and the cover story appeared to have convinced his German captors that Orr was simply another prisoner of war. SOE dealt with the complication of Orr's claim that he was a sergeant and not a private sympathetically, and arranged a temporary promotion (although he would remain on the same pay as before). Murray, as Orr's father, arranged for parcels to be sent to him through the Red Cross, as might be expected. 'Charles Orr' included references in his letters to such pleasures as hearing the sound of church bells ringing, a Christian sentiment, while Adam wished his father a 'Merry Christmas' in December, and sent him a Christmas card. The picture of Orr as a Christian was gently being reinforced.

In January 1943, Murray felt sufficiently confident that Orr's cover was firmly established to kill off his fictional father with a heart attack. Uncle Leopold Spiro was miraculously reconciled with Orr's father on his deathbed, and therefore could now take over the correspondence with his nephew. However, Murray briefed Spiro very carefully on what he could say, and gave him a set of written rules as to what should and should not go into his letters. Leopold Spiro was obviously a very sensible man however, and preferred to send any letter that he had prepared to Murray first for vetting. This became their established practice. Undoubtedly, very great care went into preserving Abram Opoczynski's non-Jewish identity, and as the months of 1943 and then 1944 went by, Murray must have been pleased with the result of his efforts. Opoczynski himself was also obviously adept in maintaining the pretence.

Using the code they were given for use in the event of capture, SOE's agents were thus able to keep in contact with their bosses through letters home. SOE in any event was concerned to do all it could for their welfare. A letter from Captain Sam Darby, an intelligence officer with the SSRF, to Leslie Prout in April 1943, gives an idea of this. Prout and Darby were concerned about the problem of getting Red Cross parcels (no doubt containing 'special items') to Jan Hellings, who had given his mother in occupied Holland as his next of kin. It was agreed that if the Red Cross could be persuaded to accept them, SOE would send Hellings parcels as if from a personal friend, and would foot the bill of £2 per parcel. Darby, who had joined the SSRF after the capture of Hellings, Winter and Orr, was particularly interested to know from Prout which POW camp Hellings was in, and commented: 'It would also help me considerably if you could see your way to forwarding to me any letters which you receive from our "old boys". The more I know about them, the more I can help them if help is needed.'

On 23 January 1944, Tom Winter wrote to Les Prout who was in England: 'Hollings [sic], Orr and myself are keeping fit, and looking forward to a return to England. Give my regards to Major Appleyard and the others of the team. Have you heard anything from Graham [Hayes]? Is he in England, or is he still away?'

All went well with Orr until March 1945, by which time Winter had finally made his escape. The German Reich was crumbling fast in the face of the advance of the Allies, and in particular at Stalag VIIIB, the Russians. From early 1945, as occupied Polish towns fell to the Russian army, efforts were made by the Germans to move Allied prisoners of war away from the fighting, in order to avoid their being liberated. In the bitter cold of winter, the inmates of Stalag VIIIB were marched from the camp, through the countryside towards Germany, in what became known later as the Long March (or sometimes as the Death March). The journey lasted many weeks and very many prisoners died along the route.

During the march, one mass of prisoners including Adam Orr was being taken south from Nuremburg to Munich. The long column offered a variety of opportunities for escape, and Orr, who had now been a prisoner of the Germans for two and a half years, decided to take his chance. On 1 April, as they were walking along the autobahn at Oppenheim, Orr and two others, Company Sergeant Major Cadman and Lance Corporal Arthur Todd, made their escape. Private Forbes Clubb, described as being of 2 Parachute Regiment (presumably 2nd Battalion, The Parachute Regiment), later reported witnessing it. However, what happened to them after that is not clear. Cadman eventually got back to England, and but there appears to be no record of what became of Abram Opoczynski once he left the column. When the war ended, extensive efforts were made by SOE to discover his whereabouts – his SOE personnel file reveals various enquiries made in September and October 1945. Eventually, it was discovered that Opoczynski had not survived. At the Durnbach War Cemetery in Bad Tolz, Bayern, about 40 kilometres south of Munich, there is a grave marked as that of Abraham Opoczynski, known as Adam Orr, of the Special Operations Executive. It records that he died on 12 April 1945, twelve days after his escape, and very shortly before the end of the war.

Chapter 14

Graham Hayes

Graham Hayes found himself in the water unwounded, with only a scratch on his chin. His first action was to try to save Gus March-Phillipps, who it seems must have been injured somehow and was virtually unable to swim. Hayes did his best to support March-Phillipps, but eventually lost hold of him, and he slipped away. Hayes himself kept afloat and despite increasing exhaustion managed to make his way along the coast, coming ashore close to Hamel au Prêtre, near Vierville-sur-Mer.

It was still dark and Hayes crawled up the beach, where he lay cold and exhausted for a while, recovering his strength as best he could. He was an immensely fit and determined young man, as he had proved many times during Operation Postmaster and since. Of those who had reached the beach and managed to evade immediate capture, Hayes was the man most likely to succeed in escaping. In his quiet way, he was very confident and self-contained, and would do well on his own.

Weighing up his options, Hayes knew that he had to find some sort of shelter before dawn. Although the Germans would not know exactly how many commandos had landed, there would be a hue and cry throughout the area for some days yet. Having rested long enough to regain some strength, Hayes made his way inland from the beach. It is highly likely that he was now unarmed, having dumped any weapons that he had been carrying in order to increase his chances in the sea. He had no way of knowing exactly where he was and decided he would have to chance making contact with one of the locals. He spoke only schoolboy French. However, this was occupied France, not Vichy France, and any intelligence from SOE would have informed him that many local people hated the German occupation, and were sympathetic to the Resistance.

Before approaching anyone, however, Hayes wanted to put some distance between himself and the coast. Therefore he walked inland for about three miles. He found himself on the outskirts of a village (in fact Asnières-en-Bessin), chose a farmhouse and knocked on its door. Had he made a bad choice, he would have had little option but to run. The door was opened by the farmer, Marcel Lemasson, and Hayes found himself in luck. Lemasson was sympathetic to the Resistance and had no wish to hand Hayes over to the Germans. The firing on the coast had been heard by everyone, and Hayes' uniform and general condition made it quite clear who he was. Lemasson welcomed Hayes into the house, and when asked, Hayes introduced himself simply as 'Graham Hayes, British Officer'. Whilst his wife cooked Hayes a meal, Lemasson himself went to wake the village mayor, Paul de Brunville, who lived nearby at the Château d'Asnières.

It was by now daylight, and to move Hayes from the farm would be dangerous. However, Lemasson was worried about the possibility of a German search of the area, and believed that the mayor, an educated man, would know what to do. Paul de Brunville was also a Resistance sympathizer and when informed by Lemasson of the situation he decided that it would be best to fetch Hayes under his own roof. He and his 22-year-old son, Olivier, went to Lemasson's home and after dark that Sunday evening they brought Hayes to the Château d'Asnières.

Soon after they were safely home a German patrol passed by on the road outside the chateau. De Brunville gave Hayes a set of civilian clothes to change into, fed him and hid him the hayloft of his barn for the time being. The next problem was how to get Hayes away – the obvious answer being to pass him over to the Resistance. De Brunville decided to contact a man called Septime Humann, whom he knew to be a fervent patriot, and on the Monday morning sent his son Olivier to see Humann in the nearby village of Jouay-Mondaye. Humann agreed to help. He had a friend called Suzanne Septaux, who lived in the village of Le Pin, many miles away near Lisieux, whom he thought might take Hayes in, and whom he believed to be a member of the Resistance. The only problem was that because of the urgency of getting Hayes out of the area, there was no time to warn his friend that he was bringing the fugitive to her. Humann told Olivier de Brunville to get Hayes to the railway station in the nearby town of Bayeux on the following morning, buy him a ticket, and put him on the 9.00 am train to Lisieux. He, Humann, would also be on that train, travelling separately, but would guide Hayes from Lisieux to Suzanne Septaux's house in Le Pin.

Olivier returned to Asnières-en-Bessin to inform his father and Graham Hayes of the plan. It was decided the best way to get Hayes to Bayeux station would be by bicycle. Olivier would cycle off ahead, and Hayes would follow at sufficient distance for it not to be obvious that the two men were together.

Anderson Manor – the Commando Camelot (*courtesy of the estate of the late Major Leslie Prout*)

MTB 344, 'The Little Pisser' (*courtesy of Chris Rooney*)

Major Gus March-Phillipps DSO, MBE
(*courtesy of Special Forces Club*)

Major Geoffrey Appleyard DSO, MC
(*courtesy of Special Forces Club*)

Captain Graham Hayes MC (*courtesy of Malcolm Paul Hayes*)

Major Anders Lassen VC, MC and two bars (*courtesy of Special Forces Club*)

Richard Lehniger, with his wife Lilly and daughter Irene, in late 1940 (*courtesy of his daughter, Mrs Irene Walters*)

Allan Williams with his mother, circa 1940 (*courtesy of Bob Harris*)

Major John Gwynne, the planning officer (*courtesy of the National Archives*)

Major General Sir Colin Gubbins DSO, MC, 'M' (*courtesy of the National Archives*)

Brian Reynolds/Bingham (*courtesy of the National Archives*)

Lieutenant Freddie Bourne, RN (*original source untraced*)

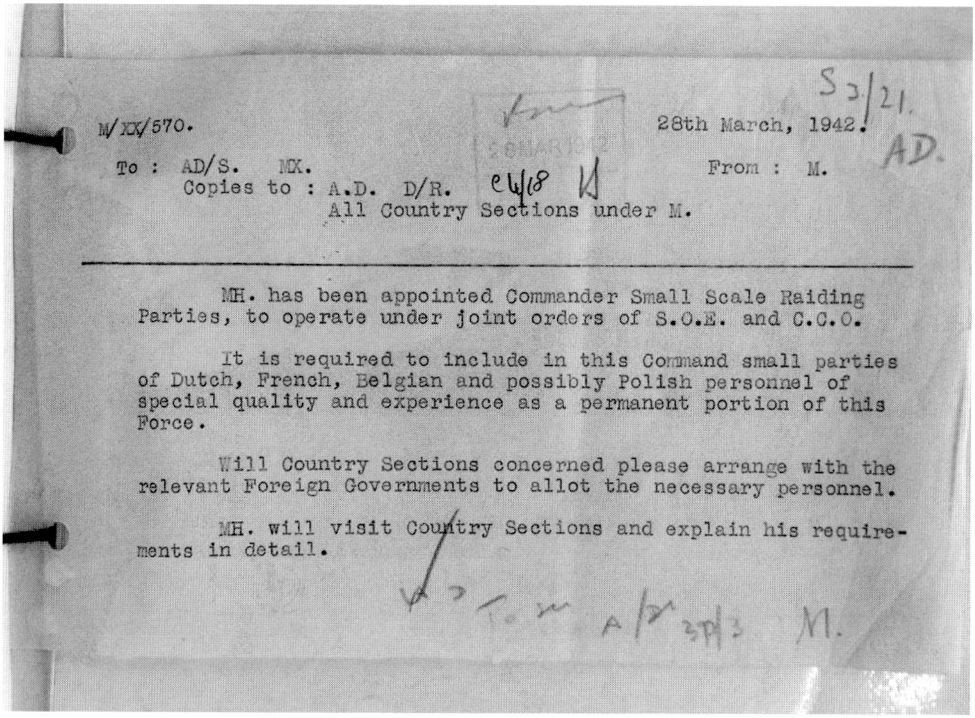

M/XX/570. 28th March, 1942.

To: AD/S. MX. From: M.
Copies to: A.D. D/R.
All Country Sections under M.

MH. has been appointed Commander Small Scale Raiding Parties, to operate under joint orders of S.O.E. and C.C.O.

It is required to include in this Command small parties of Dutch, French, Belgian and possibly Polish personnel of special quality and experience as a permanent portion of this Force.

Will Country Sections concerned please arrange with the relevant Foreign Governments to allot the necessary personnel.

MH. will visit Country Sections and explain his requirements in detail.

M's memo regarding recruitment into the SSRF (*courtesy of the National Archives*)

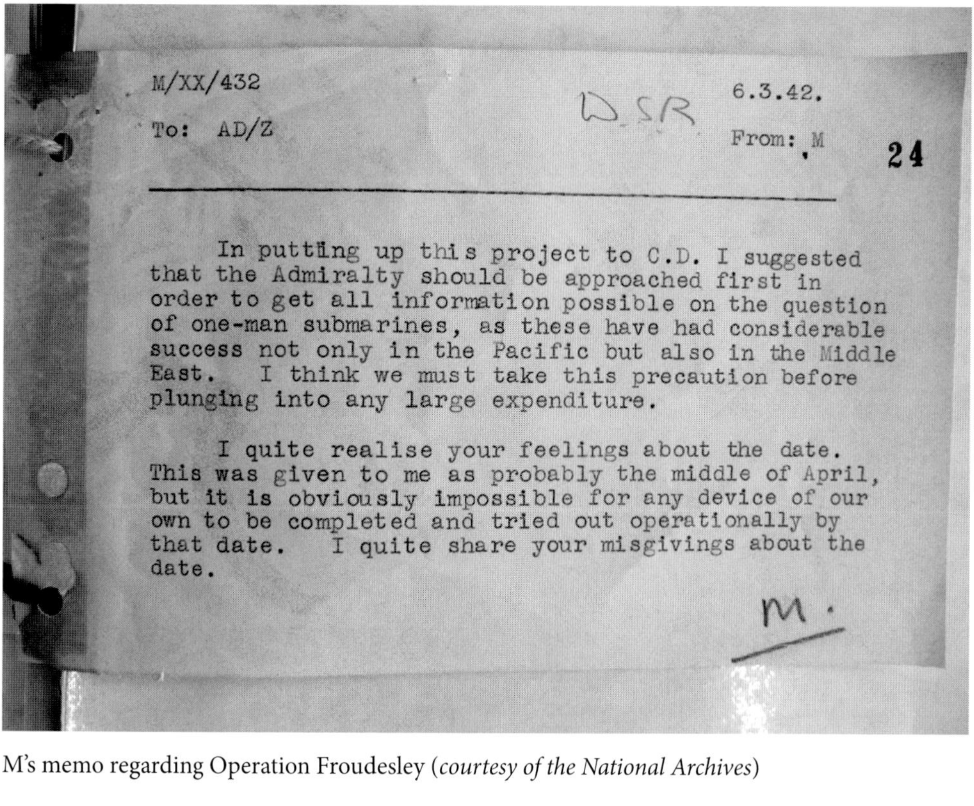

M/XX/432 6.3.42.

To: AD/Z From: M

In putting up this project to C.D. I suggested that the Admiralty should be approached first in order to get all information possible on the question of one-man submarines, as these have had considerable success not only in the Pacific but also in the Middle East. I think we must take this precaution before plunging into any large expenditure.

I quite realise your feelings about the date. This was given to me as probably the middle of April, but it is obviously impossible for any device of our own to be completed and tried out operationally by that date. I quite share your misgivings about the date.

M.

M's memo regarding Operation Froudesley (*courtesy of the National Archives*)

KNIVES, THUMB
Catalogue No. JS 188.

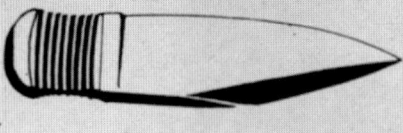 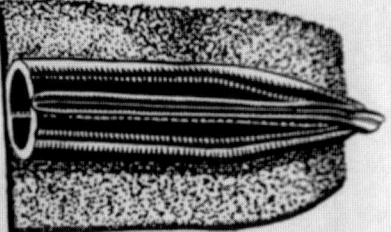

DESCRIPTION. A very small, dagger-shaped knife, sharpened for the full length of the blade along one edge, and for three-quarters of the length along the other; the remaining quarter is flattened to give a grip for the thumb. The hilt is only one inch long, and the Knife can easily be concealed in the hand.

The Knife is provided with a leather sheath, with flaps which can be sewn to the clothing.

DIMENSIONS. In sheath 4" x 2". Knife 3¼" x ¾".   **WEIGHT.** ¼ oz.

PACKING AND SPECIAL NOTES. As required.

MUCUNA
(ITCHING POWDER)

Catalogue No. NS 300.

DESCRIPTION. This powder is composed of minute seed hairs which owing to their peculiar structure cause considerable itching when applied to the skin.

METHOD OF USE. The greatest effect is produced by applying the powder to the inside of underclothing.

PACKING AND SPECIAL NOTES.
As required.
This material is supplied in foot powder tins for the purpose of camouflage.

SOE's *Descriptive Catalogue of Special Devices and Supplies* included items as diverse as miniature knives (top) and itching powder (below) (*courtesy of the National Archives*)

Colin Ogden Smith (*courtesy of the National Archives*)

Major Oswald 'Mickey' Rooney (*courtesy of his son Chris Rooney*)

Lieutenant Colonel Bill Stirling (*courtesy of the National Archives*)

Lieutenant Henk Brinkgreve (*courtesy of the National Archives*)

The SSRF went to the Lake District for training in rock climbing. Left to right: Lord Francis Howard, behind him André Desgranges, Jock 'Haggis' Taylor, unknown, Graham Hayes, Anders Lassen (*original source unknown*)

Practising dory landings, Graham Hayes in shorts at the bow (*courtesy of Chris Rooney*)

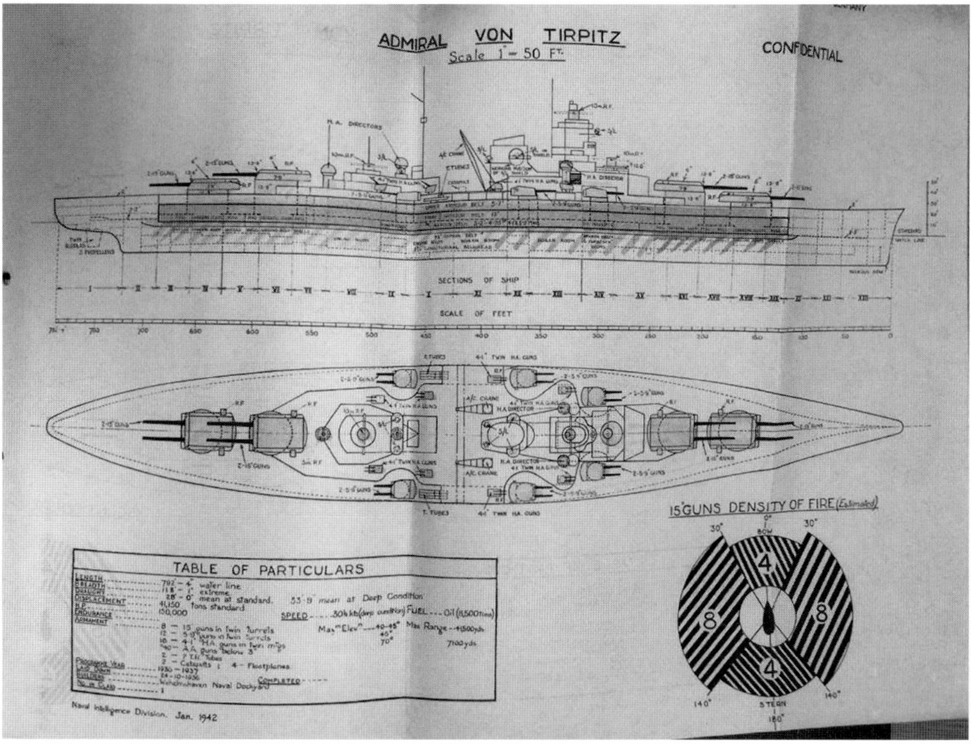

Plan of the *Admiral von Tirpitz*, taken from SOE Intelligence files (*courtesy of the National Archives*)

A Welman miniature submarine, photographed in late 1942 (*courtesy of the National Archives*)

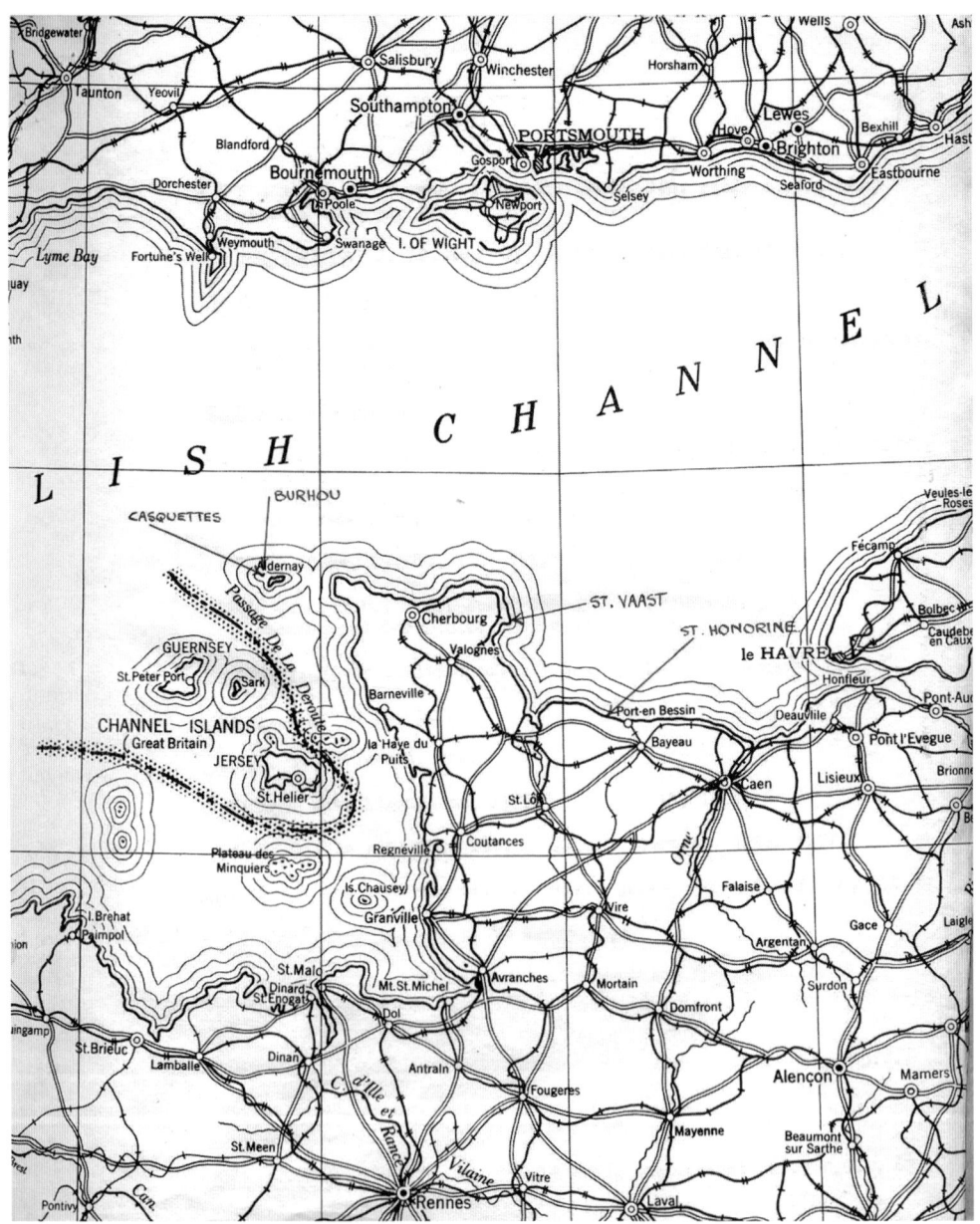

Map of the English Channel, marking raids by MTB 344 in August and September (*courtesy of the National Archives*)

Operation Barricade: the intended targets (*courtesy of the National Archives*)

Operation Dryad: Casquets Rock (*courtesy of the postcard collection of Klaus Huelse*)

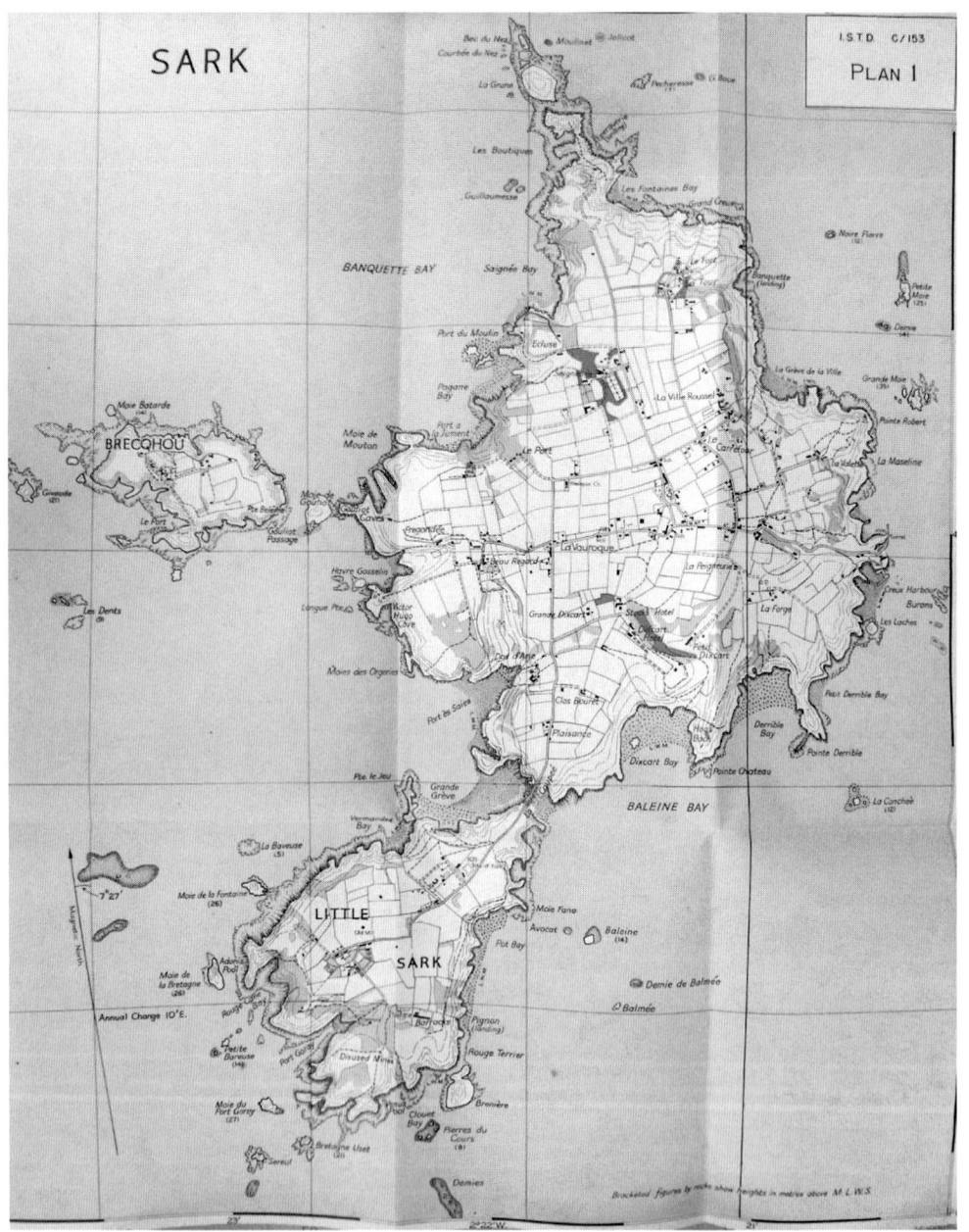

Wartime map of Sark, used for intelligence briefings (*courtesy of the National Archives*)

Intelligence photo of the Hog's Back, Sark, used for intelligence briefings (*courtesy of National Archives*)

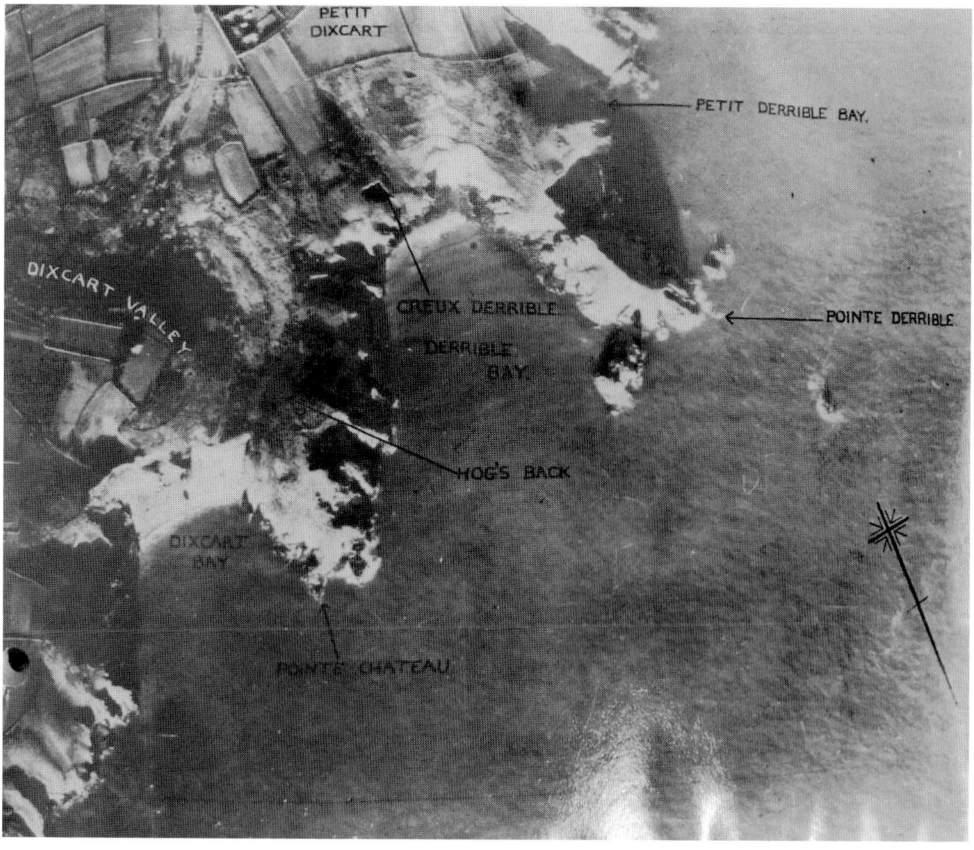

Aerial photo of Baleine Bay, Sark (*courtesy of the National Archives*)

La Jespellaire, photographed in 1979 (*courtesy of After the Battle publications*)

The annexe to the Dixcart Hotel, apparently unchanged in 1979 (*courtesy of After the Battle publications*)

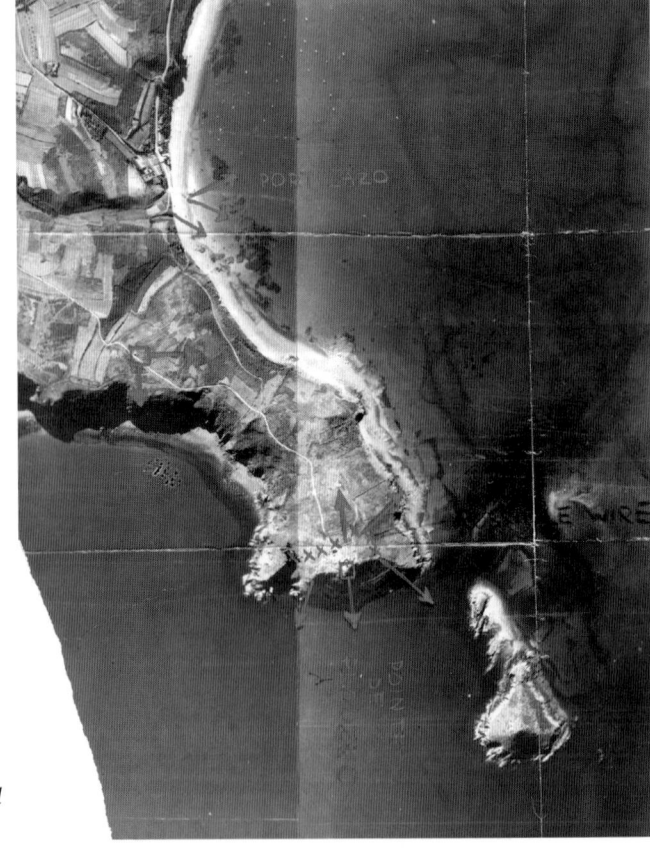

Operation Fahrenheit: aerial photograph of the Pointe de Plouzac (*courtesy of the National Archives*)

Operation Witticism: aerial photograph of St Peter Port, Guernsey (*courtesy of the National Archives*)

Operation Huckaback: intelligence photos of Herm (*courtesy of the National Archives*)

Intelligence photo of the main house for Operation Huckaback (*courtesy of the National Archives*)

Intelligence photo of Belvoir beach and Shell beach, Herm, for Operation Huckaback (*courtesy of the National Archives*)

Hayes had no papers, so if stopped by police or soldiers would be bound to be arrested. If Olivier de Brunville was seen to be connected to him, he too would be arrested and quite possibly shot. The journey was a risky affair for both men.

In the event, all went well. On Tuesday, 15 September, young de Brunville cycled, with Hayes following, to the station at Bayeux. There, still keeping apart from Hayes, Olivier bought a ticket to Lisieux and managed to slip it to Hayes. The station was busy, and there were many Germans intending to catch the same 9.00 am train. Hayes, with Olivier's help, made silent contact with Septime Humann, who passed him a copy of the local paper, the *Bonhomme Normande*. Both men took their places on the train, Humann finding a seat in a compartment, Hayes standing in the corridor outside, apparently engrossed in his paper.

It was now, perhaps, that Hayes' months of experience as a covert agent in West Africa was of greatest value to him. The crew of the Q ship *Maid Honor*, on which he had served, had become experts at pretending to be what they were not. They always travelled in plain clothes, and had on a number of occasions passed themselves off as civilians when challenged. The *Maid Honor* had carried a neutral Swedish flag, and Hayes was able to pass for a Swede, having learned a little of the language when sailing around the world with a Swedish crew on the windjammer *Pommern*, before the war. Thus, although there is no evidence that Hayes spoke very much French, he had experience of covert work and a cool nerve. Now dressed in French civilian clothes, he played his role on the train sufficiently well to excite no comment from his travelling companions. He stuck his head in the newspaper, produced his ticket when requested, and after a journey of 75 minutes they arrived in Lisieux.

Septime Humann left the train first and then Hayes, a respectable distance behind. The ticket barrier was a potential hazard, but Hayes surrendered his ticket and passed through without being questioned. He proceeded to follow Humann on foot in the general direction of Le Pin. The next danger was the checkpoint on the edge of town, but again Humann and Hayes, each still apparently walking alone, passed through without challenge. Hayes, with no papers, must have been tense and anxious until Lisieux was a good distance behind them, but he would have been too professional an agent to show it.

The two men walked on from Lisieux to Le Pin. For part of the way it seemed safe for them to walk together. Once they arrived near the village of Le Pin, however, Humann took Hayes into a small wood, where he told him to wait out of sight whilst he, Humann, visited the house of Suzanne Septaux. Humann had not had the opportunity to warn his friend even that he was coming, let alone bringing with him an English soldier. In fact, Humann had chosen well. Mme Suzanne Septaux, then aged 56, was indeed a member of the local Resistance group, and when she learned of the situation she was delighted to help. She sent her nephew, who happened to be with her, with Humann to fetch Graham Hayes, and they brought him to her house shortly thereafter. It was around midday on 15 September 1942. Hayes was to stay with Suzanne Septaux for over a month.

Thus within a little over two days of landing on the beach at St Laurent-sur-Mer, Hayes had successfully got himself into the hands of the French Resistance, and had travelled a long way from the area of the raid to a 'safe house'. It had taken considerable physical strength to get himself to Asnières-en-Bessin, and coolness and nerve to make the journey to Le Pin. He had received very considerable help from a number of French people, all strangers to him, at substantial risk to themselves. At this point the other three escapers, Burton, Orr and Hellings were still on the loose also, hoping to walk a very considerable distance south, to cross into Spain. However, just two days later on 17 September they were captured, leaving Hayes as the only free survivor of Operation Aquatint.

Once in the relative safety of Mme Septaux's home, Hayes had time to worry about the fate of his close friends and comrades. Of March-Phillipps' death he undoubtedly knew – he had tried to help him in the sea and had failed. Of the others in the landing party he knew little, save that Tony Hall had been left for dead on the beach. Hayes did not know whether MTB 344 had been sunk, which would mean his childhood friend Geoffrey Appleyard had also died, or whether it had got away, possibly with casualties on board. Likewise, the fate of his old sergeant and fellow Postmaster veteran, Tom Winter, remained unknown to him.

Graham Hayes remained with Suzanne Septaux for longer than the Resistance had intended, because he fell ill. The cause was something that the Germans could take no credit for – Hayes suffered from food poisoning as a result of a meal he had been given by his helpers. Happily, the doctor who treated him was also the head of the local Resistance group, Dr Paul Hautechaud. Hautechaud had set up his group in early 1941, and was part of a wider network which had come to the notice of the French section of M's Secret Service, SOE. In the summer of 1942, one of that wider network, Henri Frager, codename 'Paul', was smuggled to London to liaise with Maurice Buckmaster, the head of the French section, and returned in company with two SOE agents, Commander Nicholas Boddington and Mme Yvonne Rudellat. Following Boddington's assessment of the network, a formal relationship with SOE had been established.

Thus, on the face of it, Hayes had fallen on his feet. He was an SOE agent in the hands of an SOE accredited Resistance group. Its head, Dr Hautechaud, now faced the task of getting Hayes out of Occupied France, and to safety. As is well known, the French Resistance ran a number of highly successful escape lines, commonly smuggling Allied servicemen across the Pyrenees into neutral Spain. Plans had to be carefully laid, and Hautechaud had to liaise with various members of the Resistance network. In the meantime, Hayes stayed with Suzanne Septaux, in the relative safety of her fairly isolated house in Le Pin. He had been there for two weeks when he fell ill with food poisoning. He also suffered a complication with an old knee injury, and was treated by Dr Hautechaud for both conditions. It was not until mid to late October that he was fit enough to be moved on.

Hautechaud made contact with another agent called Raoul, real name Robert Kieffer. Raoul was the liaison man for the Resistance network between Paris and Normandy, and a plan evolved that Hayes should be taken to the Paris area, then taken down an escape route by train from Paris, eventually arriving in neutral Spain. A veteran of the Operation Postmaster raid in January 1942, when he, March-Phillipps and the rest of Maid Honor Force had outraged the Spanish by stealing an Italian liner and two German tugs out of the neutral harbour of Santa Isabel, at Fernando Po, Spanish Guinea, Hayes must have appreciated the irony that mainland Spain was now to be his gateway to freedom. Happily, the Spanish government had never been able to discover who was responsible for the Postmaster raid, and therefore no official blame had attached to the British.

Hautechaud understandably put the arrangements into the hands of Raoul. It was agreed that Raoul would take Hayes by train to the Paris area, and would place him in a safe house there until the necessary papers and passes could be obtained, after which an agent would take him by train and on foot to cross the Spanish border. A date of 20 October was fixed for Hayes' departure from Le Pin. Early that morning, Hayes and Suzanne Septaux were picked up by Dr Hautechaud in his car, and driven to the Cathedral Square in Liseux. He dropped them off in front of the cathedral and drove away. Suzanne Septaux stayed with Hayes – to have left the Englishman alone would have exposed him to the curiosity of any Germans in the vicinity. In company with a middle-aged woman who might well be his mother, all seemed natural. Raoul and a companion were due to meet them outside the cathedral in time to catch the 9.00 am train to Paris. The hour came and went, but there was no sign of Raoul. In fact, he and his companion were travelling down from Paris to fetch Hayes, and they had missed their train. Graham Hayes waited stoically, as Suzanne Septaux became more and more concerned. If Raoul failed to turn up, she would have to find a means to get Hayes back to the safety of her home in Le Pin. She told Hayes to go into the cathedral and to wait there – a single worshipper would attract no attention and would be left in peace.

At about 0930 hrs, Raoul appeared in the square, together with his companion, a man called Robert Goubeau, known in the Resistance simply as 'Bob'. The two men made their apologies and Suzanne Septaux fetched Hayes from the cathedral. After a hurried goodbye to his hostess of the past five weeks, Hayes followed Raoul and Bob towards the station. He was given his ticket and all three men boarded the next express bound for Paris. As before, Hayes' instructions were explicit – keep apart from your escort, and do not speak to them or to anyone during the journey. Hayes understood that Raoul and Bob were only couriers, who would take him to Saint-Lazare station, where he would be handed over to the Paris network. He would meet two men, one of whom would look after him for as long as he was to stay in the Paris area.

This journey also passed without incident, Hayes obeying his instructions. He stayed close to the two Resistance men, but never acknowledged their presence in any way. On arrival at Saint-Lazare station in Paris, all three men passed safely through the ticket barrier at the end of the platform, and then Hayes was handed over to the two men of the Paris network waiting there. They were introduced to him as 'Paul', the organizer of his escape, and 'Armand', who would house him while the details were finalized and false papers obtained for him. The meeting was brief, Raoul and Bob melted away into the crowded station, and Paul told Hayes to go with Armand, which he willingly did, no doubt relieved by his safe arrival in Paris and impressed by the efficiency of the Resistance. Armand, real name Jean-Louis Ortet, took Hayes to his home in Garches, a suburb of Paris.

Graham Hayes was now entirely reliant upon Armand, but felt no cause for concern. Everything that the French Resistance had promised to do for him so far, they had achieved with efficiency. Hayes no doubt felt reassured when, the day after his arrival in Paris, he received a visit from Raoul, who was still in the city. Raoul came to Armand's home in Garches and, during his conversation with Hayes, offered to deliver by hand any letters of thanks that Hayes might like to write to his helpers in the Le Pin area. Hayes was happy to take up the offer and wrote to both Suzanne Septaux and Dr Paul Hautechaud to inform them of his safe arrival in Paris, thanking them for all their help and kindness. As he had promised, Raoul eventually delivered those letters to their intended recipients.

Armand, who was responsible for Hayes' day-to-day care, but who perhaps had little in common with him, now took Hayes to meet an Englishwoman living in Garches, Mrs Winifred Davidson. Mrs Davidson's husband had been interned by the Germans as an enemy national, but she had been allowed to stay at liberty with her two young children. Armand took Hayes to her house and it was not long before the two became firm friends, both no doubt enjoying the opportunity to have lengthy conversations in English. Hayes told Mrs Davidson something of how he had come to be in France, and she eventually offered to write a letter for him to let those close to him know that he was alive and well. Graham Hayes had fallen for a young woman called Jane Dreyer, whom he had met during his time in Capetown, South Africa, on the way back from Operation Postmaster. She was employed there by SOE as the secretary to the head of the South African Mission, and they had come to an understanding. Mrs Davidson believed that Jane Dreyer was Hayes' fiancée. As an interned 'enemy national' in German-occupied territory, Mrs Davidson was entitled to send letters through the Red Cross to relatives and friends outside German territory, and she offered to write to Miss Dreyer on Graham Hayes' behalf. Jane Dreyer would then be able to get in contact with Hayes' family. On 27 October 1942, about a week after she had first met Hayes, Mrs Davidson sent a letter through the Red Cross to Jane Dreyer. It said simply: 'All well here. Do not worry. Graham sends his love also.' It was sent under Mrs Davidson's name, from her address at 245 Grande Rue, Garches.

Hayes' stay with Armand in Garches lasted for two weeks. During that time he met with Mrs Davidson often, and eventually told her much about what had happened at St Laurent-sur-Mer. He couldn't hide his distress at having been unable to save Gus March-Phillipps in the cold waters of the Channel, or his concern at what might have happened to Appleyard and the others. He also spoke at length about his family. Eventually, in early November, Armand told Hayes that everything was prepared for his departure. The papers Hayes needed were ready, coming apparently from a friendly police official. Two days later, Hayes went with Armand to Austerlitz railway station in Paris, to catch a train with him to Toulouse. From there, they would make their way together to the Spanish border, where Armand would hand Hayes over to a guide who would take him to safety in Spain. The false papers would only be necessary as far as the border – once in neutral Spain, Hayes could declare his true name and rank.

When Mrs Davidson said goodbye to Hayes before his journey into Paris, she was full of confidence that he would successfully complete his journey home to England. She gave him a letter addressed to her father, who lived on the edge of London, which he promised to deliver personally. Graham Hayes too no doubt set off with Armand fully confident that he would soon be back in England, or at the very least safely in Spain and out of enemy hands. Everything had so far gone so well, and the French Resistance, from the very start, had proved to be trustworthy and efficient. What Hayes could not know was that he and many of the friends that he had made since arriving in France had been duped. Raoul (Robert Kieffer), the liaison man between Calvados and Paris, was a double agent, and in truth, from the moment he had left Lisieux, Hayes had been in the hands of the enemy. Raoul's companion on the journey to Paris, Bob (Robert Goubeau), was also a double agent. Both men had been turned by the Abwehr, the German army's secret counter-espionage service, and now worked for the enemy against their own countrymen. The two men who had met Hayes upon his arrival in Paris were also enemies – Armand (Jean-Louis Ortet) was another double agent, and Paul was in fact their German handler, Sergeant Hugo Bleicher, who was bilingual and could pass as a Frenchman with ease. Everything that had happened after Hayes' departure from Lisieux had been a charade, designed to maintain the cover of the double agents, whilst gathering as much information as possible about who was working with or helping the Resistance. The Abwehr had been using Hayes, and the letters of thanks that he had written to Madame Septaux and Dr Hautechaud had been taken by Armand to Abwehr headquarters in Paris, where they were copied, before being delivered by him to their intended recipients. They would be used as evidence against them.

The story that Armand later told Mrs Davidson after he returned from his 'trip to the border' was that all had gone well, and that he had handed over Hayes to a guide at the Spanish border. That may well have been true, and a part of the careful disguise of the operation, because Hayes was later to say that he had indeed reached Spain, but that the Spanish had handed him back to the Germans. If that was true, then those in Spain who were responsible broke the laws of neutrality, as had Maid Honor Force in their attack on Santa Isabel early in that same year. Whatever the truth, Graham Hayes was returned to Paris as a prisoner of the Germans before the end of November 1942, and was incarcerated in the Fresnes prison there for many months in solitary confinement.

As the months went by, nothing more was heard of Graham Hayes. The letter that Mrs Davidson had sent to Jane Dreyer in Capetown was delayed and did not arrive until the beginning of June 1943. Miss Dreyer immediately sent a telegram to Hayes' family in Linton on Wharfe, telling them of the good news and simultaneously, under her codename of DZ.41, cabled SOE in London. M himself had been concerned to discover Hayes' fate, since he had met him a number of times and held him in high regard. Although the letter was now months out of date, there was good reason to think that Hayes might still be at large in France, perhaps working with the Resistance, or in Spain. Sadly, of course, Hayes remained in German hands.

Other British prisoners were moved in and out of the Fresnes Prison, and one or two had contact with Hayes. Flight Lieutenant Peter Waddington arrived there in late May 1943, and found himself in a cell underneath Hayes. The two men could not meet, but each morning and night they would call out greetings to each other and they were also able to 'talk' by tapping out messages in morse code. Waddington learned that Hayes had been caught in Spain and handed over to the Germans (undoubtedly a planned arrangement). Hayes did his best to cheer up Waddington, who was in low spirits after his own capture, and said that he had been well treated and had been told that he would ultimately be taken to a prisoner of war camp. Hayes asked Waddington whether, if he reached a POW camp before Hayes, he would write to Jane Dreyer. Waddington of course agreed, and memorized Dreyer's address in Capetown. In fact, Hayes left Fresnes prison first, so Waddington did not write the letter.

Whatever his German interrogators may have said to Hayes, he was never transferred to a prison camp. On 13 July 1943, Graham Hayes was taken out of his cell and shot. His body was buried in the graveyard at Ivry. His elder brother Dennis, to whom he was very close, and who himself was working in munitions, having been found unfit for military service, recalled much later that there was a moment on 13 July 1943 when he felt so dreadfully unwell that he had to stop driving and get out of his vehicle. He concluded that this must have been the moment that Graham was shot.

Nobody at SOE, or in Hayes' family, heard any more of him after the arrival of Mrs Davidson's letter in early June. When France fell to the Allies in 1944, both M at SOE and the Hayes family did all they could to find out his whereabouts, but without success. Those who had helped him in France, including of course Mrs Davidson, told all that they knew, but it was not until late July 1945 that the records of the Fresnes prison were discovered and Hayes' grave identified in the Ivry graveyard.

The execution of Graham Hayes was undoubtedly murder. However, after the war, a German report was recovered that purported to justify his execution. It was dated 12 January 1944, and was apparently prepared in answer to the Kharkov War Crimes Trial of four members of the German military by the Soviets in December 1943, following massacres in the Kharkov area. The introduction to the report reads (when translated): 'Re Counter-Action to Kharkov Fake Trial, For exploitation for propaganda purposes, the following cases come into consideration'. There follows a list of various unfortunate commandos who had been captured and shot before January 1944. The entry at number 6 on the list reads:

Landing at Port en Bessin

Death sentence on Captain Graham Hayes b. 9.7.14 in Leeds, Hayes landed near Cherbourg with a fairly large Commando on 13.9.42. On retreating his boat was shot up. He swam back to the coast, remained in hiding in civilian clothes for a month with French people, and was engaged in espionage activities. He was particularly active in trying to obtain information about landing-grounds and in trying to enlist agents. He was shadowed for some time by a V man and unmasked. He was arrested in Paris on 28.10.42. On the 22.2.43 he was condemned to death by the Court of the Commandant of Paris. Sentence was carried out on 13.7.43.

The account seems clearly untrue. Hayes was arrested on or near the Spanish border, having been taken there by a German double agent. If he had been tried and condemned to death on 22 February 1943, it seems inevitable that he would have told Waddington about that in the Fresnes prison in May 1943, when the two were in contact with each other. The most likely explanation is that Hayes was shot without trial, quite possibly under the authority of Hitler's Commando Order, which had resulted from Operation Basalt (see below) in which he took no part. After the war, lawyers argued that even the Commando Order could not be used to justify such an execution. Hitler's order related to the instantaneous execution of commandos caught behind the lines. It did not apply to men who had already been held for days or months as prisoners of war, which was Graham Hayes' situation.

Of the French double agents who betrayed Hayes and many of the French Resistance, 'Armand' was found murdered before the end of the war, possibly executed by the Resistance for his treachery. 'Raoul' was tried for treason by the French after the war, and was condemned to death. The sentence was eventually commuted to imprisonment, and he was released following an armistice in 1953. 'Bob', his companion on the train from Lisieux to Paris was also tried, and received a sentence of five years hard labour.

Chapter 15

André Desgranges

André Desgranges was separated from Winter after their arrival at Caen. As a member of the Free French Forces, he, like Jan Hellings, was entitled to be treated as a prisoner of war in the normal way. So far as SOE was concerned, Desgranges, like the others, had disappeared, and they could only wait to see if he was registered in due course as a prisoner of war. If not, it would mean that he was either dead or on the loose in France somewhere. The months passed, and as with Graham Hayes, nothing was heard from Desgranges. Then, to everybody's surprise, in early May 1943, SOE in Baker Street heard that Desgranges was free in Spain, and now in the care of SOE's escape network there.

After some time, he was smuggled out of Spain and eventually arrived at SOE's headquarters in North Africa, known as Massingham Mission, on 2 July 1943. As it happened, Geoffrey Appleyard and a number of others of the SSRF were in North Africa at the same time. Safely back in Allied hands, Desgranges was brought speedily back to London for debriefing. Despite Desgranges' excellent previous service with SOE, great care had to be taken to check the story of his escape – there was always the danger that an escaper might have been 'turned' and now be an enemy agent. In Desgranges' case, although a Frenchman, he had many British military friends to speak for him. He had been promoted to honorary second lieutenant by the SSRF and had served with distinction with both Maid Honor Force and the SSRF. He was well known to, and admired by Geoffrey Appleyard and the late Gus March-Phillipps. He was certainly not a stupid man, and had adapted well to serving with SOE.

As soon as he was back in London, on 9 July, he was interviewed by MI9, who wished to extract as much information from him as possible about his escape, and conditions in the countries through which he had passed. His account of his time in German hands and of his escape from them was dramatic. He described how after twenty days in the hands of the Gestapo, he was transferred to a prison at Wilhelmshaven. There, he was further questioned, and subjected to physical torture. He was told that if he did not talk he would be shot. Desgranges said that he had been kept in a ten-bed room on the second floor, where he was the only occupant. There were no bars on the windows. He managed to make a rope out of blankets and straw from the palliasses on the beds and, having discovered that there was a brief period of time when the sentry below would be out of sight of his window, shinned down the rope one night, pulled it down after him and disappeared into the night. It took him three nights on foot to cross the countryside and reach the Dutch border. From there, with some help from the locals, he eventually made his way to Paris. Once in Paris, he worked in the black market for a while to raise sufficient money to buy false papers in the name of Fournier, and to make his way into Spain. Having made contact with SOE there, he was smuggled into North Africa and taken to Casablanca, then to Massingham Mission.

As was their job, MI9 noted a number of queries about the accuracy of this account, which they passed on to MI5 internal security, who interviewed Desgranges on 15 July. The MI5 interrogator pressed Desgranges quite hard, to see if he could catch him out on any detail. The Interrogation Report from MI5 includes a surprising assessment of Desgranges himself, commenting that: 'Desgranges is remarkable for the slowness of his intelligence, indeed he is about the slowest witted Frenchman that I have seen.'

Desgranges was watched by an undercover agent for some days, and the report came back that he spent most of his time drinking and gregariously chatting in French to his friends. Nothing of any substance was found to his discredit. M himself weighed in with a strong personal reference in support of the Frenchman and, by 20 July, Desgranges' account of his escape was finally accepted and he was cleared for further service in the Allied cause. He asked to rejoin his friend Geoffrey Appleyard in North Africa, but was told that that was not possible. With the war in North Africa won, and with plans for the invasion of Europe well advanced, it was decided that Desgranges should be put back into France to work with the Resistance. He was sent for further relevant training (including a parachute course), and it is interesting to note that in contrast to MI5's view, Desgranges' training instructor at parachute school reported: 'Capable officer, plenty of experience. Good leader.'

In late November, Desgranges was dropped into France under yet another false name. The head of the Free French section of SOE was Lieutenant Colonel (formerly Major) Dizzy Dismore, one of Desgranges' old comrades-in-arms from Operation Postmaster. Desgranges served with the Free French section until the eventual liberation of France, following the successful D-Day invasion in June 1944. He was recommended by SOE for a decoration for his good service, and was awarded the Conspicuous Gallantry Medal in January 1945.

But there is a twist to Desgranges' story. The Gestapo Headquarters in Paris had been at the Hotel Majestic. When Paris fell to the Allies many papers were seized from the hotel, and once the war had ended, a careful and thorough check was made by the French security forces of the material recovered. In April 1946, the French authorities notified the British that Desgranges had been arrested by them. Amongst the papers at the Majestic Hotel had been a receipt signed by André Desgranges, and a Gestapo agent's card with Degranges' photograph on and the note: 'satisfactory'. On the face of it, therefore, Desgranges had been turned by the Gestapo, and had become their agent. When confronted with this by the French authorities, Desgranges changed his story. He now said that he had been arrested at the Dutch border after his escape from Wilhelmshaven, and had accepted an offer to work for the Gestapo in order to secure his liberty again. He had never had any intention of providing them with anything of value, but was simply using them to enable his return to Allied hands. Thus, said Desgranges, the Gestapo had helped him to cross into Spain (as they had Graham Hayes), with the intention that he should rejoin Allied forces and spy for them. Desgranges said that although he had accepted their help, he then in effect went back to his previous life as an energetic anti-Fascist agent for the Allies. He admitted lying to both MI9 and MI5, saying he had thought it best to keep quiet about his 'recruitment' by the Gestapo because it might have prevented him from going back into action as an SOE agent or Commando. Once his secret was out, Desgranges was held in prison by the French pending a possible trial for treason.

At this time, Major Thackerthwaite was the liaison officer in Paris for the by then defunct SOE, and he had personal experience of Desgranges' good service with SOE in France. He alerted Desgranges' surviving colleagues to his situation. In a letter to Leslie Prout on 23 April 1946, Thackerthwaite wrote:

> Unfortunately [Desgranges] is at the moment in prison. He did not tell the whole truth about his escape from Germany, fearing that he would never be sent back on similar work. The fact was he was recaptured by the Germans and only got away by promising to work for them. Unfortunately for him, his Gestapo card was found by the French authorities. Needless to say I believe his story. Had he done any work for them a considerable number of us including myself would not have been able to work in France with impunity. Naturally however, this has to be proved. Had he made a clean heart of the business, then there would have

been no trouble at all. He admits however having kept it from everyone, even his oldest friends such as Dismore and yourself. I am doing all I can for him, and have written a variety of documents. If by any chance you have anything which might help, let me know.

Thackerthwaite wrote similar letters to others, and Desgranges' British comrades now rallied round, led by his section commander in France, Dizzy Dismore. Both Dismore and M himself had written testimonials for Desgranges after he had been vetted in the summer of 1943, M saying of the Maid Honor Force/SSRF days that Desgranges had been 'one of the best members of the Force. He has a good knowledge of demolition work and is a very accurate shot with all types of small arms. He is also possessed of considerable courage and physical strength. He proved himself entirely trustworthy and always carried out his duties skilfully and without regard to his personal safety.'

M and Dismore now came to Desgranges' assistance again, together with two surviving veterans of the SSRF, Leslie Prout and Bunny Warren. All supplied excellent character references for him, and SOE drew attention to the important point that Thackerthwaite had made in his letter, namely that if Desgranges had been a double agent whilst working with the Resistance, many of his colleagues would have been arrested. Eventually, it seems that the French authorities accepted Desgranges' story, and he was cleared and set free. Accepting therefore that Desgranges' account was true, he must deserve considerable credit for fooling both MI9 and MI5 into believing that he was of such low intelligence that any inconsistencies in his original account were down to stupidity and not lying.

The sad comparison is perhaps between Desgranges and Graham Hayes. Both were captured after the same raid, and both fell into the hands of the Gestapo. Desgranges agreed to work for them, and thereby secured his release and their help on his journey to freedom. Graham Hayes would never have agreed to help the Gestapo in any way or for any reason. His fate was therefore to be taken out and shot.

Chapter 16

After Aquatint

Upon their return, Geoffrey Appleyard and Freddie Bourne went straight from Portsmouth to London to report what had happened. No doubt Appleyard was grateful for a little time to get his mind in order, before facing the rest of the men of the SSRF at Anderson Manor. In London, he reported to SOE, but not to M himself, since, as M's diary shows, he was away on leave. It is probable that Appleyard debriefed with his friend Ian Collins, who the same day wrote a short note on the lessons to be learnt from the failure of Operation Aquatint, and the way forward for the SSRF. Collins referred to the fact that MTB 344 was carrying its own dinghy, but had been unable to use it once the alarm was raised to assist in the rescue of the raiding party. He commented that in future it would be better for a raiding party to go ashore in two boats, for the obvious reason that if one was sunk there would still be a second available to get them back to the MTB. The other very relevant point that Collins made was that there should have been a pick-up point and time fixed for any of the raiding party left behind – so that the MTB could return covertly at a later time to a different place to pick up survivors. The idea was obviously sound, but one of the problems for the men of Aquatint would have been that they had landed in the wrong place to start with, and didn't know where they were. In the event, there had been no such back-up plan, and Hayes, Burton, Hellings and Orr were left to do the best they could on their own.

For Appleyard, the disaster at St Laurent-sur-Mer was a personal tragedy as well as a serious blow to the SSRF. He and Gus March-Phillipps had formed a close partnership and an even closer personal friendship, since their first meeting on the beach at Dunkirk. Graham Hayes had been his friend since boyhood in Linton on Wharfe. Both, together with many other comrades, were now dead, captured or on the run in enemy territory. Although Appleyard knew that only time would reveal what their precise fate was, he had no reason to be optimistic for any of them.

However, despite personal distress, Appleyard demonstrated now what a positive leader he was. What was done was done, and the fate of those left behind on Aquatint was beyond his control. It was most important, in his judgement, to move forward, and to plan and carry out another operation as soon as possible. Peter Kemp was later to comment: 'We had been prepared for casualties, but not for such a catastrophe as this. The death of the gallant idealist and strange, quixotic genius who had been our commander and our inspiration, together with the loss of so many good friends, all in the space of a few hours, was a crippling calamity which nearly put an end to our activities. Indeed, it probably would have done so but for the energetic reaction of Appleyard, who refused to let our grief for our comrades arrest his determination to avenge them.'

Ian Collins agreed with Appleyard's approach. He commented in his note on the operation that the SSRF was bound to face mishaps, that it was important to get them back into action as soon as possible, and that the next raid should be on the Isle of Sark on or about 20 September, a mere seven days time. Because the number of SSRF commandos had been substantially reduced by the losses on Operation Aquatint, Collins also proposed that they should be immediately reinforced, perhaps by men of No.12 Commando. Appleyard was for the time being to command the SSRF, with the rank of major.

News of the disaster gradually found its way back to the men at Anderson Manor. Those waiting there were only too aware that nobody had returned from the Aquatint raid. Anders Lassen had been away from the Manor on the night of 12/13 September, staying with his friends the Knight family, in Bournemouth. Lassen was another who was very close to March-Phillipps – in the words of others, Lassen 'worshipped him'. Lassen's mother later recorded that the Knights had found Anders to be very restless after dinner, pacing up and down and looking out of the window at the weather, and how during the night, at what proved later to be the time of March-Phillipps' death, he had cried out from his bed. When Mrs Knight went to see what was wrong, Lassen claimed that he was sure March-Phillipps had been killed.

Peter Kemp had a cottage at Spettisbury where he lived with his wife, about five miles away from Anderson Manor. On 12 September he was two days out of hospital and still on the injured list. Hamish Torrance and Brian Bingham (Reynolds) drove over from Anderson Manor to join the Kemps for dinner, but all three men were tense. Conversation was artificial and strained. After they had eaten, the men stood in the garden, looking out at the weather, and wondering whether fog in the Channel would again prevent Aquatint from going ahead. Kemp's close friend John Burton was going on the raid, and Kemp wished he could be by his side. Torrance said to Kemp before he and Bingham left that he should not phone Anderson Manor for news, promising that he, Torrance, would drive over and let him know as soon as there was any. Kemp spent a restless night, and it was not until after dark on 13 September that Torrance reappeared, bringing the desperate news that only Appleyard and Bourne had come back from the raid.

The two men had not returned to Anderson Manor until the evening of Sunday, 13 September, when they were finally able to tell their friends and comrades all they knew of what had happened. It was little enough –all eleven men of the raiding party had been left behind, but what their fate had been in the maelstrom on the beach was unknown.

On the following day, 14 September, the picture became clearer. At 1250 hrs, the German official news agency issued a communiqué saying:

During the night of 12–13 September, a British landing party consisting of five officers, a Company Sergeant Major and a Private tried to make a footing on the French Channel coast, east of Cherbourg. Their approach was immediately detected by the defence. Fire was opened on them, and the landing craft was sunk by direct hits. Three English officers and a de Gaullist Naval officer were taken prisoner. A Major, a Company Sergeant Major and a Private were brought to land dead.

This communication confirmed some of the worst fears of SOE and the men at Anderson Manor. If the report was accurate, March-Phillipps and Winter had been killed, plus one of the three privates on the raid – Lehniger, Orr or Hellings. However, the reference to 7 men brought some hope. It sounded as if the Germans were unaware that the raiding party had in fact comprised 11 men, and that therefore 4 must have got away.

In the very early hours of the following morning, 15 September, another communiqué was received from Berlin. This was not specific as to numbers, but stated: 'Several British officers were killed, including one Major.' It was some time before it was finally confirmed that three men were dead, March-Phillipps, Williams and Lehniger/Leonard.

Some weeks later, Appleyard described the effect that the loss of March-Phillipps had on him: 'His death was a tremendous blow to me ... Gus meant a very great deal to me, and he was my closest personal friend. We had been together for over two years and the occasion on which he was killed was the one and only occasion in all that time that we were not actually alongside each other.'

Lilly Lehniger and her daughter Irene had been living since May in Yeovil, Somerset, near enough to Anderson Manor for Richard to have been able to visit them. Once the news of her husband's death had reached her, amid the devastation of her personal loss Lilly now faced a difficult and uncertain future as an 'alien' widow with a very young child. Happily, after the war, the Commando Association provided financial support for the schooling of Richard and Lilly's child, Irene.

For Marjorie, Gus March-Phillipps' young widow, the news of his death was equally devastating. She was away at Ringway, Manchester, doing her parachute training at the time. Before going off on Operation Aquatint, Gus had rung to say goodbye, but she had missed his call. She never spoke to him again. Gus and Marjorie had been married for a little under five months. A short while later, Marjorie discovered that she was pregnant. She and Gus had conceived a baby girl in the days before Operation Aquatint, and she had gone on her parachute training course in total ignorance of her condition. Henrietta March-Phillipps was born on 15 June 1943, never to meet her father.

Chapter 17

Operation Basalt

In accordance with Collins' recommendation (approved by M and by Mountbatten), a small detachment from E Troop, No. 12 Commando (the 'Irish' Commando), was immediately sent to Anderson Manor to re-enforce the SSRF. They were Captain Philip Pinckney and five other ranks, amongst them Bombardier Redbourn and Horace Leonard 'Stokey' Stokes. More were to follow in due course. No. 12 were hardened and experienced commandos, who themselves had previously raided on the French coast and in Norway. Some of their men had taken part in the St Nazaire raid in March 1942. Nonetheless they were immediately subjected to specialized night-time training by the SSRF, though there was very little time before the next operation was due to take place. The target was to be the small island of Sark.

The raid on Sark, to be known as Operation Basalt, had been planned for some time. Appleyard himself knew the island well, having holidayed there with his family before the war, and on weekend leave he took the chance to view again a cine film they had taken during their holiday. Like all the Channel Islands, Sark was now occupied by the Germans, who were believed to keep a significant garrison there. SOE was able to draw on information in pre-war guide books to the island in order to supplement Appleyard's knowledge and there were, of course, maps and aerial photographs. Also, one of the prisoners taken at the Casquets Lighthouse, the wireless operator Reineck, had supplied quite detailed intelligence about the island. He had said that the garrison comprised 200–300 men, all German infantrymen but apparently quite recent recruits and still undergoing training. They were armed with rifles and light machine guns, and three or four artillery pieces.

Winston G. Ramsey, in his book *The War in the Channel Islands* (1981), records that the actual German strength on Sark at the time was one heavy machine gun section, one light mortar group, and one anti-tank platoon, all from 6 Kompanie of the 583 Infantry Regiment. There was also a five-man engineer unit working on alterations to the small harbour. The island was under the command of Oberleutnant Herdt. The fixed defences comprised anti-tank guns, flame throwers, and almost 1,000 mines laid in 22 separate minefields. At night there was a curfew at 2200 hrs for soldiers and residents alike, after which time the island would be patrolled by at least one 7-man patrol. The small harbour at Creux was to be avoided. It was guarded, including by armed Customs officials, and there was a tunnel leading from it through the cliff towards the main part of the island. The tunnel was gated and the gate was closed at night. Where the tunnel emerged on to the road across the island, a barracks was being built. The SSRF would have to find another way on to Sark.

One of the new recruits, Bombardier Redbourn, described preparations for the raid: 'One day [18 September], we were called in to Major Appleyard. On the table stood a model of Sark, together with a dozen aerial photographs. All morning we received instructions what to do.' As was the practice of the SSRF, thorough briefings took place on the morning of the raid, and the afternoon would then be free for the men to rest, or to make whatever personal preparations they wished. In the evening, an army lorry would arrive to take them to Portland, and off they would go. There was a two-night slot available for Operation Basalt, the 18/19 and 19/20 September. If the weather proved adverse, the raid would have to be put off until the next favourable phase of the moon. The raiding party was to consist of 12 men, 7 of them from the SSRF, including Appleyard (who was still not fully fit, but insisted on leading the raid), Lassen, both Colin and Bruce Ogden Smith, Dudgeon and Young. Pinckney, Redbourn, Stokes, Corporal Flint and one other newly arrived from No. 12 Commando joined them.

The objectives of the raid were similar to before. If at all possible, prisoners were to be taken and brought back to England for interrogation. Intelligence materials were to be seized. Where appropriate, some casualties were to be inflicted on the enemy, although not if that gratuitously endangered the operation. Sark is a very small island, and since it was apparently heavily garrisoned, a silent execution of the entire raid was the preferred option. Certainly, if shots were fired, they would be heard all over the island and the garrison could be expected to react. For No. 12 Commando, it was simply a new adventure, but for the men of the SSRF, it was to be much, much more. This was their chance to avenge their lost commander and comrades, and to prove to the enemy that they were still an effective unit. Only six days had passed since the disaster of Aquatint, and the wounds of loss were still raw. Nerves, always taut before any operation, were now stretched almost to breaking point.

By the evening of 18 September, it was clear that the weather would not be good enough for them to go that night. The operation was postponed for 24 hours. On the evening of the next day the weather was still far from ideal, but Appleyard decided that they should go, and take their chances. Even if conditions proved to be too difficult for a landing on Sark, they could at least carry out a useful reconnaissance. An army lorry took the SSRF to Portland, where they embarked on the Little Pisser, with Freddie Bourne as always in command. The dozen passengers, faces blacked and carrying full kit, crowded together on the MTB as it headed out to sea at 2159 hrs. The journey was rough and noisy, the engines roaring as they pushed the MTB through the water at full speed – some 30 knots or more. The silent approach would come later. Redbourn did not enjoy the bumpy ride, and commented on the 'ear-splitting noise from the engine [that] is in my opinion even worse than the noise from an aeroplane engine.' It was difficult to talk, and the men tried to keep their minds from dwelling on the dangers that they were about to face.

The weather worsened as the MTB approached the Channel Islands. It took the SSRF more than two hours to reach the coast of Sark – its lighthouse was spotted at 0020 hrs. As they closed on the island, the engines were reduced in power to semi-silent and then silent. Their intended landing point was Derrible Bay, but it soon became clear that the sea was running too strongly to allow them either to land the raiding party by Goatley or, if they did, to give the raiding party any chance of a safe return to the MTB. Time was also too short by now for much to be achieved on the island, even if they had been able to land.

Reluctantly, Appleyard gave the order to withdraw and return to Portland. Their journey had been of some value – they had circled much of the island, and now knew a lot more about the sea's currents and the possible hazards of any landing. After another uncomfortable ride, the MTB arrived back within the safety of Portland Harbour at 0530 hrs. For the men of the SSRF, it had been a tough and unsatisfying night. When Appleyard submitted his written report on the night's operation, he signed it poignantly as '2nd in Command, SSRF' through respect for his much loved late commander, although he knew by now that March-Phillipps was dead, and that he himself was in command.

M had been away over the weekend of March-Phillipps' death, apparently returning to his desk on 16 September. At 1700 hrs on 21 September, his desk diary records that he had a meeting with Appleyard. It must have been a sombre one, for M had known March-Phillipps well, and had greatly admired his achievements. Also, he still had March-Phillipps' young widow Marjorie on his staff. However, M was always very positive, and no doubt gave Appleyard much to encourage him for the future. M followed this up by making the trip out to

Anderson Manor on the weekend of 26/27 September, and spending time with all the men of the SSRF. M was a genuine leader and fully understood what Appleyard and the others were going through. His visit was much appreciated by all.

The SSRF had to wait another 13 days for the next suitable phase of the moon. Sark remained their primary target. For the new recruits from No. 12 Commando, the wait did at least provide more time for training and assimilation into the unit. For the rest, it was just further frustration and impatience. Finally, on 3 October, the go-ahead was given for another attempt on Sark. After a day of briefing and then rest, the SSRF left the haven of Anderson Manor and set off for Portland on the usual army lorry. They started much earlier than before, since Appleyard wanted to make sure that, provided they were able to land, they would have plenty of time on the island. MTB 344 left the quayside at Portland at 1903 hrs. On board were the same personnel as before, seven of the original SSRF and five of No. 12 Commando. They were accompanied by a Captain Warre, of what Appleyard recorded as the M. E. Raiding Group. This time the weather was fair and the sea was smooth, with only a light swell.

They passed the Casquets Rock, scene of their earlier triumph, at 2053 hrs, but stayed well clear and out of sight of it. At 2117 hrs, MTB 344 dropped its speed to 10 knots, the quietest it could manage whilst still using the main engines. Thirteen minutes later, the Sark lighthouse was spotted on the starboard bow. Bourne took his boat round the north-eastern and eastern coast of the island until, at 2220 hrs, they calculated that they were positioned 4 miles due east of the southern tip of Sark. The main engines were then cut, and Bourne steered towards the still invisible island on the MTB's silent auxiliary engine. The plan was to drop anchor in Baleine Bay, at the south-east end of the island.

The outline of Sark loomed up when the MTB was still some two and a half miles out from the coast. Steering now by eye and landmark, as well as by compass, the SSRF crept nearer and nearer to the island, dropping their speed to between one and two knots. They eventually dropped anchor in 6 fathoms of water, about 2 cables away from dry land. The two obvious landing points for the raiding party were at Dixcart Bay and Derrible Bay (inevitably referred to in the Operation Basalt reports as Terrible Bay). Dixcart offered an easy shingle beach, Derrible a mainly sandy one, but then a steep and difficult cliff path. It was not known whether either beach had been mined by the enemy. However, the two bays were divided by a promontory known as the Hog's Back, which ended in a high cliff at Pointe Chateau, jutting out into the sea. Recent reconnaissance from the air had suggested that there might be a new enemy machine-gun post on top of Pointe Chateau, with a field of fire that covered both Dixcart and Derrible Bay. If there was such a post, it would spell disaster for a landing on either beach, and was likely to lead to a repeat of the horrors of Operation Aquatint.

Appleyard had spent much time studying guide books about Sark. In one of them, long out of print, he had found a reference to the existence of a route down from Pointe Chateau to some caves at the foot of the cliff below. The old book described it as a long and difficult climb down, and there was of course no guarantee that the route was still passable. Appleyard himself was still not properly recovered from his broken ankle. However, it seemed likely that any gun on Pointe Chateau would not be able to cover an attack from directly beneath it, and certainly any approach from that direction should take the enemy by surprise. As with their raid on Casquets, the most difficult route might prove to be the safest. Surveying the land from the MTB, Appleyard decided that the route up the cliff of Pointe Chateau was the one they would try first. If that proved impassable, their second attempt would be at Derrible Bay.

The Goatley landing craft was launched at 2312 hrs, paddling as silently as possible towards the rocks at the foot of Pointe Chateau. The journey was not a difficult one, and landing was made on the rocks at 2320 hrs, Anders Lassen acting as bowman and skilfully ensuring that they all landed dry. Almost immediately, however, the raiding party realized they had not actually reached the mainland of Sark. The rock on which they had landed was divided by another small sea gully from the cliffs. Muttered curses spread throughout the party as they faced the task of crossing this further obstacle. Two unnamed volunteers swam the gully, in order to ensure a secure and dry landing for their comrades, who re-embarked on the landing craft and crossed the gully dry-shod. Once it was confirmed that they had finally reached the mainland, Appleyard issued his orders. Second Lieutenant Young was given the difficult and unhappy task of remaining at the bottom of the cliff to guard the boat. He was to remain with the landing craft at all times, and if the party did not return by a given hour, he was to leave and return to the MTB. To Anders Lassen, the best stalker and silent killer, Appleyard gave the task of scaling the cliffs and reconnoitring the expected enemy machine-gun post. It was now 2330 hrs. Four and a half hours had passed since they had left Portland.

Lassen disappeared up the cliff into the darkness, and the others followed more slowly. As the old guide book had warned, the ascent was initially very steep and difficult. The darkness, loose rock, shale and the need for silence all contributed to a very dangerous climb. The men of the SSRF were up to it, however – even Appleyard with his injured ankle managed to make the ascent.

After gaining 150 feet in height the gradient eased somewhat, and eventually the route became a steep path climbing through rocky gullies, leading to the crest of the Hog's Back. Appleyard noted that if going up the cliff was difficult, going down it again with a number of prisoners would be even harder. At least, however, they were now familiar with the route.

Anders Lassen climbed on ahead. He knew that if he encountered the enemy, he was to observe, and to shoot only as a very last resort. As always he was carrying a commando knife and would be quite happy to use that if he could. He reached the top of the cliff well before the others, and silently scanned the crest of the ridge. He saw no one. Moving forward, he quickly searched the end of the promontory. There were barbed wire entanglements but there was no enemy machine-gun post. The coast was clear. In fact, the aerial reconnaissance had been partly right – there was a gun. Happily, it was an ancient Elizabethan cannon, lying incongruously on the ground without a mounting, facing out to sea, Any visitor to the island will still find it lying there today. Once he was satisfied that the immediate area was safe for his comrades, Lassen moved down the path along the Hog's Back towards the interior of the island. He scouted all the way to the end of the ridge and saw no sign of the enemy. Quickly, he returned to join the others.

Despite the difficulty of the climb, Appleyard and all his party reached the top of the cliff by midnight. When Lassen rejoined them, reporting that the coast was clear, Appleyard led his men on towards the centre of the island. Their primary target was a group of cottages known as Petit Dixcart where, their intelligence had informed them, enemy troops were billeted. To get to it, they needed to find their way along the Hog's Back, then drop down the side of the valley to the hamlet. They had been warned that there was at least one mobile enemy patrol on the island at night, and remained totally alert to any sound or movement. In the dark, it was difficult to make out what any more distant shapes were, and as Appleyard led his men along the ridge, they spotted what they thought were a Nissen hut and radio mast, beside an old mill. Instantly, the SSRF went to action stations and moved forward to carry out what they hoped would be a silent attack. The opportunity to seize radio logs and codebooks was too good to be missed. Appleyard's own suspicions were confirmed when he saw what he believed to be a group of enemy soldiers standing nearby – a chance to take prisoners or wipe out an enemy patrol. That way they might quickly achieve their objectives and retreat to their boat.

It was too perfect to be true. Appleyard halted his men in easy range of the enemy soldiers and crawled forward himself to check out the darkened figures. As he drew closer, he was puzzled by the total lack of movement on the enemy's part. He began to doubt his own eyes. His night vision was by now very good, but why were these men standing so still? Moving even closer, he could finally see the answer. What he and his men had discovered was a firing range, and the 'enemy soldiers' were well-dressed target dummies. His only half-suppressed laugh carried back to the men who, until he returned to tell them what he had found, were totally confused. Further inspection showed that the 'Nissan hut' was in fact the butts end of the shooting range, with the 'soldier' dummies standing nearby. The radio mast turned out to be a flag pole. It was a good joke, and the tension with which his men had readied themselves for action was released by hearty (if suppressed) laughter. In truth it demonstrated the difficulties that the SSRF so often faced in the dark in strange territory. They rarely knew for certain what awaited them as they rounded a corner, or approached a building. Bombadier Redbourn later commented: 'All the time we were peering into the darkness and we felt the excitement, the loneliness and the fear that can grip a man when he does not know what the next moment will bring.'

Appleyard now led his men in the direction of their primary target, Petit Dixcart. They dropped left off the ridge, down towards the bottom of the valley that ran up from Dixcart Bay. They had deliberately left the path, but now found themselves fighting their way through thick gorse and bracken as they made their descent. Reaching another path at the bottom of the valley, they closed on the cottages of Petit Dixcart at 0115 hrs. Redbourn recalls that at one point on the way, a German patrol passed by. Appleyard was at the front of the small column of SSRF, and Pinckney was at the rear. Rapidly when they heard the approach of the enemy, the SSRF dispersed off the path into the darkness and undergrowth, and the Germans passed by unaware of their presence. Ambushing a patrol up on the lonely heights of the Hog's Back, close to the boats, would have been an acceptable risk, but doing so close to Petit Dixcart, where there was thought to be a small garrison, would have been foolhardy.

Once the danger had passed, the SSRF moved close to the cottages. Keeping the main party under cover, Appleyard sent two men to scout the houses and discover if they were occupied. Each of the cottages proved to be empty. The intelligence was bad. Presuming that it was Wireless Operator Reineck who had supplied the intelligence, either it was out of date, or Reineck had not in truth been as helpful as he pretended to be. The secondary target was a nearby house called La Jespellaire, which again was said to contain a number of German soldiers. La Jespellaire was a detached house, standing in its own grounds at the top of a hill above Petit Dixcart. It did not take long for Appleyard and his men to find it. For a while Appleyard kept all his men under cover whilst they studied the house for any possible activity or sentries. They saw no movement. A reconnaissance party of three was then sent to check the windows, doors and outbuildings. All the doors and windows were found to be locked, and the outbuildings contained only a single horse. However, there was a set of French windows on one side of the house that looked easy to force.

It was now 0150 hrs. The SSRF had been on the island of Sark for well over two hours. Already they had twice prepared to attack targets which proved to be fruitless, and had dodged an enemy patrol. Now Appleyard gave orders for a third attack. They would storm La Jespellaire through the French windows, disperse to all parts of the house, and capture or kill any enemy troops inside. The whole party advanced stealthily on the building, with a variety of lethal weapons at the ready. Quickly they forced the French windows by breaking the glass, burst in and spread out on both floors of the house. Men were immediately posted in defensive positions on the ground floor, in case of a reaction from elsewhere on the island. Appleyard was one of those searching the first floor. He and another man crashed through the door into one of the bedrooms, to find a single occupant, a lady who had been fast asleep in bed. She turned out to be the only person in the house. Again, the intelligence given to the SSRF had proved to be bad.

The lady was the owner of La Jespellaire, Frances Pittard (née Mardon). Mrs Pittard was English and in her forties, the daughter of a Royal Naval Volunteer Reserve commander resident in England, and the widow of the local doctor. She was awoken unexpectedly in the middle of the night to find two commandos with blackened faces, and heavily armed, in her bedroom. Very much to her credit, she recovered from that considerable shock almost immediately and, as Appleyard apologized and explained, Mrs Pittard made clear that she would help in any way she could. Geoffrey Appleyard immediately ordered all but one of his men out of the house, instructing them to set up a defensive cordon around the building. Then he sat down with Mrs Pittard, who gave him a very thorough briefing on the affairs of the island. She spread out a map of Sark, showing him where the German troop dispositions presently were, and provided Appleyard with copies of the local newspaper and other German-generated pamplets. Significantly, she also provided him with evidence of a recent German declaration to the effect that all local men over the age of sixteen who had not been born in the Channel Islands, or did not have residency there, were to be deported to the European mainland, and consigned to German labour camps. Some had already gone. During their lengthy discussion, Mrs Pittard gave Appleyard detailed information of all sorts, from German strongpoints to local rations. She also told him that the beach at Dixcart Bay had definitely been mined by the Germans, and it was believed they had also mined the beach at Derrible Bay. It was just as well that Appleyard had decided on a direct approach up Pointe Chateau.

Geoffrey Appleyard was obviously keen to know where he and his men might capture some German prisoners to take home with them, and Mrs Pittard suggested the annexe to the Dixcart Hotel, in Dixcart village. The annexe was a single storey beside the main building, with a separate entrance. Provided the raid could be carried out silently it should prove an easy target. However, if the alarm was raised the Dixcart Hotel was next door and another, the Stocks Hotel, was only a short distance away, also inhabited by Germans. Appleyard was clearly impressed by Mrs Pittard, and offered her a passage home in the MTB 344. She, however, refused, saying she preferred to stay on Sark, having lived in the Channel Islands all her life, even though she appreciated that there were likely to be German repercussions against locals and probably herself after the raid. Instead, she wrote a letter to her father, and asked Appleyard to deliver that back to England for her.

Locals on Sark today suggest that Mrs Pittard guided Appleyard and his men to the Dixcart Hotel, and that after the raid, her small footprints were found by the Germans in the area of the hotel. It may well be true that she did so, but Appleyard makes no mention of it in his debrief report. By the time he had finished talking to Mrs Pittard, the SSRF had overstayed their expected departure from the island by an hour, and Appleyard sent a runner back to Pointe Chateau to signal the MTB to wait for them. Appleyard decided that the annexe of the Dixcart Hotel was now to be their target. As it happened, he knew the hotel, having stayed there with his family ten years before. He remembered in particular a yew tree in the grounds, under which his younger brother Ian had found a halfcrown coin during the holiday, a memorable event for a young boy! The family cine film that he had seen again shortly before the operation was now going to become very useful. However, he also knew that building was a riskier target than either Petit Dixcart or La Jespellaire, being situated in the Dixcart valley a mere 500–600 metres from the main village, where inevitably many more Germans would be stationed. If the attack became noisy, the SSRF would be vulnerable not only to counterattack from the main hotel at Dixcart, and from the nearby Stocks Hotel, but also from the village. Nonetheless, the SSRF had yet to exact revenge for the disaster of Operation Aquatint, and Appleyard and many of his men were eager to do so.

It did not take the SSRF long to cover the relatively short distance between La Jespellaire and the Dixcart Hotel. The men passed through the grounds of the hotel and paused, out of sight, within a short distance of the adjacent annexe. German records say that the annexe was 500 metres from the coast, and 400 metres from the company reserve strongpoint (presumably in the nearby village of St Marguerite). Lassen and Redbourn were sent forward to reconnoitre the low building, alert as always to the possible presence of sentries.

They discovered that there was indeed a sentry on duty, an Obergefreiter called Peter Oswald. Anders Lassen crept up noiselessly behind him. Oswald could not have been expecting any trouble. Sark was a peaceful backwater, many miles from the British mainland, and the Dixcart Hotel was some distance inland from the coast. To him, it was just another night, and another spell of guard duty. It was to be his last. Lassen attacked swiftly and silently, giving Oswald no chance to resist, and killed him with his knife. All that the waiting commandos heard was a muffled groan from the darkness, then Lassen returned to announce that the coast was clear. Lassen had begun to avenge the death of his friend and mentor, Gus March-Phillipps.

Appleyard now gave the order to attack the annexe. His small group burst through the unlocked door to find themselves in a lighted but empty room. A door led off it towards the bedrooms. Wasting no time, the men of the SSRF rushed through into the small corridor, and divided up, kicking open the doors of the five or six single bedrooms. Inside they found a total of five German soldiers, all of them asleep in bed. The shock and surprise was total. Redbourn even had difficulty in waking the German he found, who when the light in his room was turned on and the bedclothes stripped back, simply pulled them back over himself and tried to go on sleeping. Only when he eventually opened his eyes and saw the blackened face of the commando who was threatening him did he come to his senses. Redbourn then laid him out with his knuckleduster, to ensure that he remained silent while the room was searched.

Five prisoners were taken, all of them dressed only in night clothes. They surrendered without any fight. They were the members of the Pioneer Corps Engineer Unit who were working at the small harbour – Obergefreiter Weinrich, and Gefreiters Esslinger, Bleyer, Just and Klotz. Their clothes, lying in the bedrooms, were searched for weapons and for anything that might be of value, and paybooks and papers were seized. Appleyard then had to decide whether they were able to take all five prisoners back to the boat. In the raid on Casquets, the SSRF had successfully captured and returned home with seven German prisoners. This situation was, however, very different. On Casquets, they had captured the entire garrison for the island. Here on Sark, there were a large number of enemy troops who, if alerted, would do their utmost to kill or capture the men of the SSRF, and to prevent them from returning to their boat. In any event, it was a long and difficult journey back to where Graham Young and the Goatley were (hopefully) still waiting for them. However, amongst the things that the SSRF never lacked were nerve and ambition. Perhaps, on this first operation after his death, Appleyard paused to consider what March-Phillipps would have done. If he did, the answer would have been to 'take the lot', which was exactly what Appleyard decided to do.

By 0245 hrs, the search for intelligence materials had been completed, and the five prisoners were ushered outside and under cover of the nearby trees. Until this time they had remained separated in their rooms, and it was only now that they were able to assess the strength of their captors and to collectively gather their wits. Each man was still in his nightclothes and, on Appleyard's orders, their hands had been tied together to discourage escape and to make it easier to escort them over the considerable distance to the end of the Hog's Back. There is some evidence to suggest that Appleyard's party was reduced to only seven at the time of the entry into the annexe. Twelve men had landed, Young had been left with the Goatley, and a messenger had been sent back to him from La Jespellaire. That should have left Appleyard with nine men at his disposal, but it may well be that others had been detached to guard the retreat route. The group at the Dixcart Hotel certainly included Appleyard himself, Pinckney, Lassen, Dudgeon (who spoke German), and Redbourn.

Whatever the precise mathematics, the five prisoners were not grossly outnumbered. Once outside the annexe of the Dixcart Hotel, they could see that Appleyard's squad was a small one. Nearby in the Dixcart Hotel and Stocks Hotel, Obergefreiter Weinrich and his German companions knew that many of their comrades were sleeping. The village was also within shouting distance. The prisoners hands were tied, but they had not been gagged, and their legs were free. The temptation became too strong for one Gefreiter, and he decided to make a break for it. In the darkness, what followed was chaos. Appleyard later reported that the German attacked his guard and then, shouting loudly for help and trying to raise the alarm, ran off towards the main hotel building. Three more of the Germans followed; only Obergefreiter Weinrich remained passively beside his guard. Shouts and blows could be heard in the darkness, then the first of a number of shots rang out.

Accounts of exactly what happened outside the annexe to the Dixcart Hotel not surprisingly vary. Appleyard, in his official report, states that the first man to attempt to escape was caught almost immediately, 'but, after a scuffle, again escaped, still shouting, and was shot.' This was probably Gunner Redbourn's prisoner. Redbourn later recalled:

> I was having so much trouble with my prisoner. He had freed his hands – we were struggling – and he was getting away from me. I bowled him over with a rugby tackle. We rolled over and he got free again. He was a much bigger fellow than I was, but I managed to knock him over again, and we lay struggling among some cabbage plants. One of the officers shouted loudly above the din: 'If they try to get away, then shoot them.' Captain Pinckney's prisoner broke free and set off towards the hotel, shouting at

the top of his voice. Captain Pinckney chased after him and shot him. I had had more than enough with my prisoner. I couldn't manage him and so I had to shoot him.

Appleyard's report continues:

Meanwhile, three other prisoners, seizing the opportunity of the noise and confusion, also started shouting and attacking their guards. Two broke away and both were shot immediately. The third, although still held, was accidentally shot in an attempt to silence him by striking him with the butt of a revolver. The fifth prisoner remained quiet and did not struggle. There were answering shouts from the direction in which the prisoners had attempted to escape, and sounds of a verbal alarm being given.

It was Lieutenant Patrick Dudgeon who had tried to silence his prisoner by striking him with his revolver. The gun went off, shooting his prisoner in the head. Anders Lassen also ended up with his prisoner dead on the ground. In total, Appleyard recorded that four Germans were shot, in addition to the sentry whom Lassen had killed with his knife.

Naturally, the shots, shouts and screams had by now fully awakened the occupants of the Dixcart Hotel, and presumably Stocks Hotel as well. Lights had started to go on in the buildings, and the SSRF tensed in expectation of enemy fire. Lassen asked for permission to throw the grenades that he was carrying through the lighted windows, but Appleyard refused, saying: 'No, keep them, we might need them later on.' He knew it was likely that they would now have to fight their way off the island.

Appleyard and his men retreated at speed, dragging their only remaining prisoner, the terrified Obergefreiter Weinrich, with them. They stayed under cover, avoiding the paths, running and scrambling their way back up through the gorse bushes on to the Hog's Back. Anders Lassen took up the rear, covering their retreat as best he could. The going was extremely tough, and made more difficult by the need for as much silence as possible. Fortunately for the SSRF, the island of Sark is crossed by paths rather than roads, and it apparently took the enemy some time to assemble the necessary foot patrols to pursue them. They did not know how many enemy troops had landed – whether perhaps this was a full-scale invasion by the British. The Germans were an occupying force, and could not count on help from the locals, particularly following their decision to deport some of the local men to labour camps on the mainland.

The alarm had been raised as soon as shooting broke out outside the Dixcart Hotel. Klotz, the only man who had escaped from the SSRF, was found nearby, apparently completely naked. The Kommandant, Oberleutnant Herdt was informed, and began to organize a search operation. Herdt sent a squad of soldiers under the command of a Leutnant Balga towards the Hog's Back to look for the retreating commandos, all the strongpoints on the island were alerted by field telephone, and at 0325 hrs, Herdt despatched a customs boat with a crew of five, armed with a machine gun, to search Derrible and Dixcart bay. These beaches and bays were the obvious departure point for any craft that had brought the commandos to Dixcart.

The retreating SSRF had left obvious tracks through the undergrowth behind them which the Germans were able to follow. Winston G. Ramsay records that a number of items of British kit were found dropped or abandoned along the way, including two commando knives and a magazine for a sub-machine gun, as well as a pistol, torches, wire cutters, several toggle ropes, and a woollen hat and scarf.

Having reached the crest of the ridge, Appleyard was apprehensive as to what he would find at the end of it. Would the boats still be there, or had they gone, or been discovered? Would there be a German reception committee waiting at Pointe Chateau? Unbeknownst to Appleyard, his courier had actually lost his way in the undergrowth going up to the Hog's Back, and arrived there at the same time as the rest of the party. No warning had therefore been delivered to Graham Young to continue to wait at the bottom of the cliff with the Goatley. Happily for the SSRF, both Young with the Goatley and Freddie Bourne in the MTB had waited, even after they heard the firing from the Dixcart Hotel. For Freddie Bourne, the memory of Operation Aquatint was still raw and he was not prepared to leave the SSRF behind as long as any other option remained. He had resolved to stay in position until the approach of daylight forced him to leave. All the same, time was running very short.

Appleyard and his party reached Pointe Chateau at about 0310 hrs. It was long past their intended departure time, and the moon was now bright in the sky. Appleyard was able to see the shape of the MTB, still waiting in the bay. The moonlight, although dangerous in many ways, greatly helped their descent down the cliff to the sea. When Appleyard and the others reached the base of the cliff, they found Young and the Goatley waiting for them. They bundled their prisoner into the landing craft and set off for the MTB. The paddle took them only ten minutes, but for every second of it they were watching the cliffs and the beaches for any sign of pursuit. Happily there was none. At 0345 hrs, they were welcomed back on board MTB 344 by Freddie Bourne, and quickly put out to sea. The journey home passed without incident, and the men of the

SSRF spent the time cracking poor jokes to uproarious laughter, as they allowed the tension of the past few hours to ease.

At 0605 hrs they sighted Portland Bill, and just 28 minutes later they entered the harbour. A lorry took the SSRF back to Anderson Manor, whilst Obergefreiter Weinrich was handed over directly to MI9, and taken immediately to London for interrogation. Thankful, and probably very surprised to be still alive, he proved to be an extremely valuable source of information.

The British all felt the raid had been a great success. Good intelligence had been obtained, as well as a German prisoner for interrogation, up to five Germans had been killed in accordance with Churchill's 'butcher and bolt' objective, the island's garrison had been taken entirely by surprise, and the SSRF had returned without a single casualty (although Appleyard's ankle was causing him real problems). The morale of the SSRF received an enormous boost. For them it was 'normal service resumed'. On his return, Lassen proudly showed Ian Warren, one of his room mates at Anderson Manor, the bloodstained knife with which he had killed the sentry.

Appleyard's official report of the raid was completed on the day of their return. It was endorsed by Lord Louis Mountbatten, the Chief of Combined Operations, and presented to the war cabinet, chaired by General Sir Alan Brooke, on 6 October 1942. They were delighted with the success of the raid, and with the intelligence obtained. The success of the SSRF raids was having a very unsettling effect on the German garrisons in the Channel Islands, and was tying up extra troops. When Prime Minister Winston Churchill came to hear of the raid, and its background, he asked to see Appleyard in his room in the House of Commons, where he personally congratulated him, as did General Sir Alan Brooke, the Chief of the General Staff, who was also present. Shortly afterwards, Churchill made a stirring speech, making direct reference to the work of the SSRF: 'There comes from out of the sea from time to time a hand of steel which plucks the German sentries from their posts with growing efficiency.' More tangible reward followed. Appleyard was awarded the Distinguished Service Order and Dudgeon (whose performance on Operations Dryad and Basalt had particularly impressed) was awarded a Military Cross, as was Anders Lassen.

Not surprisingly, German reports of the raid were different to that of the British. Naturally, they had had ample time after the raid to assess their casualties. According to their reports, only three Germans were in fact killed: Obergefreiter Oswald (the sentry), Gefreiter Esslinger and Gefreiter Bleyer. Gefreiter Just was injured but recovered. Gefreiter Klotz escaped apparently unharmed but, according to German sources, 'naked'. Thus it seems that of the four who made a break for it at the Dixcart Hotel, two died and two survived. The German High Command investigated the affair, and the Kommandant of Sark, Oberleutenant Herdt was relieved of his command. Herdt had apparently been ordered to billet the engineer unit at the barracks of the central reserve, and had disregarded that order. In contrast, Gefreiter Klotz was presented with a watch to mark his successful escape from enemy hands.

As the German investigation developed, the valiant Mrs Pittard came under suspicion, as she had appreciated that she might. Whether the Germans did find her footprints in the vicinity of the Dixcart Hotel is not clear, but they gathered enough material to satisfy themselves that she had helped the raiding party in some way. At one stage the Germans threatened to deport all the inhabitants of Sark from the island, leaving only the German garrison, but in the end their action against civilians was more modest. Mrs Pittard was deported to the neighbouring island of Guernsey, where she was imprisoned. Happily, after just a few months she was freed and allowed to return to her home on Sark. The two joint owners of the Dixcart Hotel, Miss Duckett and Miss Page (who had apparently slept through the whole incident), were interrogated at length, and they too were apparently deported for a while to Guernsey, but eventually released. The local paper, the *Guernsey Star* announced that 13,000 extra mines were being laid on Sark, and that all cliffs and beaches would be closed to residents. The clifftop on the Hog's Back was amongst those areas sewn with mines.

However, there were other consequences to Basalt. Adolf Hitler was increasingly worried and irritated by the raids and the effect they were having on his troops' morale. A propaganda battle was also going on between the British and the Germans, both feeling it was important to win the hearts and minds of the neutral nations. When Hitler was briefed on the details of Operation Basalt, he decided to take drastic action. Three days after the raid, on 7 October 1942, the German Government published a communiqué which can be translated as follows:

> Another incident took place on October 4 on the Channel Island of Sark. Early in the morning, sixteen British attacked a German working party made up of one NCO and four men. The Germans were bound with thin but very strong cord while in their shirts, and prevented from putting on any other clothing. When the German soldiers resisted, the NCO and one man were shot or bayoneted. One other German soldier was wounded. This is confirmed by a sapper who succeeded in escaping. The questioning [of the sapper] has resulted in the conviction that the tying of prisoners is being carried out according to orders ... From October 8th at

12 noon all British officers and men captured at Dieppe will be put in chains ... In future all sabotage and terror tactics by the British and their accomplices, who behave like bandits rather than soldiers, will be treated as such by German troops, and will be ruthlessly exterminated wherever they appear.

The Dieppe raid in August 1942 had been a disaster for the Allies, and many prisoners (mostly Canadians) had been taken. In accordance with Hitler's order, they were now shackled with chains, an obvious breach of the Geneva Convention on the treatment of prisoners of war. The Allied reaction was to announce that an equal number of German prisoners held by the Allies in Canada would also be shackled. That aspect of the row rumbled on for some time, and shackles were used by both sides.

Although he had not been on the Dieppe raid, but had been captured on 13 September 1942, about a month after it, Tom Winter was one of those who was shackled. In early October, he was still in the hands of the Gestapo, and he later commented that Hitler's order to shackle prisoners: 'probably saved my life for I was still under interrogation by an SS unit. Their officer, and I can still see his delighted expression, said: "You tie our prisoners up. We have something for you now." With that he sent me away to a camp to be chained because that was the order from Berlin ... yet this was an outfit that thought nothing of rubbing people out.' Winter went on to say that at first, prisoners in the camps were tied with string, because there were not enough chains to shackle them properly. Chains eventually arrived. Hellings and Orr, who arrived in the same camp as Winter, were also shackled. Their camp, Stalag VIIB, contained a large number of Canadian prisoners from the Dieppe raid.

The British Government had intended to keep the Basalt raid a secret, but once the German allegations had been published, it felt bound to reply. A summary to be found in the British Government intelligence file on Operation Basalt comments on a 'storm of libellous allegations against the Allies' by the Germans in the recent past, of which their communiqué regarding the Basalt raid was the latest. The propaganda war was being carried on by way of Government communiqués published in national newspapers. On the day following the German communiqué, 8 October 1942, the British press carried articles supposedly rebutting the German allegations. In a time of war, the press was supportive of the Government's efforts, and each newspaper presented matters in a way that would appeal to its own readers. The *Daily Telegraph* headed its article with the words: 'Germans deport Channel Island Britons – Sark Raid Revealed Labour Round-up – Enemy Threat to Chain

Dieppe Men Today'. At the other end of the market, the *Daily Mirror* told its readership:

> A small scale raid was made last Saturday night on the island of Sark. It was one of many such operations which are successfully and frequently carried out and about which nothing is normally said. But since the enemy have from ulterior motives announced the raid with the addition of inaccurate details, the facts are now issued. The main purpose of this raid was to obtain first-hand information about the suspected ill-treatment of British residents in the island. These suspicions have been confirmed by the seizure of a proclamation ... this states that all male civilians (a) not born in the Channel Islands, and (b) not permanently resident there, between the ages of 16 and 70, have been deported to Germany, together with their families. This deportation took place last week..... . eleven men of Sark were ordered to go last week, but two committed suicide, and only nine left. The total British raiding force consisted of ten officers and men. We suffered no casualties. Five prisoners were taken, of whom four escaped after repeated struggles, and were shot while doing so. One was brought back to this country. He has confirmed the deportations, and has stated that they were forced labour.

This article was based entirely upon what Geoffrey Appleyard had learned from Mrs Frances Pittard, and the newspapers and pamphlets that she had given him. The piece was deliberately slanted – it was not true that the main purpose of the raid was to find out more about German ill-treatment of British residents. Nothing was said at this stage in answer to the allegation that the German prisoners had had their hands tied on the Sark raid. However, as Appleyard and those who had served in the Maid Honor Force already knew, truth is a servant to convenience in all-out war.

However, the question of tying the hands of prisoners had to be addressed at some stage. Having published a somewhat 'diversionary' article on 8 October, a press war raged over the next few days. On 9 October, the *Daily Telegraph* reported: 'Although the War Office has made it clear that no German prisoners have ever been tied – the charge on which Berlin has based its reprisals – it was pointed out in London yesterday that there is nothing in the Geneva Convention of 1921, which Britain and Germany both signed, against the tying up of captives in the process of catching them – the rules do not deal with conditions during action or in circumstances where it might be essential to prevent a prisoner from being a source of danger.'

Then on Sunday, 11 October, the press carried the fuller story of what had actually happened on the Sark raid. The *News of the World* said:

> The raid on Sark was carried out by a party of ten officers and men. Seven of the party captured five Germans. The hands of the Germans were tied in order that arms might be linked with the captors. No orders, written or otherwise, had been issued, but the prisoners had to be taken past a German-occupied barracks on the way to the boats, and precautions were therefore necessary. In spite of the precautions, four of the five German prisoners of war broke away, and had to be shot to prevent them raising the alarm.

The commentary in the Government intelligence file on Operation Basalt points out that it is the duty of a prisoner captured during operations to try to escape, and that the German prisoners were only two fewer in number than their captors (confirming the size of Appleyard's party at the Dixcart Hotel). At the time of the Basalt raid there were believed to be up to 300 German troops billeted on the island of Sark, and tying the hands of the prisoners in those circumstances was not a measure of excessive severity. Considering the journey back to their boat that the SSRF intended to make with the prisoners, it was logical that each should be tied in such a way that he could be controlled by one of his captors. The party had difficult terrain to cover between the Dixcart Hotel and the rendezvous, including the climb up to the Hog's Back, and the descent of Pointe Chateau. Thus the tying of the prisoners hands was necessary.

Obviously, if a prisoner attempts to escape, he may be appropriately restrained – it is perfectly possible for an erstwhile prisoner to become a combatant once more. The German prisoners from the annexe of the Dixcart Hotel had colleagues not far away, and knew if they could escape, or at least raise the alarm, they would have every chance of avoiding a future as a prisoner of war. The Geneva Convention simply did not contemplate the situation in which the SSRF had found themselves. One of their main objectives was to take prisoners back to England and clearly, having taken prisoners (albeit a rather ambitious number of them), the last thing they wanted to do was to shoot them.

The operational order for Basalt, and other SSRF operations, included the following: 'The responsibility for the safe custody of prisoners of war remains yours until the return of your forces to England or such time as prisoners are evacuated from the scene of operations. They should be put ashore as early as possible on the return of your force, where they will be met by representatives of MI9 [intelligence], who will take them over.' Prisoners were a valued intelligence asset.

Sadly, Hitler remained enraged, and did not stop at the shackling of prisoners. On 18 October 1942, he issued his murderous 'Commando Order' (as it became known). In the introduction to the order, Hitler stated:

> For a long time now our opponents have been employing in their conduct of war, methods which contravene the International Convention of Geneva. The members of the so-called Commandos behave in a particularly brutal and underhand manner; and it has been established that those units recruit criminals not only from their own country but even convicts set free in enemy territories. From captured orders it emerges that they are instructed not only to tie up their prisoners, but also to kill out-of-hand unarmed captives who they think might prove an encumbrance to them, or hinder them in successfully carrying out their aims. Orders have been found in which the killing of prisoners has been positively demanded of them.

The body of the order read:

> From now on all men operating against German troops in so-called Commando raids in Europe or Africa are to be annihilated to the last man. This is to be carried out whether they be soldiers in uniform or saboteurs, with or without arms; and whether fighting or seeking to escape; and it is equally immaterial whether they come into action from Ships and Aircraft, or whether they land by parachute. Even if these individuals on discovery make obvious their intention of giving themselves up as prisoners, no pardon is on any account to be given. On this matter a report is to be made on every case to Headquarters for the information of Higher Command.
>
> Should individual members of these Commandos, such as agents, saboteurs etc., fall into the hands of the Armed Forces through any means – as, for example, through the Police in one of the Occupied Territories – they are to be instantly handed over to the S.D [Sicherheitdienst – the Security Service]. To hold them in military custody – for example POW camps etc., – even if only as a temporary measure, is strictly forbidden.
>
> ... I will summon before the tribunal of war all the leaders and officers who fail to carry out instructions – either by their failure to inform their men or by their disobedience of this order in action.

Further instructions were given that in every case, the execution should be kept secret, the bodies should be buried in unmarked graves, and no report should be made to the International Red Cross as to the fate of those executed.

The men of the Special Air Service (SAS) were later to pay a high price as a result. Hitler was determined that his order should be carried out if commandos were caught behind the lines, and following the invasion of Italy in 1943 and the Normandy landings of 1944, his order was enforced many times. As it happened, two of the raiders from Operation Basalt were themselves to suffer the effect of the order: Captain Philip Pinckney and Lieutenant (later Captain) Patrick Dudgeon, each of whom was captured and executed hundreds of miles behind the German front line in occupied Italy in the autumn of 1943*.

---

* See 'SAS in Tuscany' by Brian Lett, Pen and Sword 2011

Chapter 18

Operation Facsimile

Meanwhile, the SSRF got on with its job. Major John Gwynne, the planning officer at Anderson Manor, had been dying to get involved in the action himself, particularly since the death of Gus March-Phillipps. Peter Kemp described him as 'a teetotaller and vegetarian, obstinate, unwearying and fearless, he fretted constantly under the restraints of his sedentary occupation; eager to lead an operation in the field, he was always planning for himself some desperate adventure into enemy territory. With his lean, dark, ascetic face, gleaming eyes, and thinning almost tonsured hair, he had the look of some medieval inquisitor; he always shaved in cold water.'

At the end of September, Gwynne saw his opportunity to be involved. The SSRF had lost many of its experienced men and Gwynne, with Appleyard's approval, put himself forward to command a raid into France. He spoke good French. The raid would be called Operation Facsimile, and would be rather different to anything the SSRF had done so far. A small SSRF party would be landed near Beg an Fry on the north coast of Brittany, and would carry out an attack on Morlaix aerodrome. After the attack, the party would exfiltrate across the border to Spain, and from there find their way back to England. On 1 October, before the second attempt at Operation Basalt took place, the CCO, Lord Mountbatten, had approved the plan, and suggested a date of 6, 7, or 8 October.

By 6 October, however, the target had changed. The raid was now to be on the Gael aerodrome, again on the north coast of Brittany, but on the western side of Cap Frebel. The SSRF raiding party would consist of 5 men – 2 officers and 3 other ranks – and Gwynne would lead it. Having landed, the party would lie up near the airfield for a week, living off rations. At a suitable moment, it would attack and destroy as many of the aircraft as it could, using plastic explosive. Although it was anticipated that the garrison at the airfield would be under strength, the SSRF were warned that it might number as many as 640 men, and therefore orders stipulated that 'battle will be avoided if possible'. The German 17 Infantry Division and the 6 Panzer Division were also both believed to be within the general area of the airfield. The plan was to watch, to creep onto the aerodrome covertly, attach plastic explosive bombs with six-hour delayed fuses to as many planes as possible, and then to retreat to deep cover to watch the resulting show. Having done maximum damage, Gwynne's party would cross the border into Spain and hopefully return from there to England. They would carry sleeping bags, cookers and rations for eight days per man, and were expected to supplement these with local produce – fruit, vegetables, nuts and so forth. Gwynne was finally to get a real slice of action.

The raiding party would not use MTB 344, but would sail from Dartmouth on an MGB, number 312, which was also assigned to the SSRF. The period within which the raid should take place was moved back to 10–20 October. The Naval OIC, Dartmouth, was ordered to keep the SSRF informed of any Allied naval movements that might affect their passage, as well as the latest information on enemy movements. Fighter cover would be provided. The plan was that an additional boat party of 6 members of the SSRF would accompany the raiding party to sea, under the command of Appleyard.

Thus, only a few days after Operation Basalt, the SSRF were ready to go again. Gwynne and the raiding party, together with Appleyard and the boat party, were fully briefed during the day on 10 October, and waited anxiously for the weather reports that would decide if they could go that night. The answer was no, conditions at sea were unsuitable. The same held for the next two nights. On 13 October, the weather was better, but other naval activities in the Channel took priority, preventing the raid from taking place. The weather then changed again for the worse, and the nights of 14 and 15 October were unsuitable. For six days now, the SSRF had been keyed up to go. The night of 16 October was in reality the last chance, since thereafter the state of the moon would have made any cross-Channel raid very difficult, and would have compromised Gwynne's party once on French soil.

As the day of 16 October passed slowly, it looked as if John Gwynne would finally be able to lead his first raid. The weather seemed good enough, and when they assembled in Dartmouth shortly before 1700 hrs, Appleyard took the decision to sail. They left Dartmouth, and passed the Dart buoy at 1723 hrs. However, once they reached the open sea, the weather began to worsen, with the wind rising to force 5–6. The sea got up, and it became impossible to steer a true course in the MGB. At 1845 hrs, Appleyard reluctantly decided to abort the operation and return to harbour. The correctness of this decision was confirmed 45 minutes later when, battling against heavy seas, a pipe in the hydraulic steering gear of the MGB burst. Eventually, a very dispirited SSRF party limped back into Dartmouth Harbour at 2100 hrs.

Reluctantly, Appleyard now called the whole operation off. It would be some time before the moon would again enter a suitable phase, and by that time most of the leaves would be off the trees. The cover that Gwynne and his party had hoped to use in the vicinity of the Gael aerodrome would be gone. Tree cover made an enormous difference to covert warfare in Europe, and once the branches were bare, Appleyard acknowledged that a raid would have to wait until the following spring. Despite the apparent success of Operation Basalt, it was in other ways a frustrating time for the SSRF, and in particular for John Gwynne.

However, Gwynne did eventually get his wish to see some action. He was transferred to Tunisia in early February 1943 as a part of Brandon Mission there (see later), organizing French guerrillas and carrying out operations behind enemy lines, and between July and November of that year served as a British liaison officer working with Greek partisans behind the lines in the Balkans.

Chapter 19

Expansion

Despite the setbacks, October 1942 proved to be a good month for the SSRF overall. Winston Churchill remained much impressed by what they had achieved. On 13 October an order was issued that commando raids across the Channel should be intensified. The SSRF was officially recognized as a successful and effective force, and should be expanded. March-Phillipps and Appleyard had always intended that the SSRF should grow from its humble beginnings once it had proved itself, and now it did. Four more large houses were commandeered: Inchmery, at Exbury in Hampshire, Wraxall Manor, near Dorchester in Dorset, Lupton House in Devon, and Scorries House, Redruth in Cornwall. Anderson Manor would remain the headquarters of an expanded SSRF.

New personnel were assigned to the Force from No. 45 Royal Marine Commando, No. 4 Commando, the French Commando, and No. 12 Commando. Appleyard was confirmed in his rank of major, and the newly promoted Lieutenant Colonel Bill Stirling was brought in to command the enlarged force.

William Joseph Stirling was 31 years of age, 6ft 5ins tall, and came of a well established military family. His father was a brigadier general, and his brother, Lieutenant Colonel David Stirling, is generally credited with founding the Special Air Service. The family lived at Dunblane in Scotland, and Bill Stirling had been educated at Ampleforth College in Yorkshire, where he was three years junior to Gus March-Phillipps. He had then been commissioned into the Scots Guards. He served with Peter Kemp on HMS *Truant* in April 1940, and later joined SOE. He had been appointed to join YAK mission in the Middle East in January 1941, under the command of Ian Fleming's elder brother, Peter. The plan was for YAK mission to set up a school to train foreign nationals (particularly Italians) as agents, to be returned to work behind enemy lines in their own countries, but it failed due to a lack of suitable recruits. Stirling had transferred to other duties on 13 March 1941, after only a few months with the mission, and remained in the Middle East for some time. The autumn of 1942 found Bill Stirling as a major, nominally on loan to the Ministry of Supply. M was keen to have him back in SOE, and began the process of securing his transfer in October. His promotion to lieutenant colonel followed. M described him thus: 'A capable and efficient officer who has a quiet and determined way with him, a good initiative and pertinacity. A good disciplinarian. A very good knowledge of infantry weapons, tactics etc, and an excellent trainer.' Stirling officially rejoined SOE on 17 October 1942, as Commandant of Station 62 – that is, the SSRF at Anderson Manor.

A new intelligence officer, Captain Sam Darby, was also appointed to join the SSRF. He was officially described as the security officer for Anderson Manor, and was in charge of maintaining the secrecy of operations as well as gathering intelligence for briefings. Darby was 28 years old, and something of an intellectual. After graduating from New College, Oxford, he had taught at Winchester College for a year, before moving to Bromsgrove School in his native Midlands. He had joined the intelligence corps in October 1940, and SOE in January 1942. One of his jobs was to ensure there were no leaks of information from Anderson Manor – not the easiest of tasks in the informal atmosphere that prevailed there. There had been concerns, not from M but from those outside SOE, when so many agents had been killed and taken prisoner on Operation Acquatint, that there might have been some sort of leak. Also there were worries that since the SSRF was such a relaxed, informal force, their personal security might be lax also, and they might have taken revealing personal documents with them on Aquatint, that the enemy would now have in their possession. M assured SOE's critics that in order to ensure they were not inadvertently carrying something that would provide intelligence to the enemy, all his men were, and had been as a matter of routine, thoroughly searched on the dockside before they boarded MTB 344 for a raid. However, the appointment of Darby to the SSRF was no doubt intended to help quieten those critics.

To Anderson Manor now came more experienced members of No. 12 Commando, to join Captain Philip Pinckney and his men. Two new officers arrived – Captain 'Mickey' Rooney, and Lieutenant Gilchrist. Each brought six other ranks with them. Peter Kemp, now fit again, together with Bingham and Sergeant Nicholson, were appointed to train Rooney's squad, but it was hardly necessary. Kemp commented: 'Rooney, a powerfully built, self-confident officer, who knew his men intimately and commanded their implicit obedience, had little to learn from me. In fact, apart from pistol shooting, and movement at night, he and his men knew more about the business than I.' Peter Kemp had been appointed to command the landing party on the next raid, Operation Fahrenheit, and was to take Rooney's squad with him, so that they might be 'blooded' in SSRF work. Over the two weeks following Rooney's arrival, training concentrated on night work on land and water, on developing night vision, and on the skills of silent movement.

All this time, Appleyard's broken ankle still had not healed properly, mainly due to the fact that he was not prepared to rest it for long. His exploits on Operation Basalt certainly hadn't helped, and at the beginning of November, he received orders from above that he must sort it out. He was sent to the military hospital at Millbank, London, where he was given the option of either a month's bed rest at the hospital, or a plaster cast on his leg. Not surprisingly, Appleyard opted for the cast and, as he put it in a letter home: 'I went up the steps of the hospital at a run, and came down two hours later a cripple and on crutches.' Despite the plaster on his leg, however, Appleyard could still go to sea, albeit that for the time being he could not scramble on to enemy soil. Only a few days after his hospital visit, he was preparing the SSRF for their next raid, Operation Fahrenheit.

Chapter 20

Operation Fahrenheit

On Operation Fahrenheit, Peter Kemp would command the landing party, which would include 'Mickey' Rooney's section. A second raid, Operation Batman, was to follow. This would involve Colin Ogden Smith as leader of the landing party, together with Lieutenant Gilchrist and his section. Thus all three new sections from No. 12 Commando would have been blooded.

The target for Operation Fahrenheit was a promontory on the Brittany coast called the Pointe de Plouezec, about 15 miles north-west of Saint Breuc. The SSRF were to attack a signals station which was positioned on the promontory. The building was an old semaphore station, one of a series of such stations which had lined the French coast since the mid-nineteenth century. It now used more modern forms of communication. Kemp recalled that the briefing for Fahrenheit took place at Anderson Manor on 5 November 1942, some days before the intended date of the raid.

For once, there was no scale model of the target area for them to inspect, though there were plenty of maps and aerial photographs. Photographs had also been taken of the coastline from the sea by submarine. In addition, there was local intelligence from French sources describing the layout of the signals station, and its defences. A local man called Claude Robinet (alias Claude Rivière) had apparently gained access to the station in the summer of the previous year. He later escaped to England, in January 1942, in company with four other Frenchmen, and passed on what he had learned about the signals station to the British authorities. The objectives of the raid included, as usual, the taking of prisoners. The signals station was to be attacked, general intelligence was to be gathered, and a reconnaissance of the area was to be carried out. The possibility of an armed invasion of the French coast had been under consideration ever since Dunkirk, but with the United States of America now very much a part of the war it was a far more realistic prospect, and the requirement for intelligence about landing conditions and defences was becoming much more urgent.

According to Kemp, the briefing information was as follows: the signals station was perched on top of steep cliffs at the end of the Pointe de Plouezec, which jutted out north-eastwards from the bay of Saint Breuc. Both the north and east faces of the Pointe de Plouezec were defended by concrete gun emplacements containing at least one mounted gun. There was apparently a small shingle beach on the southern side of the promontory, from which a narrow path appeared to lead up the cliff to the headland above. From there it would be possible to follow a track to the signals station itself. This was defended by a single belt of barbed wire, and within it a small concrete guard house, with a garrison believed to consist of about 12 men. Local intelligence said there were no mines or booby traps laid in the vicinity of the signals station – an important piece of information since the attack was to be made, as always, in the dark.

Freddie Bourne and the Little Pisser would carry them from Dartmouth to the French coast. Ten men would land, 3 'veterans' from the SSRF, Kemp, Bingham and Nicholson, and 7 'new recruits' from No. 12 Commando, Rooney, Sergeants Joe Barry and Sam Broderson, Lance Sergeant Sid Evans, Corporal Ellis Howells, and Lance Corporals Percy Cotter and Ronald Roberts. They would not use a Goatley on this raid, but a Nicholson 18ft Dory landing craft. Bingham would be the appointed coxswain for the Dory and Kemp would command the landing party, with Rooney as his second-in-command. Appleyard would command the raid, but would remain on MTB 344 whilst the landing party were ashore.

In addition to the usual weaponry, the landing party would be armed with a Bren machine gun (carried by Sergeant Nicholson), a smaller Sten submachine gun fitted with a silencer (carried by Sergeant Broderson), and two new type grenades, called the PE (plastic explosive) No. 6. These were packed with plastic explosives which gave a very heavy blast on detonation. It was hoped that they would provide an effective way of clearing a route through the barbed wire.

As always, the most powerful weapon that the SSRF would possess was surprise. The operation was to take place during a suitably dark period of the moon, on a night between 9 and 13 November. Included in the briefing was the order that if prisoners were taken, none should have their hands tied, whatever problems that might cause to their captors. The lessons of Operation Basalt had been learnt.

Bill Stirling finished the briefing by impressing that he wanted no casualties in the SSRF party. He was fully aware that the new team from No. 12 Commando, under Rooney's command, were eager to prove themselves, and he took Kemp and Bingham to one side, telling them: 'Rooney and his chaps are very keen and will obviously seize any opportunity for a fight. Naturally we want to inflict casualties and take prisoners, but not, I repeat, at the cost of losing men ourselves; it is not worth it at this stage. If, when you get there, you don't think that you can fight without losing men, I promise you I shall be quite satisfied with a recce.' With the dreadful exception of Operation Aquatint, the SSRF had not lost a single man during its actions, and Stirling clearly wanted to avoid unnecessary risks on what, in any event, was going to be a particularly difficult raid. Not long after this raid, official policy announced that if on an operation it appeared that the element of surprise had been lost, the SSRF should immediately withdraw and not proceed with the operation – surprise was acknowledged as being essential to success.

Having been briefed on the operation, it was now left to Kemp and Rooney to work out the details of how they would mount the actual attack on the signals station. Presuming that the intelligence was good, Kemp decided that they would beach the Dory above what would be a retreating tide, and all 10 men of his landing party would climb to the top of the cliffs. There, he would post Sergeant Nicholson and a second man with the Bren gun to protect their rear and the route back down to the beach. The remaining party of 8 would divide into 3 groups, and follow the path to the signals station – Kemp would take one man up the right-hand side of the path, Rooney would take 2 men up the left side, and 2 men would follow in the rear. They would crawl forward over the last few yards, and Kemp and Rooney would take out the sentries with knives, or if necessary Sergeant Broderson would use his silenced Sten. They would then attack the signals station main building, with Rooney's party taking out the small guard house as they went.

If all went well, and the enemy were taken by surprise, the remainder of the small garrison might surrender, and prisoners could then be obtained. They would retreat rapidly, and be away before any reinforcements could cross the promontory from mainland France to reach them. It was a good plan. Both Kemp and Rooney knew, however, that in reality everything could be very different. Both men were keen to get into action, Kemp after his enforced layoff through injury, Rooney on his first operation with the SSRF.

It was in fact not until five days later, at about midday on 11 November, that the raiding party set out. Weather conditions were now suitable, and the moon still dark. By this time, plans for the follow-up raid on the Cherbourg Peninsula, Operation Batman, had also been approved. It was intended that the

SSRF should have a busy month. The Operation Fahrenheit party was taken, by lorry as usual, to Dartmouth, where Freddie Bourne and MTB 344 awaited them. They stopped en route at the new base that had been acquired for them at Lupton House, another splendid country estate near Paignton, where they ate a hurried meal and changed into their operational clothing. Then they were whisked down to the quay at Dartmouth to find MTB 344 waiting for them, her engines already running. Stirling and Sam Darby, the intelligence officer, were there chatting with Freddie Bourne.

After a brief exchange of greetings and farewells, the SSRF took to sea at about 1745 hrs. It was a fine evening and became a fine night as the Little Pisser sped on her way, picking up speed once clear of land, and reaching 28 knots into a Force 3 wind. It was a long crossing, and Rooney's men went below and mostly curled up and went to sleep, always the sign of a seasoned commando. Appleyard remained as ever on the bridge with Bourne, and Kemp joined them there, cold and soaked by spray. As he grew even colder, Kemp stopped worrying about the operation, finding himself too numb for coherent thought. It was a dark night, and he was unable to make out any horizon. Navigating as they neared the French coast proved difficult, and an hour was lost searching for their first and vital landfall, the lighthouse at the Roches Douvres. Finally, they identified it at 2200 hrs, and Appleyard was able to set a course for Saint Brieuc Bay and the Pointe de Plouezec.

At 2330 hrs, with the sky now clear and full of stars, they were close enough to sight the Pointe de Plouezec, and switched immediately to their silent engine. At 0010 hrs, they dropped anchor off the point. On a clear night such as this, the low-lying profile of MTB 344 was essential for concealment. Rooney and his men filed noiselessly on deck, the dory was launched, and the 10 men of the landing party set off for the shore. It was now that their nighttime training proved its worth. They boarded and rowed silently and efficiently. Appleyard and Bourne were to hear and see nothing more of any of them for nearly two hours.

It took about 15 minutes for the dory to reach the shore. Once the beach came into focus, Kemp realized they had their first problem. It was not shingle, as had been advised. It was no more than a series of rocks and boulders at the foot of the cliff. The tide was receding fast, and if they left the dory grounded on the rocks, they would find it nigh on impossible to launch it again after the raid when the tide was out. Kemp took his men ashore to establish a beachhead, and sent Rooney to recconnoitre the cove to discover if there was anywhere safer where they could land the dory. Rooney reported back that the conditions all round the cove were the same. Since a speedy and effective exit was essential to the success of the operation, Kemp made the only decision he could: a man must be left with the dory, to keep it afloat and ready to depart at any time. The man he chose was Bingham, the coxswain. Thus the attacking party was immediately reduced from to 9, against the 12 expected soldiers at the station.

Things got worse, not better. Kemp led the remaining men off on what was, according to the aerial photographs, a path to the top of the cliffs. It soon became clear that either the path didn't exist, or else it was proving impossible to find in the dark. The cliff was very steep, and about 50ft (15m) high, and the SSRF were reduced to scrambling up the rockface as best they could. Any semblance of a formation was lost, and the slippery wet grass and shale made silence impossible. The men winced as they clambered upwards to the sound of falling shale, rock and debris, and even for Sergeant Joe Barry, an expert climber, the going was difficult. Thick gorse pierced their clothes and tore at their hands and faces. If there was an enemy patrol at the top of the cliff, it seemed certain that they would be heard and would emerge at the top to face a maelstrom of gunfire. The climb took 20 minutes – ample time for the enemy to gather themselves in force at the top of the cliff.

Miraculously, and no doubt only because of the background noise of the sea, when Kemp, and then Rooney, edged their way over the lip of the cliff, they found that there was no reception committee waiting, and that their arrival on the Pointe de Plouezec was apparently still unnoticed. All nine of the SSRF crawled on to the cliff top, and lay absolutely still. They found themselves about 100 yards from a track leading to the signals station, that they had been able to see on the aerial photographs. For a while, Kemp kept his men where they were, whilst they caught their breath and had a careful look around. All seemed quiet. Then, at his signal, the SSRF rose and moved swiftly and silently across the flat open ground between the clifftop and the track. They reached the track without incident, and found themselves about 150 yards from the barbed wire that surrounded the signals station, and the guard house.

Kemp now noticed that Rooney was standing apparently frozen, staring fixedly at two small noticeboards beside the track. He moved closer to see them – each read *Achtung! Minen*. According to the signs, they had just walked straight through a minefield. The local intelligence received at their briefing had told them there were no minefields or booby traps in the area. Were the signs just a bluff, or was the intelligence wrong or out of date? The presence of mines would explain the absence of any enemy patrol along the clifftop. Also, Kemp of course registered that if they had come across a minefield, they would have to cross it again on their return, to descend the cliff to the waiting dory.

While he considered their options, Kemp sent Rooney forward along the track with Sergeant Barry to reconnoitre the enemy's defences, which from what he could see included a concrete pillbox. Rooney returned with a report about half an hour later. It was not very encouraging. Two coils of barbed wire surrounded the signals station and blocked the track, and there were two alert sentries by the entrance to the complex. However, the suspected pillbox had turned out to be merely an old and deserted observation post. As a precaution, Barry had severed the telephone wires that led from the observation post to the signals station, scaling a telegraph pole, and cutting out lengths of the wiring. There had not been time to cut the wires that led back towards the mainland. Rooney also reported that the guardhouse was on the left, not the right-hand side of the track.

Kemp decided that the best plan was to try to circle round the wire to a point further away from the sentries, and to cut the wire and enter the complex there, thus coming on the sentries from behind. It would mean cutting across open ground behind the *Achtung! Minen* signs, but the SSRF had been briefed that there were no mines, and they had crossed the 'minefield' already without mishap, so hopefully the signs were just a bluff. If, of course, Kemp was wrong, and somebody stepped on a mine, they would be not only caught in the middle of a minefield but also exposed to the fire of an alerted enemy. Kemp decided that he had to take that risk. He himself would lead, and they would go in single file, stepping in each other's footsteps. Kemp ordered Sergeant Nicholson and another man, Percy Cotter, to remain with the Bren gun beside the path, to cover their backs and their possible retreat. He then led the remainder of his men off on the level ground to the left of the track.

Kemp did not get very far. Crouching down and moving very slowly, he peered at the ground in the darkness, trying to make out any irregularity that might indicate the presence of a mine. Despite these precautions, after a few paces Kemp very nearly did tread on a mine. Thankfully, it appeared to have been laid carelessly, with little attempt at concealment, under a small lump of turf. Turning very slowly and carefully, Kemp signalled to his men to halt where they were, and called forward Rooney and Lance Sergeant Evans to have a look. Evans, who had some experience of mines, declared it to be an anti-tank mine, on account of its size. There seemed, however, to be no point in sewing anti-tank mines on top of the Pointe de Plouezac, and therefore, if Evans was right, it was possible that it was merely a 'show mine' placed in an obvious position as a deterrent. However, Kemp decided that he could not take that risk, and ordered his men to return the way they had come to the track. Happily, all regained the track without setting off any explosions.

The only options now were retreat or a frontal attack. Kemp had Stirling's words ringing in his ears – 'if you don't think that you can fight without losing men, then I will be quite content with a recce.' But to simply turn around and go home would have left a very bitter taste in all their mouths. They had in any event to risk crossing the minefield again on their return, so they could lose men whether or not they attacked the signals station. After a short discussion with Rooney, Kemp decided to attack. They could at least blow the wire and kill the sentries, before retreating if necessary when the rest of the garrison turned out.

Kemp now divided his men into three sections, as he had originally planned. Nicholson and Cotter, with the Bren gun, remained where they were. Kemp himself took Sergeant Broderson (with the silenced Sten) and advanced on the right side of the track. Rooney, with Sergeant Barry and Corporal Howells, advanced up the left-hand side. The remaining two men of the SSRF, Evans and Roberts, formed the rear party. They would all approach as close as they safely could before dropping to the ground on Kemp's signal. They had rehearsed the movements many times at Anderson Manor, so very little had to be said now. Rooney carried one of the new type of grenade, the PE No. 6, which he would throw to explode and breach the wire, and hopefully also kill the two sentries. Then they would launch their full-on attack, cause as much damage as possible, and get the hell out of it.

Unfortunately, it was now a very still night. As the SSRF crept slowly forward along the path, they could soon hear the voices of the two sentries chatting to each other. Kemp recalls that even Sergeant Broderson's breathing sounded like a steam engine to him. However, the SSRF were practised at moving silently in their felt-soled boots, and so long as the sentries kept talking, there was at least some cover for any slight sounds that they made. Whenever they stopped speaking, the SSRF stopped moving, and remained still until the conversation started up again. In this way, Kemp got to within 30 paces of the two sentries, before dropping down on to his stomach. The others also sank silently to the ground. Kemp and Rooney crawled forward inch by inch, until they were within a mere 10 paces of the sentries. There they came upon a trip wire slung across the track. Kemp concluded that they were as close as they were going to get without being noticed. He lay still, hoping that the sentries might move away from the track, perhaps to do their rounds of the complex.

Fifteen minutes passed. The tension mounted. The sentries chatted on, seeming to have no inclination to move away. Rooney decided that there was nothing to be gained by waiting any longer, and reached for his PE No. 6 grenade. To arm it, he had to unscrew its top, and as he did so, there was an audible click. The sentries, just a few yards away, heard it and were instantly alert. They stopped talking and as Rooney threw the grenade, one of them cocked his rifle. He was too late. A split second later there was a tremendous bang and flash of light as the grenade exploded, shattering the quiet of the night. Back on the MTB 344, Appleyard and Bourne heard the explosion and knew that the action had started.

Rooney and Kemp were so close that they were shaken by the blast from the grenade, but unhurt. Moans and screams came from the two German sentries, both mortally wounded and badly burned by the explosion. Rooney was first to his feet, bursting forward through the remains of the barbed wire, and Sergeant Barry and Kemp were close behind him, as all the men of the SSRF rushed forward. The two sentries were put out of their misery by a burst of machine-gun fire. The guardhouse was found to be empty, so Rooney, Kemp and the others made for the doorway of the signals station itself.

In the courtyard outside the main building, they were fired on by a single German who loomed up out of the darkness, but they fired back, Sergeant Barry's Tommy gun eventually putting the enemy soldier out of action. Another soldier fired on them from a doorway to the main building, but he too was shot down. Lights within the building were rapidly dowsed, and those inside began to organize their defence and a counterattack. Within seconds, heavy fire began to pour down from the darkened doorway and windows. The advantage of surprise had faded away quickly, and the odds against the SSRF had now lengthened. Time was running short, and it looked as if there were still 7 or 8 of the German garrison inside the building, who were now reacting by firing back. Across the promontory on the mainland, there would doubtless be reinforcements, and it would not take long for them to reach the signals station. Since the taking of prisoners now seemed impossible, Kemp took the decision that it was time to go.

Kemp gave the signal and he and his men raced from the compound, collecting a rifle and stick grenade from the dead sentries on the way, then ran back down the track to where the Bren gun party were waiting impassively for them. They were quickly swallowed up in the night, and the fire from the signals station became ineffective. Kemp was praying that they sustained no casualties now, because a descent at speed down the cliff was going to be dangerous enough without the additional burden of any wounded. Back they went through the minefield, quickly this time, trying to stick exactly to the route that they had taken on their way in. Miraculously perhaps, no mines exploded. All 9 men reached the edge of the cliff in one piece, Nicholson still watchfully bringing up the rear with his Bren gun.

Their descent down the cliff to the rocks below was neither orderly nor elegant. They slipped and slid down the gorse and shale-filled gullies leading to the beach, achieving their descent a great deal faster than the ascent. Noise no longer mattered, speed was of the essence, Desultory firing continued from the direction of the signals station, but it seemed for the moment that the enemy, not knowing how many were in the force that had attacked them, were staying within the perimeter of the complex, and not yet attempting pursuit. A number of Verey signal lights had been fired in the air, no doubt to alert anyone on the mainland to the attack who was too deaf to realize what was going on.

Reaching the rocks below, Kemp was thankful to see that Bingham and the dory were still there. Because of the difficult conditions, Bingham had spent much of the last two hours standing up to his waist in water, despite the cold of the November sea, to keep the dory afloat and under control. Eventually he had found a small sandy spar where he could drop a kedge anchor. Once he heard the grenade go off, and the subsequent firing, he had readied the boat for departure. Kemp, Rooney and the others now climbed rapidly into the dory and took their places, and Rooney called the roll – two men were missing, Cotter and Howells.

'No casualties,' Stirling had said. Kemp and Rooney both believed that all members of the attacking party had safely reached the top of the cliff, so they would either have to wait or go back to find the missing men. A magnesium Verey flare shot up into the sky, illuminating the cove and the waiting dory. The men winced in the light, believing that the Germans were bound to see them now. They waited for guns to open up on their flimsy craft from the top of the cliffs, but nothing happened. Gradually, the bright light faded in the sky and the comforting darkness enveloped them once more. At last, the remaining two men came tumbling out of the darkness, and clambered on board. It seems that Cotter had got stuck on the way down the cliff, and Howells had gone back to help him.

Bingham now pushed off and they began to row furiously towards the MTB. The agreed signal to indicate that they were returning and all was well, three green flashes with their signalling lamp, was sent to the waiting MTB. The journey to the Little Pisser took a mere eight minutes, and Appleyard and Bourne were delighted to welcome the entire raiding party back on board at 0328 hrs. They had been gone just over three hours. Inevitably, when the firing had started on land, the minds of both Appleyard and Bourne must have gone back to the last time they had waited together off the coast of France for the return of a raiding party – the ill-fated night of 12/13 September, when not a single man had returned.

As Kemp's men clambered aboard the Little Pisser, more Verey lights shot up into the sky from the Pointe de Plouezac. Appleyard and Bourne decided that now the alarm had been raised they should head out to sea with all possible speed, avoiding Guernsey or any other German positions from which a pursuit might be launched. Bourne opened up the engines and MTB 344 did not fail them, but kept a steady 28 knots per hour all the way back to the relative safety of British waters.

A landfall was made at 0720 hrs, and they entered Dartmouth Harbour at 0800 hrs. Stirling and Darby were waiting for them on the quayside. Darby, the intelligence officer, had with him a squad of Field Security Police to escort any prisoners that Kemp and Rooney had captured into the hands of MI9, for immediate interrogation. Darby was not pleased when told what was obvious, namely that the SSRF had returned empty-handed. His response was to say to Kemp, perhaps in his schoolmaster's manner: 'Go straight back and get some!' Stirling, however, listened to Kemp and Appleyard's reports and announced that he was quite satisfied, saying to Kemp: 'You were fully justified in breaking off the action when you did, in view of the score at the time; I will say so in my covering report. It is bad luck that you couldn't take any prisoners, but you must have given the enemy quite a shock, which is one of your objects.' Bill Stirling was as good as his word, and later reported that Kemp had been right to withdraw when he did. When the reports of the raid eventually reached Prime Minister Winston Churchill, his comment was simply: 'Good'.

Back at the signals station, the Germans still did not know who had attacked them. It seems they were unaware of the retreat by the SSRF down to the cove, or the departure of MTB 344. Reinforcements duly arrived from nearby Port Lazo and Paimpol, but the defenders of the station were unable to tell them much – their attackers were either local 'terrorists' (the French Resistance) or Allied commandos, they did not know which. The following day there were systematic and rigorous searches of all the local houses, but of course nothing was found and because of their uncertainty the Germans took no reprisals against the local population. Rumours abounded – one apparently said that the garrison of the signals station had got drunk and started fighting with each other, resulting in shots being fired and casualties sustained. The German military investigators, of course, knew that this was not true. They recovered two magazines from an English pistol at the scene, and believed the remnants of the grenade that Rooney had thrown to be of French manufacture – it was obviously not German. The official conclusion eventually was that the attack had either been by British commandos, or by French saboteurs armed with English weapons. As always, the official report concluded that 'the attackers were repulsed … the garrison behaved with determination and courage.' Thereafter, the defences of the signals station were strengthened.

Back in England, the SSRF were given an excellent breakfast at the YMCA in Paignton, their morning tea laced with their rum ration. They were then driven back to Anderson Manor, arriving in time for lunch. There was no rest for either Appleyard or Kemp that afternoon, however. Both had to write their reports of the operation – a summary that would find its way to Prime Minister Churchill, and a detailed report for Combined Operations Headquarters and for M at SOE. Kemp records that he was writing his reports well into the evening.

Chapter 21

Operation Batman

The object of the SSRF's next raid was to land on the Cherbourg Peninsula, and as always to gather intelligence and to seize prisoners for interrogation. The operational order specified that the raid was to be carried out on the first suitable night after Operation Fahrenheit had been completed: the window of opportunity would close on the night of 17/18 November. The landing was to be made at Buchy, near Pointe Jardeheu. The SSRF would, as usual, use their preferred vessel, MTB 344, under the command of Freddie Bourne, and Appleyard would travel with the raiding party, but would not land. It was Colin Ogden Smith's turn to command the raiding party, and he would have with him Lieutenant Gilchrist and his section of six men. As always, photographs of the intended target area were supplied, taken both from the air and from a submarine, together with maps, and as with Fahrenheit the briefing was given early, so that the men had plenty of time to train for their specific objective. One of the reasons why Bill Stirling had not been concerned at the failure of Operation Fahrenheit to bring back any prisoners was that Operation Batman was to follow immediately.

Operation Fahrenheit was completed on the early morning of 12 November. Freddie Bourne and his crew were allowed a few days' rest, as Batman was scheduled for the night of 15/16 November. MTB 344 would pick up the SSRF from Portland. For the chosen men, the daytime of 15 November passed slowly, until finally it was time to board the army lorry that would take them to Portland. Gilchrist's men were all experienced commandos, but this was the first time they would see action with their new comrades of the SSRF, and they were anxious to do well.

At Portland, they boarded the Little Pisser, and set off at 2145 hrs. The weather was overcast, and there was some coastal fog and a wind of Force 2–3, but the sea was smooth with only a slight swell. Landfall was made on the

French coast two and a half hours later. However, visibility was poor, and it was very difficult to see the coast well enough to identify any landmarks. The situation was even worse after the moon set at 0050 hrs, and it became exceptionally dark. It was not until 0125 hrs that Appleyard and Bourne were able to identify their exact position. They then calculated that they were still more than an hour from the intended landing area. They would have to creep up the coast, parallel to it, on their silent engine, which even with MTB 344's low profile would bring a grave risk of detection by RDF (radar) or by observation posts. To make matters worse a strong breeze had sprung up from the north, creating a choppy sea that would make landing and departure very difficult for the raiding party under Ogden Smith. If the wind strengthened further while they were on land, it would be impossible for them to return in their dory to the waiting MTB.

Both Appleyard and Bourne had ample experience of the frustrations of these raids, and Stirling's order to avoid taking unnecessary risks and losing men still applied. The memory of Operation Aquatint remained fresh. Shortly after 0125 hrs, Appleyard aborted the raid and gave orders to return home. His decision was soon justified as the wind strengthened, and they suffered a wet Channel crossing back to Portland, which they reached at 0520 hrs.

Reporting to Combined Operations Headquarters, Bill Stirling commented: 'I consider that the right decision was taken in view of prevailing conditions. Abortive operations of this nature are of value in training both Naval and Military personnel.'

Nonetheless, the sense of frustration undoubtedly remained with Gilchrist and his section. Pinckney had accomplished Operation Basalt, Rooney had accomplished Operation Fahrenheit, and of 12 Commando detachment, only Gilchrist's men had yet to see action with the SSRF.

As winter set in, the opportunities for small-scale raiding by the SSRF became more and more limited. When the leaves fell from the trees, there was far less natural cover on land for raiding parties, but the main problem was the sea. The Little Pisser was the SSRF's preferred vessel because of its unusually low profile, but with that came an inability to perform in high seas. If the wind was much stronger than a Force 3, MTB 344 would be in some difficulty, and certainly not able to maintain its speed. Additionally, the Channel was becoming much more crowded with other special operations as plans for the eventual invasion of Europe progressed. Small-scale raids were regarded by many as low priority. However, Mountbatten had approved further raids in the batch of proposals that Stirling put before him at the end of October 1942, which had yet to be carried out. Perhaps the most ambitious of them was called Operation Witticism.

Chapter 22

Operation Witticism

The first operational plan for Operation Witticism is dated 4 December 1942, although it had been approved in principle long before that. The idea was as daring as it was simple. Four men of the SSRF would be transported by MGB as close as possible to St Peter Port, Guernsey, and would then use canoes to paddle in to the harbour and place limpet mines on as many enemy ships moored there as they could.

On this occasion two MGBs were to be used, not the usual MTB 344, and they would be under the command of a friend of Appleyard's, Lieutenant Commander Robert Hichens DSO, DSC, RNVR, who would be loaned to the SSRF for the purpose of the raid. Appleyard held a planning meeting with Hichens on 1 December, in order to perfect the operational plan. The time period for the operation was between the nights of 7/8 and 13/14 December, and it would be launched from Portland. A detailed intelligence briefing pack was prepared, in which were some rather attractive pre-war photographs of the harbour and its shipping, much of it small yachts. It was believed that the current occupants of the harbour included a number of German E boats, as well as enemy merchantmen.

Bad weather prevented the operation from taking place during the first intended period. Conditions had to be suitable not only for the MGBs to make the covert crossing to Guernsey, but for the canoeists to successfully paddle into the harbour and place their mines. However, Lord Mountbatten himself expressed a strong desire that the operation should be rescheduled for the next suitable phase of the moon, saying: 'I am most anxious that this operation should be carried out if possible, as apart from the actual damage done to enemy shipping at St Peter Port on this operation, we should learn some useful lessons which may open up possibilities of similar raids on other targets on the French, Belgian and Dutch coasts'.

The next suitable phase of the moon was between the nights of 2/3 and 13/14 January 1943. Another operational order was produced for a fresh briefing and again Commander Hichens was made available to command the naval side of the operation. MGB 112 would carry the raiding party, MGB 111 would act as escort. According to his father, Appleyard was called away from the celebratory party for the DSO that he had received after Operation Basalt, in order to attend a planning meeting with Hichens. He was invested with his DSO in the morning by King George VI, but went almost straight from the palace to meet with Hichens, not returning to his own party until midnight, by which time most of the guests had gone. It is interesting to note that when invested in December 1942, Appleyard was officially described as 'Lieutenant (temporary Captain) (acting Major)'. He had started the year as a lieutenant, had been promoted captain upon return from West Africa in February, and promoted to major following March-Phillipps' death in September, but as often happened in wartime, official confirmation of his promotions dragged a long way behind the promotions themselves.

The operational briefing for January indicates that the SSRF commander on Operation Witticism was to be Lieutenant I. R. 'Bunny' Warren (the Yorkshireman whom March-Phillipps and Appleyard had first met in Freetown, Sierra Leone, and who had eventually badgered his way into the Small Scale Raiding Force in the Spring of 1942). The attack was to be carried out in two canoes, launched between a quarter and half a mile from St Peter Port, in the middle of the night. They would attack shipping on the Northern Quay within the harbour with specially designed limpet mines, then paddle back to MGB 112 and depart.

Bunny Warren and his men waited anxiously at Anderson Manor for a day of good weather. Finally, on the morning of 8 January, conditions looked ideal, and the operation was given the go-ahead for that night. However, during the afternoon the wind got up, and although Warren and his men took the lorry to Portland and duly embarked on MGB 112, once in mid-Channel the weather worsened still further, and the decision was reluctantly taken to turn back. Frustrated and tired, Warren and his men returned to Anderson Manor. Over the next few days, they waited but the weather did not improve. Finally, on 13 January, the SSRF stood down, and Lieutenant Commander Hichens and his men were released back to their regular duties. On 14 January 1943, Operation Witticism was formally cancelled.

Chapter 23

Huckaback, Backchat and Pussyfoot

Increasingly, as plans for the invasion of mainland Europe progressed, the nature of cross-Channel operations changed. It became necessary for agents to be landed along the enemy coast to infiltrate and gather information, and for that it was desirable that the enemy defences were relaxed and inefficient. One of the original objectives of the SSRF had been to force the enemy to tie up as many troops as possible along the Channel coast and in the Channel Islands, and to make them nervous of unexpected raids. Now, the opposite was true. A 'butcher and bolt' regime could be counter-productive. Also, traffic in the Channel became busier, with operations connected to the future invasion taking priority. It became increasingly difficult for the SSRF to get clearance to take either MTB 344 or the less popular MGBs 111, 112 or 312 (all of which rode higher on the water) across the Channel. Then on 14 January 1943, the SSRF's favourite vessel, MTB 344, had to be taken out of service for a thorough refit. It had been working hard for over six months. The overhaul was expected to take three to four weeks.

There were further conflicts of interest with the Secret Intelligence Service (SIS), otherwise known as MI6. As the senior international secret service, SIS complained that Mountbatten's Combined Operations and M's SOE both got in the way when it was carrying out its activities in France and Norway. The dispute reached the Chief of Staff Committee of the War Cabinet, where Mountbatten stoutly defended the small-scale raids, but in January the Chiefs of Staff ruled that 'where the proposed activities of SOE and SIS and minor raids clashed in any area, SIS would normally be given priority.'

Also, SOE was still not very popular with the Regular Services, and in any event, most of its efforts were now concentrated on its networks of agents throughout Occupied Europe, rather than commando work. The question became 'what to do with the SSRF?'

Despite the problems, an ambitious programme for raids had been set for the month of February 1943. However, the temporary loss of MTB 344 meant a further significant restriction on the work that 1SSRF (as it was now known) at Anderson Manor could undertake. The 1SSRF had been provided with two MGBs in place of MTB 344, but a report dated 14 January setting out a revised February programme made the comments: 'Two MGBs have to be used for each operation for safety reasons, owing to their low speed, and they can be picked up by RDF (radar) far more easily than the smaller MTB 344. Their silhouette is so much larger than MTB 344. They cannot safely approach within half a mile of the coast. This means that many of the operations we have in view are not practicable ... the only targets which can be strongly recommended ... are on the Brittany Peninsula, which is not so strongly covered by RDF.'

For reasons set out in the next chapter, in February 1943, a significant number of the members of 1SSRF stationed at Anderson Manor were posted to North Africa. They included Lieutenant Colonel Bill Stirling, Major Geoffrey Appleyard, Captain Philip Pinckney, and Lieutenants Anders Lassen and Patrick Dudgeon. Peter Kemp, promoted to Major, took over command at Anderson Manor. Despite that departure of a number of its founder members, the SSRF continued to carry out some raids from England in the early months of 1943. Major Peter Kemp still had Leslie Prout, one of the originals of Maid Honor Force, with him, although Prout had suffered extensively from illness in 1942 and was not yet fit for action. Amongst the new recruits to Anderson Manor after March-Phillipps' death had been Captain Pat Porteous VC, a cheerful and courageous 25-year-old who had won his VC in the ill-fated attack on Dieppe, and he also remained at Anderson Manor. Additionally, of course, there were the units in training at the other bases of the SSRF.

The first of the raids carried out by the remaining men of the 1SSRF was Operation Huckaback, on the island of Herm. This had been originally planned for late December/early January, together with two other operations, Inhabit and Backchat. The intention then was that all three raiding parties were to be transported by MTB 344. Three separate sections of the SSRF were to carry out the raids. The objectives were the usual ones: to capture enemy prisoners, to obtain information from the local population, and to generally gather intelligence on the islands. One of the questions that it was hoped Huckaback would answer was whether Herm could be used for artillery support for an invasion of the island of Guernsey.

The operational order dated 27 December 1943 specified that the three operations should take place between the nights of 30/31 December and 13/14 January. Huckaback was to sail from Portland. However, December and January were bad months for weather, and it proved impossible to carry out the raid during that period of the moon. On 14 January, Operation Huckaback was formally cancelled, only to be resurrected by an operational order of 30 January 1943, intended for a three-night period commencing on the night of 9/10 February. The raids were now to be simultaneous, since the available time period was very short. The 'Little Pisser', MTB 344, was undergoing its overhaul, and therefore three MGBs would be used, numbers 312, 317 and 326. Forty-two men of the SSRF and No. 4 Commando (who were now attached to the SSRF) were to be used on the three MGBs under the commands of Captain Graham Young, Captain Pat Porteous VC, and Captain A. Hesketh Pritchard. Again the raids were frustrated by the weather, and a formal cancellation order was issued on 16 February.

A few days later, on 21 February 1943, Operation Huckaback was resurrected yet again, together with Operation Backchat. It seems that Inhabit was now abandoned. The first raid would be Huckaback on Herm, to be followed later by Backchat. The period allotted was between the nights of 25/26 February and 3/4 March. On the second night, 27/28 February, the weather finally proved good enough for the operation to be given the go-ahead. Happily, MTB 344 was back in action with Lieutenant Freddie Bourne at the helm. His navigator would be Lieutenant Vann RNVR, whom Geoffrey Appleyard had trained as his substitute before leaving for North Africa. Vann had been with the SSRF at the outset, and had taken part in the very earliest attempts to raid the Casquets lighthouse.

The Huckaback raid was to be mounted by a party of 10 officers and men of No. 4 Commando, attached to the SSRF, under the command of Captain Porteous and a Lieutenant Thompson. They would be accompanied by Captain W. Hewitt of No. 1 Bombardment Unit, whose task was to assess the potential to land and use artillery on the island. As was now the practice, the operational order included the clear direction that 'instructions reference no manacling of prisoners and that no string or wire will be taken on operation must be stressed particularly to all personnel.' There was a nervousness that, if and when they discovered that the raid had taken place, the enemy would try to manipulate the facts for propaganda purposes, as they had done with Operation Basalt. The operational order also specified that particular emphasis was to be placed on the capturing of a German infantryman, samples of German wire and German weapons and documents, but the primary purpose remained to make an artillery survey of the island. The plan was that the SSRF should land by dory soon after midnight, and remain ashore for no more than four hours.

Herm had been owned at the outbreak of the war by Sir Percival Perry, who had done his best to preserve the natural beauty of the island. Its population had always been small (48 persons were recorded on the 1931 census), and in fact the island had been cleared of residents by the Germans following the occupation. It was believed that only a German anti-aircraft battery now remained on the island, around 12 to 14 individuals, possibly together with the caretaker for the big house, Mr Le Page.

As usual, the SSRF drove by lorry from Anderson Manor to Portland, from where they sailed on MTB 344 at 1900 hrs. The wind was a north-easterly Force 2, and the sea was relatively calm. The crossing passed without incident, and at 2200 hrs Bourne stopped the main engines and crept forward on the silent auxiliary. They dropped anchor off Herm at 2245 hrs, and the landing party embarked in their 18ft dory ten minutes later. It was a dark night, and the moon was due to rise shortly before 0300 hrs. The landing place chosen, a shingle beach in a small bay surrounded by cliffs, was reached without difficulty and the party landed successfully.

As always, they were alert to the possibility of an enemy presence, but encountered no resistance on the beach. The cliffs, however, proved a problem. According to their usual practice, the SSRF had chosen a landing point that the enemy would not expect due to its apparent inaccessibility. The cliffs were about 100ft high and made of soft clay. They presented real difficulty and three unsuccessful attempts were made to scale them. Finally, a route was discovered up the bed of a small stream in the middle of the western cliff. Porteous climbed it first carrying a rope, which he then used to pull up the remainder of the force. A sentry was positioned at the top of the cliff to guard their retreat and Porteous led his party to Belvoir House, above Belvoir Beach. Whilst Captain Hewitt surveyed the beach to judge its suitability for landing artillery, Porteous, leaving Lieutenant Thompson and two men to provide covering fire if necessary, forced an entry into Belvoir House, but found it unfurnished and abandoned. The SSRF had with them a number of propaganda leaflets, which they left in prominent positions along the way. They also chalked the letter C on various walls and buildings, although the significance of that is not clear. Curiously, it was apparently not intended that their visit should remain a secret.

The party re-formed and moved on, initially bypassing the largest house on the island, known as the Chateau, and making their way across an overgrown golf course to Shell Beach. This beach is over half a mile long, and is a unique site for ancient shells of creatures no longer found in the Northern Hemisphere. They found no sign of any enemy activity on that part of the island either, and no wire, mines or defensive positions. Hewitt's survey of Shell Beach led him to conclude that artillery could indeed be landed there. The sandy ground around the beach was turf-covered, and wheeled or tracked vehicles would have no difficulty crossing it.

The party now divided again, Thompson taking two men to search the nearby 'Old Tower of Herm' which was deserted, and Porteous turning his attention to the Chateau and its surrounding buildings. The Chateau itself and three nearby houses were entered and all found to be abandoned. The only sign of any German occupation was a notice in the back yard of the Chateau, which appeared to place the building and its surrounds out of bounds to all troops. It was indeed the only sign of any German presence on the entire island that the raiding party saw. They encountered neither German not Channel Islander. There was a small collection of houses around the harbour, but time was now running short, with the moon due to rise at 0256 hrs. Having completed the search of the Chateau, Porteous decided that it was time to go. He rendezvoused with Lieutenant Thompson's party, and they returned to the sentry who was guarding their route back down to the beach. Using the rope, they descended without great difficulty to where they had left the dory. They left the island at 0225 hrs, and quickly regained the relative security of MTB 344. They had been on dry land for about three and a half hours.

The journey back to Portland was uneventful and they docked at 0540 hrs. Porteous duly reported his findings, as did Captain Hewitt. Porteous concluded that there were Germans on Herm, but that they must be billeted in the houses around the harbour, and that there were no defensive works of any kind on the north or east coasts. Hewitt reported that Belvoir beach was unsuitable for the landing of artillery because of the difficulty presented by the surrounding terrain, but that Shell Beach was suitable. He noted that there were fields on the part of the island that they had surveyed that were suitable for the siting of artillery batteries, and that there were a number of acceptable observation posts including the Old Tower.

Almost immediately after Huckaback had been completed, the second operation, Backchat, was launched, taking advantage of the favourable weather and the same phase of the moon. Operation Backchat had originally been conceived back in the summer of 1942 as an operation for No. 12 Commando. Then it was planned that a squad of 60 commandos – E troop under the command of Captain Philip Pinckney (later of the SSRF) – would land on the French coast at Anse de St Martin, on the north-west corner of Cherbourg Peninsula. An operational order was issued, dated 14 July 1942, and it was intended that the operation should be carried out between 21 and 24 July, at the same time as the SSRF's Operation Barricade. Five landing craft were to be used, with two MGBs as escorts. The object was a 'butcher and bolt' raid – to capture and kill as many enemy as possible.

Both the original Backchat and Barricade had had to be put off, and although Barricade was carried out a few weeks later in August, Backchat remained on the back-burner until December 1942, when it was resurrected as one of the three operations intended for end December/early January, but on a very much smaller scale, and for reconnaissance purposes only. Like Huckaback, it was cancelled due to bad weather conditions, resurrected, and cancelled again, before being finally resurrected on 21 February 1943. This time, it went ahead.

Operation Backchat set out from Portland on the evening of 1 March 1943. Freddie Bourne and MTB 344 were again the transport.

According to the operational order, the raiding party was to be a small one, comprising four men under the overall command of the SSRF Commando, but on loan from the 2 Special Boat Section (2SBS) who were based at Green End Lane House, Tichfield Haven in Hampshire, including Lieutenant Smee and Second Lieutenant McClair. In the event it appears it was even smaller, just two men of 2SBS, with Second Lieutenant McClair in command. As with Operation Huckaback, Lieutenant Vann, Appleyard's understudy, was the navigator.

MTB 334 sailed from Portland at 2000 hrs, arrived off Pointe de Jardhen and made landfall at 2205 hrs. Bourne then switched to the auxiliary engine, and began the approach south along the coast towards Anse de St Martin. However, for the first time it seems that the Little Pisser was spotted from the French coast, and at about 2330 hrs, while they were still short of the intended landing point, two searchlights suddenly came on, and firing began from a number of guns positioned close to the lights. Shrapnel exploded in the air above the MTB, and soon two small ships were seen nearby, which were presumed to be enemy patrol vessels. The decision was taken for MTB 344 to abandon its mission, and make full speed for Portland, which it promptly did, arriving safely home at 0200 hrs. McClair and Smee returned to their base at Tichfield Haven the same day.

Although the decision to abort the mission was approved in due course as the correct one, there was discontent at the performance of Lieutenant Vann, the SSRF navigator. The Brigadier Commanding, the Special Service Brigade (of which both the SSRF and 2SBS were a part) reported:

> We should leave navigation to the Royal Navy (except perhaps in the case of Major Appleyard, who is rather an exceptional person) and I do not think that the practice of the SSRF navigating their own MGBs will normally work. When I first joined the Special Service Brigade, I was inclined to advocate an optimum situation in which we, as seabourne raiders, would possess our own navigators, thereby becoming completely self-contained units which would stand or fall on our proficiency in every aspect of a raid. I have since come to regard this utopian conception as

impracticable, and feel that I must now recommend that in future navigation of all raiding craft must be the sole responsibility of the Royal Navy ... The navigator [on Operation Backchat] was Lieutenant Vann RNVR ... who is, in fact, Appleyard's understudy ... I personally know little of the navigational problems discussed [on Operation Backchat], but it would appear to me as an unqualified observer, that the undesirable navigational procedure adopted by Lieutenant Vann arose through his having less self-confidence and experience than Major Appleyard.

Before that report was written, a decision had been made to visit the island of Herm for a second time. The new operation was called Pussyfoot and the operational order, dated 23 March 1943, states that a party of 10 officers and men of the SSRF should visit the western side of Herm (that part that Porteous and Operation Backchat had not had time to reach), should reconnoitre the hamlet there, and should obtain information and take prisoners. Pussyfoot was to take place on the first suitable night between 29/30 March and 11/12 April, and the raiding party would travel from Portland on MTB 344. There was to be a sister operation, entitled Catswhiskers, that would take place on the neighbouring island of Brechou in the same period. Yet a third operation was proposed called Kleptomania, a similar raid on the island of Ushant, for which it was suggested that the SSRF should be given a time slot at the end of April/beginning of May, but it appears that this was never approved. Operation Pussyfoot set out from Portland at 1945 hrs on 3 April. At 0407 hrs the next morning it returned to Portland. The weather, this time apparently thick fog, had defeated them.

The difficulties that had frustrated Stirling and Appleyard a few months earlier persisted. There was intense competition for the use of the sea lanes and, in addition, by 19 April 1943, all MGBs had been assigned to other duties. Perversely, although with the coming of spring the weather could be expected to improve, the dark hours of the night, so valuable for the journeys by MTB 344 to and from the landing areas, and so vital for the operations on land, would rapidly shorten. One of the problems with the proposed Operation Kleptomania was the shorter nights. The plan was that a squad of 14 SSRF should attack machine-gun positions on Ushant and destroy a cable-head there, taking prisoners if possible. However, the island was 120 miles from Falmouth, and a lengthy journey time would be required to get there and return. By the end of April/beginning of May, when it was intended that the operation should be carried out, there would be a mere six and a half hours of darkness available. The commandos would have a maximum of two hours ashore and much of the journey in each direction would have to be made in partial or full daylight.

As a result of these and other operational difficulties, the SSRF in England was formally disbanded on 19 April 1943. In truth, it had outlived its purpose. The reason why Bill Stirling and Geoffrey Appleyard had left for North Africa in February was that, in their view, the future of small-scale raiding lay in the Mediterranean and the Aegean. M now recalled his remaining agents from their shared role with Lord Louis Mountbatten's Combined Operations, and brought them fully back under his own control. Some of the men of 12 Commando (including Philip Pinckney) had already gone to North Africa, others (such as Oswald 'Mickey' Rooney) returned to 12 Commando. Amongst those who remained at Anderson Manor were Peter Kemp, Colin Ogden Smith, Brinkgreve and Reynolds/ Bingham. Of those, three were now assigned alternative roles within M's secret service – in due course Kemp was sent to the Balkans, Ogden Smith eventually went to France, and Brinkgreve to the Netherlands. Bingham/Reynolds took a naval commission in the name of Bingham, and returned to the exciting activities crossing the North Sea that he had enjoyed before joining SOE. Of the four, only Peter Kemp survived the war.

Chapter 24

Confusion in North Africa

It is clear that from late 1942, the minds of some, including Bill Stirling, had been on the possibility of moving a part or all of the SSRF to North Africa, where Stirling's younger brother David was doing good work with 1SAS, and where the relative calm of the Mediterranean might provide for better sea raiding than the British Channel. The many frustrations of trying to operate the SSRF in domestic waters around Britain are made clear in the previous chapters. With United States involvent in the war, the campaign in North Africa was under joint Allied command. The idea of an invasion of Vichy French North Africa had been under discussion throughout 1942, and the decision had been taken in July 1942 that there should be an invasion that autumn, under the overall command of the American General Dwight D. Eisenhower. The invasion was to be known as Operation Torch.

Simultaneously to the planning of Operation Torch, SOE began negotiations in August to open an advanced base of their own in North Africa. It was to be a self-supporting base that would provide its services both in support of Torch, and the intended later Allied invasion of Europe from North Africa. By November, arrangements were in place for SOE to open its North African base under the codename Massingham Mission.

Operation Torch began in early November 1942, when three seaborne landings took place at Casablanca, Oran and Algiers, and the Allied force fought its way east into Tunisia. On 17 November, the advance party for Brandon Mission arrived, and set up a base at Cap Matifou, about 25km from Algiers, and a sister mission, Brandon Mission, was set up for the specific purposes of assisting Operation Torch. Brandon Mission, under the command of Lieutenant Colonel Young, ran a number of special detachments behind enemy lines in Tunisia, employing many Free French agents. Their activities were entirely separate from those of David Stirling's 1SAS Regiment. It was Brandon Mission that Major Gwynne joined in February 1943.

However, according to the Massingham Mission war diary, in December 1942 the US Lieutenant General Kenneth Anderson, who commanded the mixed British and American force that had landed at Algiers, expressed disappointment with Brandon Mission's work, and as early as 18 December 1942, announced that he had decided to ask whether Colonel Bill Stirling of the SSRF and some of his detachment might be sent to him. British High Command duly consented to this, and indicated that the SSRF should receive reinforcement from the commandos. M visited Massingham Mission in North Africa in early 1943, arriving on 25 January and staying for nearly six weeks in preparation for the expected invasion of Europe. He too initially agreed to the American request.

However, SOE's Lieutenant Colonel Young, who commanded Brandon Mission was obviously not pleased at Anderson's criticisms, or the request for a fresh unit. Just how it came about that that Lieutenant General Anderson knew of and asked for the men of Anderson Manor is not entirely clear. His request for them seems to have coincided with Bill Stirling and Geoffrey Appleyard's enthusiasm to go to North Africa. Back in England, by January, the impending loss of MTB 344 (even if only temporary) undoubtedly contributed to Stirling's wish to find a more profitable war zone than the Channel. For long stretches of time the Brittany Coast was closed to the SSRF, and they were having difficulty in finding suitable targets even when the weather was good enough.

It seems likely that Bill Stirling, even though he had only been in charge for two months, had begun to put the word about that he felt the SSRF might be more productively deployed in North Africa, and that this had reached the ears of Lieutenant General Anderson, perhaps through Stirling's brother, David. Although early in 1942, M had agreed to share control of the SSRF with Mountbatten's Combined Operations, he had not particularly enjoyed the experiment, and was not very keen to repeat it by loaning some of the SSRF to Lieutenant General Anderson. Furthermore, he obviously did not wish to lose experienced men such as Appleyard and Lassen from his Secret Service. However, Massingham and Brandon were SOE missions, and if the SSRF was attached to one or other of them, M would retain overall control.

The British General Alexander met Eisenhower and Lord Mountbatten of Combined Operations on 16 January 1942, and the three agreed to create a new force to operate along the same lines as David Stirling's 1SAS. Initially, the agreement was that this force should consist of 200 commandos, under the command of General Eisenhower. The men of the SSRF, with their special skills, were an obvious choice for the new unit. The agreement was announced by Mountbatten to Major General Haydon in London, on 20 January 1943. One of his comments was: 'Most important that Commander [of the new force] should co-operate with [David] Stirling, and therefore be likely to get on with him.' Bill Stirling, David's elder brother, might therefore have seemed perfect for the new command, but there were actually some concerns about this. Apparently, two of the principal commando leaders in North Africa, Lord Lovatt and David Stirling, were currently not getting on at all well together, despite being cousins, and it was thought that if David's brother Bill arrived with a new force it might make things even worse – as someone pointed out, 'it would mess up the whole thing if the commanders of these two forces fought.'

General Alexander, General Eisenhower and High Command in the Middle East and North Africa were very keen to increase the number of long-range sabotage raids of the type that 1SAS had been so successfully carrying out, and were enthusiastic about the prospects of amphibious raids. At this time there was already a fledgling amphibious unit within 1SAS, under Lord Jellicoe's command. Alexander and Eisenhower wanted to start organizing and training a proportion of David Stirling's 1SAS for full-time amphibious work – hence the attraction of the SSRF as a part of the new force.

The two generals now wanted a detachment of the SSRF to come from England, to be placed under Eisenhower's direct control. The SSRF was asked on 20 January 1943 to provide two good officers, 'first to train and then to take part in operations with [David] Stirling's men.' They were to build up the amphibious unit. Major General Haydon, at Combined Operations in Whitehall, expressed himself firmly against the idea of the new force from the start. Nevertheless, the decision was taken to send a detachment of 50 British commandos as soon as possible to North Africa. That would include about half of the SSRF men stationed at Anderson Manor. Bill Stirling was determined to take command of the force, and when his brother David was taken prisoner behind enemy lines at the end of January 1943 and shipped to a prison camp in Italy, the objection that there might be some sort of personality clash with Lovatt faded away.

Two officers from the SSRF, Philip Pinckney and Anders Lassen, were provided as the requested advance guard to help with immediate training. They flew out in early February 1943 to Cairo, where they were formally attached to the strength of 1SAS, now under the command of Major V. W. Street. Lassen was signed on with effect from 22 February 1943, Pinckney from 9 March. Bill Stirling also travelled out by air not long afterwards, together with his either his Administrative Officer, Captain Barkworth, or Patrick Dudgeon – records vary, but both ended up with what was to become 2SAS in North Africa. It was left to Geoffrey Appleyard, still the Operational Commander of the SSRF, to bring out the main body of men and equipment by sea. The main body was divided into two parties: Appleyard, together with a team of 12, travelled as the advance party, and the second party of 34 men followed shortly afterwards. Peter Kemp took over operational command of the remaining men of the SSRF at Anderson Manor, together with a Major Horning.

Not everybody was happy. The Massingham Mission war diary for February 1943 shows that SOE in North Africa and the Middle East increasingly suffered misgivings about the impending arrival of the SSRF. The diary records that although initially London had understood that the detachment of the SSRF would come under the orders of Eisenhower himself, that position was now changing. M was at Massingham during February, and he was concerned that Allied Force Headquarters (AFH) in North Africa were in fact now much less anxious to have the SSRF, as they foresaw a shortage of available sea transport, and therefore thought that there would be very limited scope for the SSRF to achieve anything.

Shortly after this, M reported back to London that AFH had apparently changed its mind altogether about having the SSRF, and would now like just one officer, nominated by Combined Operations, to come out and study the possibilities fully before the main party was despatched. The Massingham war diary emphasized that if the party came out and there was no specialized work for them, AFH would simply use them as reinforcements for the commandos, a suggestion with which M was very unhappy. He viewed his trained agents as specialists, and in no way ordinary commandos. M was quite willing for Stirling to come out to recconnoitre the situation, but did not want any larger party such as Appleyard's to arrive only to be absorbed into the commandos. M went so far as to obtain an assurance from Combined Operations that his men would not be used in this way, but nonetheless was not entirely comfortable with the situation. Later, on 4 March 1943, Sir Charles Hambro, the overall head of SOE at this time (M assumed overall control in September 1943) issued a clear directive saying so far as the SOE were concerned they 'did not wish their party to be absorbed into or lent to commandos on any account whatsoever.'

Stirling and Barkworth had already left England by air (as had Lassen and Pinckney), but it was promised that on arrival Stirling would confer with M (who was still in the Middle East) before M returned to England. Appleyard, with the two parts of his detachment, had been preparing to leave England, and in the event did so before any orders to the contrary arrived. On 17 February, Massingham Mission was informed that Appleyard's party had already left the UK by sea, and that the rest of the SSRF detachment, 4 officers and 30 other ranks, would be on their way by 19 February. It seems that with M absent from

England, his control over the movements of his agents was not as effective as it might have been. Also, it is quite clear that Stirling and Appleyard were keen to get out to North Africa, where they believed that the 'real war' was going to be over the next few months.

Things became even more difficult when on 19 February, too late to prevent the sailings, M received a message suggesting that Appleyard's departure might seriously affect the leadership of the SSRF remaining in England. The suggestion had been that Horning should take over the planning role at Anderson Manor (Gwynne had already joined Brandon Mission), but Horning was said to have no navigational experience in planning and carrying out special operations. Bill Stirling would have to give up overall command of Station 62 if he remained in North Africa, since he obviously could not command it from there, so Appleyard's presence would be sorely missed. M decided to tell Stirling to send Appleyard back to England as soon as he had arrived and handed over his party. Horning could then go out to North Africa to replace him. Appleyard, once back at Anderson Manor, could ensure the SSRF's future as a unit there.

Thus the officers and men of the SSRF arrived in North Africa to find confusion awaiting them. The situation was not nearly as rosy as they had hoped and been led to believe. There was no immediate work for the SSRF to do. One result of the capture of Bill Stirling's brother David at the end of January was that 1SAS was in a state of flux. The Massingham Mission war diary for 2 March 1943 records that M did indeed order Bill Stirling (who had now arrived) to send Appleyard back to England as soon as he had landed and handed over his party, but that did not happen. There was a power struggle going on at the highest level. M himself left for England on 7 March.

By this time Massingham Mission appears to have become very hostile to the SSRF's arrival. Bill Stirling was recorded in their diary as being sadly disillusioned at the situation he found, partly (claims the diary) through his own fault and partly owing to Combined Operations' excessive enthusiasm to get the SSRF out to North Africa, when in fact there was no appropriate work for them. The Massingham diary comments that there was really little future for Stirling. AFH were apparently grumbling that the SSRF had been thrust upon them, and again threatening to send them forward to Army Group Headquarters to be put on general operational duty. Army Group themselves took the view that since the SSRF had been sent to North Africa, they would have to try to use them, but only on the First Army front and quite independent of 1SAS. There was no opening for raids by sea. All this was exactly what M had feared and tried to avoid. The Massingham Mission diary comments that they all could offer the SSRF was work on the same lines as

Brandon Mission (behind the lines in Tunisia), for which they were much less well-fitted than the Brandon agents.

To make things worse, Bill Stirling now fell out badly with Lieutenant Colonel Young, the CO of Brandon Mission. It was because of the Mission's alleged shortcomings that the SSRF had first been requested. Now that the SSRF party had arrived, some coordination between them and Brandon Mission had to be set up, in relation to any work they were to do. A meeting was arranged on 17 March, at which Lieutenant Colonels Young and Stirling were both present. It was agreed that the units would work separately, but that proper liaison was to take place between them. However, problems quickly arose. Amongst them was the question of recruitment or secondment of personnel. The Massingham Mission war diary records:

> Colonel Young was specially summonsed in the middle of operations to a conference at 18 Army Group Headquarters which had on 28 March taken over control of all Brandon's operations outside 1st Army and 2nd US Corps area. Here, a special directive allotting definitive objectives and areas to the SSRF and Brandon was discussed and agreed to. Colonel Stirling [in Colonel Young's view 'a really bad piece of work'] made allegations concerning Brandon's treatment of the Arabs. Colonel Young had no difficulty in refuting these allegations and eventually Colonel Stirling withdrew them. It was also agreed that Brandon should retain six French personnel who were claimed by the SSRF.

Eventually, it was decided that Stirling's command, whatever was found for it to do, would comprise those men of the SSRF who had travelled out with him, plus possibly a small detachment of 1SAS. For the veterans of Operation Postmaster, such as Appleyard and Lassen, the situation must have seemed very similar to what had happened to Maid Honor Force when they first arrived in West Africa. Their presence had not been popular with the local West African commanders and for a long time they had been kept twiddling their thumbs, unable to carry out the work for which they had been trained.

On 16 March, M, now in London, asked Massingham Mission whether Appleyard had yet left for home. He made clear to them that if he hadn't, Stirling should be contacted again and given a direct order that Appleyard was to return to England. On 25 March, Massingham cabled London to confirm that Lieutenant Colonel Young had given M's order to Stirling, in the presence of Appleyard. In spite of this, Appleyard was still in North Africa. It is clear that there was a power struggle going on in which Geoffrey Appleyard was the pawn. He was a distinguished and highly trained officer, and M was not the only commander who wanted his services. Bill Stirling was putting some noses out of joint (notably those of Massingham Mission), but pleasing others. In a report dated 17 March 1943, Lieutenant Commander Curtis of 30 Commando Special Engineering Unit (SEU) is quoted as saying: 'Colonel Stirling and Major Appleyard of the SSRF are within two hours by road and very close liaison has been made from the sharing of stores upwards. Colonel Stirling is in very high favour with Commander in Chief Mediterranean, and with Military and Planning authorities in Algiers. He looks after the SEU's interests in that direction and the SEU do liaison work for him at Bone. The SSRF has given instructions to the SEU in the recognition of and avoidance of booby traps and in handling the double-ended dories.'

The Massingham Mission war diary for April 1943 continued to be unflattering about Bill Stirling as he began to build up his unit in North Africa, reflecting the continuing conflict of wills. The relevant entries in the diary read:

> Colonel Young was told that Stirling had no war or operational experience whatever, and that foreign volunteers whether in uniform or not were SOE's job and not the SSRF's ... Stirling was not to take personnel from Brandon. He had apparently disobeyed General Gubbins' direct order to send Appleyard back to England. Gubbins had taken matter this up with the CCO [Mountbatten], and a further wire was being sent. Stirling had no authority from Gubbins to interfere in Brandon's activities in any way whatever. Massingham were warned that it was now evident that Stirling was playing quite unscrupulously with the Army Group and probably to the detriment of Brandon and Massingham. It was essential that they should contact Brandon in the near future and make sure that their own preparations and proposals with AFH were not interfered with.

M was still trying to get Appleyard back to England. On 23 April 1943, Massingham Mission was told that Combined Operations (Mountbatten) had now wired to AFH asking for Appleyard's immediate return. However, that was later varied to a return by 15 May, and it is clear that London eventually lost the power struggle. In May, Appleyard's return was again deferred, and the war diary records: 'At Major Appleyard's own request it was arranged in London that he should remain in his present appointment until the invasion of Sicily as General Gairdner had asked. [Lieutenant General Charles Gairdner was in command of the British 6 Armoured Divison, which had taken part in Operation Torch.] General Gubbins trusted that, if required, he would be returned without further delay or discussion.' It seems Geoffrey Appleyard had been making himself extremely useful in North Africa and the Middle East for some time, and in fact the SSRF in England had been officially disbanded in his absence. On 18 May 1943, Appleyard's SOE personnel file records that he was to remain in North Africa for the duration of Operation Husky, the invasion of Sicily.

Following David Stirling's capture at the end of January, 1SAS was reorganized on 19 March 1943 into two parts – the Special Boat Squadron (SBS), under Lord Jellicoe, and the Special Raiding Squadron (SRS), under Paddy Mayne. Pinckney and Lassen, the first members of the SSRF to arrive, who had been signed on to 1SAS's nominal role, were initially posted on 27 March to 'Holding Unit, Special Forces', but before the end of April both were signed on to the SBS. It is said that Lord Jellicoe specifically asked for Lassen. The constitution of the Special Forces Units in North Africa and the Middle East appears to have been exceptionally confused throughout the summer months of 1943, and undoubtedly the personnel involved in actions by the SRS, SBS, and 1SSRF/2SAS frequently overlapped. One difficulty which adds to the confusion is that the initials SBS could be used for the Special Boat Section or the Special Boat Squadron. In May 1943, Bill Stirling, despite resistance from some quarters, set up his new force 2SAS, taking with him the likes of Appleyard and Dudgeon, although for a while Appleyard remained on the books of SOE and therefore was still officially M's man. Bill Stirling's objective was to run his regiment much in the way of his brother David's 1SAS.

Thus, finally, the team that Gus March-Phillipps had put together, first as Maid Honor Force and then as the Small Scale Raiding Force, ceased to exist. March-Phillipps himself was dead, Graham Hayes was a prisoner of the Gestapo in Paris, Geoffrey Appleyard became nominally a part of 2SAS, and Anders Lassen joined the SBS. The original 'James Bonds', so admired by Ian Fleming, had spread out and gone their individual ways. The two still at liberty, Appleyard and Lassen, ceased to be secret agents of any sort, and returned to full time commando duties.

Chapter 25

Geoffrey Appleyard

Geoffrey Appleyard had travelled out by ship to North Africa with the first contingent of SSRF from Anderson Manor. They sailed from the Clyde in mid-February 1943. Captain Roy Bridgeman-Evans, whom Appleyard had interviewed and recruited after Gus March-Phillipps' death, was his second-in-command during the voyage. The two men shared a cabin and became good friends. Bridgeman-Evans wrote later to Appleyard's father to describe their first meeting: 'It was Geoffrey who interviewed me. I wish I could explain my feelings better – Geoffrey's eyes were so blue and looked so very straight at me – I know I had the feeling that he summed me up right away and that if I told a lie, he would have known it right away. When I walked out into Whitehall [the interviews were always held at Room 98, Horse Guards], I was saying to myself: "I would follow that man anywhere" – I had only been with him fifteen minutes.'

Geoffrey Appleyard himself does not appear to have been troubled by the tug of war that was going on in relation to his services and those of the SSRF as a whole. He enjoyed a peaceful voyage, undisturbed by enemy action, and arrived either at the end of February or very early March. Appleyard described the force as 1SSRF, which had been the title given to the men of 62 Commando at Anderson Manor after the expansion that followed March-Phillipps' death. Appleyard was keen to keep the force together, even if that meant for the time being that he was detached from M's command.

One of those who travelled out with him was a Canadian, Lieutenant John Cochrane of the 75 Toronto Scottish Regiment. Cochrane had been separated from his wife and family when he was posted to England in 1940, an unhappy experience shared with many servicemen. In his case it was particularly poignant, since he left behind a wife pregnant with their first child. On 21 January 1941, Cochrane had received a telegram from home to tell him the child had been born, which read: 'Due severe attack of influenza four pound incubator baby boy born January 13. Expected to live. Recovering nicely.' Cochrane's son, Michael, did survive, but due to the fortunes of war was not seen by his father until after his fourth birthday.

One of Cochrane's concerns for his family was financial – he wrote home that 'English pay and allowances are pitifully small.' However, he was happy to have joined the SSRF and wrote from on board ship to say of Appleyard: 'He's a naturally born leader and I for one would follow him anywhere. Everyone has the greatest confidence in him. His rank doesn't matter a damn to him.'

Once arrived in North Africa, 1SSRF settled in to a new base, which was on the coast near to Philippeville in Algeria, 40 miles north of Constantine, and initially managed to stay more or less intact. Certainly, on 19 April 1943, John Cochrane was still writing home using the address of 1SSRF. Like many others, Appleyard believed that Philippeville was an ideal camp for them, describing it in a letter home as: 'a most delightful place, right on the sea amongst the sand dunes about ten miles from the nearest town. A really healthy spot (all in tents of course) and an excellent training area ... wonderful surfing and great fun with the boats for training in surf work, and the length and height of the surf is about Newquay standard.'

However, as the weeks and months went by, the various special forces in North Africa changed and re-formed, whatever M's wishes may have been. As Bill Stirling put his plans into effect, 1SSRF became a part of the new 2SAS. Philippeville remained their base, but despite its beautiful setting it eventually became clear that the area contained a deadly secret that was to hamper 2SAS on later operations. Appleyard's assessment of a 'really healthy spot' could not have been more wrong. Major Roy Farran DSO, MC, one of the officers of 2SAS, described it later: 'In spite of the beautiful scenery surrounding our camp at Philippeville, it had been the beauty of a fickle jade, for the undergrowth had hidden a dangerous malarial swamp.' Malaria, that devastating recurrent illness, affected many of the soldiers of 2SAS on operations in 1943 and 1944. Appleyard, when he and Stirling selected their Philippeville base, was no doubt reminded of the base that the Maid Honor Force had set up at Lumley Beach in Sierra Leone, another beautiful spot in a malaria-ridden area. The Maid Honor Force had suffered from malaria, but not to the extent that it was to affect 2SAS.

However, the dangers of malaria were initially not appreciated, and for Appleyard and 1SSRF/2SAS the early days in North Africa were a time of optimism. Appleyard wrote home: 'As regards prospects, they are good, and things will be very busy soon ... We can do such a really useful job here and there is so much co-operation and keenness that we may get the whole party out if we can persuade London that to go the whole hog for this end can be of much greater value. After all, this is where the war is now and is going to be in the future. If the home end is definitely to go on, then I shall return to run it [Appleyard had clearly received M's order], but will greatly have profited by the experience here.' With Italy now the next likely Allied target, there was indeed potentially much work to be done by the SSRF. They would no longer have to face the crowded waters between England and France.

Having settled into their new camp in March, Appleyard at once began to subject his men to vigorous training in the local conditions. Days of marching across the African countryside followed, under the weight of 65lb packs. Even Appleyard himself commented: 'I think this is the toughest thing physically I have ever done.' Bridgeman-Evans, now second-in-command of what was becoming known as A or No. 1 Squadron, 2SAS, was greatly impressed by the care and attention to detail that Appleyard put into the planning of training exercises and operations alike: 'He started teaching me how to plan operations. His detail in planning amazed me. Most of our operations were to be weight-carrying ones and he had the Quartermaster weigh every item of equipment, even down to a box of matches. Every exercise was planned as an operation and carried out as such. I am convinced that his successes were due to this meticulous planning, on which he insisted.' Undoubtedly, planning had been a significant part of the success of Appleyard's partnership with Gus March-Phillipps – Gus had had the inspiration and vision, Apple made it all work with detailed and methodical planning.

Between March and July, Geoffrey Appleyard and the men of 1SSRF were gradually transformed into a part of 2SAS. In a letter home dated 25 June 1943, Appleyard described how he was now in command of A Squadron of 2SAS. A Squadron comprised 12 officers and 156 men, and the Regiment as a whole was 450 men, under the overall command of Bill Stirling. Appleyard was Operations Officer for the whole of the Regiment, responsible for the planning, laying on and execution of all the Regiment's operations. He supplied his family with a new official address for 2SAS, explaining that '2 SAS stands for 2nd Special Air Service Regiment, and all ranks are now parachute trained, although that is by no means our only means of entry. I am personally more interested in the other way, as that is where my personal experience is … George Jellicoe is with us with a detachment from 1SAS, and has been here about a month. I greatly admire George, he is one of the best.' Jellicoe's detachment from 1SAS was now a part of the SBS, although the distinctions between the units became increasingly blurred.

It is difficult to identify which operation was officially the last performed by 1SSRF, and which the first performed by the emerging 2SAS. However, SOE's records show that Appleyard remained officially 'on their books' until 1 July 1943, and M always intended to have him back into his Secret Service as soon as he was released from other duties.

Appleyard was very busily employed in both the planning and execution of operations from the moment that he arrived in North Africa. Whether technically raids by 1SSRF or by 2SAS, they exhibited essentially the same character, one inherited from the SSRF's days at Anderson Manor.

Chapter 26

La Galite

The first operation for 1SSRF in North Africa was planned for early April 1943, a night-time raid on the Italian-held island of La Galite, off the coast of Tunisia. It was important to Allied plans to know more about the geography of the island and about its Italian garrison, believed to number 350 men. In the usual SSRF style the raid would be by landing craft from the sea, but the raiding party would be considerably larger than it had been in Anderson Manor days, comprising 40 men.

According to Bridgeman-Evans, his second-in-command on the raid, Appleyard's plan was to land his 40 men covertly, and to secure the central high point of the island. They would then take an Italian prisoner, and send him to the Italian CO with a message demanding the surrender of the island's garrison, the alternative being that the town of La Galite would be shelled both from the high ground that they held, and from the sea. The latter threat would be pure bluff, since the SSRF would have no artillery, and there was to be no naval presence out at sea. However, the Italians were not believed to have much will to fight left and Appleyard, who had of course been March-Phillipps' pupil, felt this ambitious plan could work. If not the SSRF would have to leave as they had come, by sea.

The raiding party was to travel by surface vessel to within a short distance of La Galite, and then to proceed in small landing craft to the island. It was hoped that the raid would come as a complete surprise to the Italian garrison.

The operation was the culmination of several weeks of hard training. As always, the men in camp at Philippeville were tense before the raid, which typically for the SSRF was a venture into relatively unknown enemy territory. Appleyard delivered a thorough briefing and the chosen men embarked on the lorries that would take them to the harbour where their craft awaited – no longer MTB 344, or its commander Lieutenant Freddie Bourne. Appleyard travelled in a jeep at the head of the small column. This was to be an important operation for him – his first in North Africa, where 1SSRF wanted to establish its reputation and identity as an independent force. Appleyard intended, as always, to lead by example.

The little convoy travelled at speed. The raiding party had only one wish – to get on with it. There had been enough planning and waiting. As Appleyard's jeep sped along the road, he suddenly heard a shot, and felt a searing pain in his left shoulder. It took a moment or two to realize what had happened. A US soldier in the back of a lorry travelling in the opposite direction had been taking pot shots with his .45 pistol at opportunistic targets, probably the kilometre stones beside the road, and Appleyard's speeding jeep had come from his blindside into the line of fire. The bullet had passed through Appleyard's shoulder from behind, and lodged in the dashboard of the jeep. The US lorry continued on its way, the driver oblivious to what one of his passengers had just done.

Fortunately, the bullet had passed through Appleyard's shoulder without hitting bone, and the wound was a clean one. Only the muscle had been clipped. Nonetheless, a gunshot wound with a .45 bullet is no minor injury. The little convoy came to an abrupt halt. Since they were going on an operation Appleyard had a full medical kit with him, and a shell dressing and sulphonamide powder were immediately applied to both sides of the wound. They then drove on to the nearest military unit they could find that had a medical officer. There Appleyard was given an anti-tetanus jab, and offered an ambulance to the nearest field hospital.

In Hollywood, and in the modern James Bond films, the hero often gets shot in one of the less vital parts of the body, and simply gets up and carries on. Real life is different. Appleyard was not in the midst of a battle, nor yet on an operation. He had suffered the shock and pain of an unpleasant wound, and faced a long and testing night operation in enemy territory for which he was no longer fully fit. Any normal soldier would have handed over command to the competent and well-briefed Roy Bridgeman-Evans. Appleyard refused to do so. He declined the offer of an ambulance to hospital, and drove on for another three hours to their embarkation point, where he presented himself to his own unit's medical officer, Lieutenant Robb MC. Robb, a field surgeon of considerable experience, duly patched and strapped him up, and allowed him to carry on. Appleyard's left arm was painful, and for most purposes useless, but he was determined to lead the raid. After all, he had led the Basalt raid with a broken bone in his ankle. Despite the considerable pain, Appleyard was able to maintain a complete outward control and calm that reassured his men throughout the operation.

The weather too was against the SSRF as they set off for La Galite. Heavy seas on the voyage to the island badly damaged one of the landing craft, with the result that the plan to land all 40 men (and to demand the surrender of the Italian garrison) had to be abandoned. Nonetheless, Appleyard, Bridgeman-Evans and a small party managed to land from the remaining craft, and spent four hours in the darkness reconnoitring La Galite. They succeeded in avoiding enemy patrols, and gathered valuable up-to-date information about conditions on the small island. Appleyard gave no outward sign of suffering from the wounded shoulder, but Bridgeman-Evans commented that at one point when Appleyard had laid a hand on his arm, he could feel it trembling from the pain – yet Appleyard's voice was as steady and as natural as if they had been on an exercise. The party successfully re-embarked in the landing craft, rejoined its mother vessel, and turned for home.

Appleyard's wound healed quickly, and he became busier and busier as the planned invasion of Italy approached. Allied forces were massed in North Africa, and the gallant island of Malta remained in British hands. In order to clear the way for an invasion of Italy through Sicily, the Italian islands of Lampedusa and Pantellaria, both of them heavily garrisoned, would need to be captured. Therefore intelligence about those islands was vital. Appleyard found himself frequently in the air, flying from one high level planning meeting to another, or carrying out reconnaissance. Regularly, he would be flown to Malta, and from there take a party of SSRF or 2SAS on a raid.

His regular vessel was now a submarine, which would carry his party from Malta to the vicinity of whichever island was that night's target. The submarine would then surface, and Appleyard would take his men by landing craft to the shore. Appleyard had of course worked from the submarine HMS *Tigris* early in his career with SOE, off the coast of France. Now he exhaustively tested the various types of landing craft available, and eventually decided that the best one to use from a submarine was the RAF inflatable rescue dinghy. These were well suited to being transported in a deflated condition in cramped quarters. They could then be inflated as the submarine surfaced, and launched over the side. On return to the submarine, they would usually be punctured and sunk.

Chapter 27

Pantelleria: Operation Snapdragon

The rocky island of Pantelleria was heavily fortified, and reputedly garrisoned by 13,000 Italian troops. It was known as 'Mussolini's island fortress'. The Allies intended to assault and capture Pantelleria as early as possible in the month of June. Therefore, it was of high priority that as much detailed intelligence as possible was obtained about the fortifications and disposition of troops. Geoffrey Appleyard and 1SSRF/2SAS were assigned the task, on what was named Operation Snapdragon.

Appleyard selected a raiding party of 8 men, which included the Canadian John Cochrane and 6 other ranks, including Sergeant Leigh and Trooper Herstell. They set off from Malta on 24 May 1943 in a submarine. Cochrane recalled that it was the *Unshaken*, under the command of Lieutenant Jack Whitton, RN. The submarine eventually arrived off the coast of Pantelleria, where Whitton and Appleyard spent 24 hours surveying the island and its coast by periscope. Apart from gathering general intelligence about defences, Appleyard was looking for a suitable landing point for the raiding party. Following SSRF principles, he eventually chose a high and difficult cliff as an appropriate spot, upon the established basis that it would be the least expected point of attack from the enemy's point of view. As always, surprise would be all important. The cliff looked impenetrable at first sight, but Appleyard was confident that he had identified a way up it. Once on land, the objectives would be to survey the island for the best possible landing places for Allied assault troops and, most importantly, to assess the enemy's true strength, about which there was little good intelligence. An Italian prisoner would be highly valuable if one could be taken and successfully brought back on board the submarine.

Appleyard had planned the operation meticulously, as always. Each stage of the proposed raid was carefully timed, since it was vitally important to return to the submarine and to be submerged before dawn broke. Lieutenant Whitton had clear orders not to risk his ship by waiting too long for the return of the raiding party. The timing was also designed to fit with the state of the moon. The raiding party would land in darkness, but then carry out its work on the island by the light of a rising moon. Acknowledging the real danger of what they were about to attempt, Appleyard decided they would wear shorts, so that in an emergency it would be easier to swim for the submarine. An emergency signal to bring the *Unshaken* back to the surface at all possible speed had been arranged – two grenades thrown into the sea.

The submarine surfaced at the given time about half a mile off the coast, and two rubber dinghies were launched, each containing 4 men. The *Unshaken* then submerged again. The raiding party experienced no difficulty in reaching the shore. Appleyard posted a sentry at the bottom of the cliff to guard the dinghies, and in the pitch dark began to scout for what he believed to be a climbable route up the cliff, which was about 100ft high. The party had one false start, then found what appeared to be the route that Appleyard had spotted previously. Cochrane described the climb to the top of the cliff: 'Then began the hardest climb any of us had ever experienced – we pulled ourselves up completely by instinct, and every foothold was an insecure one, the rock being volcanic and very porous, crumbling away under our feet. By what seemed to be a miracle, Geoff finally got us safely to the top – covered in scratches.' It took them about 45 minutes to complete the climb.

Gathering their breath at the top, the raiding party could make out a path running along the gorse-covered clifftop, not far from its edge. As Appleyard began to crawl towards it, the sound of voices from an enemy patrol reached them. The patrol was clearly coming their way. The SSRF froze where they were, hoping that in the darkness the patrol would pass by. Cochrane, who had only just hauled himself over the lip of the cliff, experienced the unpleasant feeling of the ground moving under him as he tried to stay as still as possible. He realized that he was lying on an unstable part of the cliff, which was actually beginning to crumble under his weight. The sounds of the patrol were now much closer – it was obviously going to pass along the clifftop path a very short distance from where he and the others lay. Cochrane did not dare to move. He felt himself slipping slowly, back over the cliff. Meanwhile Appleyard, the nearest man to the path, was lying a mere three feet from the patrol, protected only by the gorse. Those of the raiding party who were able to silently readied their weapons.

Just as the Italian patrol came level with Appleyard, a large stone slipped out from beneath Cochrane and fell towards the rocks 100ft below. It landed with a crash. To the men of the SSRF it seemed as if the patrol must hear it, but miraculously, they showed no signs of doing so. They were relaxed and chatting amongst themselves, and if they did hear the sound of the falling rock, they paid no attention to it, but passed contentedly on their way. As soon as the coast was clear, Cochrane hauled himself up on to safer ground, and Appleyard gathered the men together for further orders.

The first objective was to find and secure a prisoner. However, knowing now the difficulty of the cliff descent that was to come, Appleyard changed the plan. Originally it had been intended to cosh the prisoner and render him unconscious, so that he might be lowered by rope to the beach below. Some of the party carried rubber-covered coshes for the specific purpose of knocking a man out. That now seemed totally impracticable, and instead Appleyard suggested that when the prisoner was taken, he should be half-strangled into a state of total subjugation, and thus cowed he would climb down the cliff himself, under orders from his captors. Such an approach might work with an unhappy, conscripted Italian soldier.

Appleyard ordered Cochrane and two others to remain where they were, and to guard the clifftop where the 'path' led down to the rocks below. He then took the remaining three men with him in search of a lone sentry whom they might take prisoner. Very shortly afterwards, the Italian patrol returned along the path, close to where Cochrane and his companions lay concealed. It became clear then that the purpose of the patrol had been to change the sentries. The raiding party had simply been unlucky in the timing of its arrival at the top of the cliff. The patrol passed by without incident.

Appleyard and his small group had also taken cover whilst the patrol passed by. Then they heard the voice of an Italian sentry singing, very close by. He now became their target. The four commandos crept slowly towards him. It was vital that he be taken out in silence, since there were obviously other sentries in the vicinity and the patrol was not long gone. Cochrane says that it was Appleyard himself who made the move to silence the sentry. Whoever it was (and it would have been typical of Appleyard to take the lead), in the darkness the lunge for the sentry's throat was inexact, and he gave out a scream before being silenced beneath a pile of four strong commandos.

Appleyard thrust his fist down the man's throat to prevent him from screaming again, which was effective, save that the Italian not unnaturally bit him. Sadly, the single scream had been enough to raise the alarm. Another sentry came running towards them from apparently no more than 50 yards away. One of the four commandos, Trooper Herstell, with only the cosh intended for silencing the sentry in his hand, rushed towards him in the hope of overpowering him, but was met with a burst of fire to the abdomen and was mortally wounded. The shooting alerted the entire Italian guard – Appleyard and his remaining two companions shortly found themselves under enemy fire, and began to fire back.

Cochrane later attested that their small party accounted for at least four of the enemy before Appleyard decided that the odds were impossible and shouted the order: 'Every man for himself!' Over the cliff the six surviving members of the SSRF went, and miraculously all of them reached the bottom more or less intact. Only Sergeant Leigh suffered any damage, an injury to his knee as he fell a part of the way down the cliff. The sentry at the bottom of the cliff had kept the two rubber dinghies safe and secure, and the commandos rapidly boarded and paddled out to sea. Their submarine was underwater, so Appleyard hurled two grenades into the sea as the given emergency signal. Despite the considerable activity on the island, where Verey lights were exploding into the sky and machine guns firing apparently at random, the *Unshaken* came rapidly to the surface and the commandos quickly climbed aboard. Members of the *Unshaken's* crew slashed and sank the rubber dinghies, and the submarine speedily disappeared again beneath the waves. Only the unfortunate Herstell had been left behind on the island of Pantelleria. His body was never recovered, but he is commemorated on the war memorial at Medjez el-Bab in Tunisia.

The *Unshaken* made a safe passage away from Pantelleria. She kept a rendezvous with three MTBs and their fighter escort some distance from Malta and the men of the SSRF were whisked back to Malta itself. From there, Appleyard was flown almost immediately to a debriefing meeting back in North Africa. Even though the operation had not been a complete success, Appleyard had valuable information on the island and its coastline, and could make an assessment of the relative vigilance of its sentries and patrols. Roy Bridgeman-Evans, who had not been on the raid but who saw Appleyard (briefly) and his team when they arrived in Malta commented: 'They had been fighting fit when they started. They looked like death when I saw them.'

Submarines were not designed to carry extra passengers in any numbers, and conditions on board were cramped and unpleasant. A part of the training for 1SSRF/2SAS had been to know how and where to keep out of the way of the crew when travelling by submarine. According to one SAS/SBS veteran, J Keith Killby, sometimes the commandos would have to sleep in the torpedo tubes. It was also Killby's experience that the fact that it was carrying a number of extra passengers would reduce the air quality on a submarine.

Pantelleria surrendered to the Allies on 11 June 1943; Lampedusa surrendered on the following day. A lot of good work by the erstwhile SSRF had contributed to the Allied intelligence that preceded these events and enabled a campaign that forced each island into submission. The next target would be Sicily.

By late June 1943, however, the curse of malaria had begun to significantly affect the operations mounted by the SAS/SBS from Philippeville. A contingent including Killby and the Canadian John Cochrane set off on a raid called Operation Hawthorn, with the intention of attacking enemy planes at airfields on the island of Sardinia. Sadly, when the expedition arrived at Algiers on 29 June 1943, to embark on the submarines HMS *Severn* and *Saracen*, a number of the men were already suffering so badly from malaria that they had to be turned back at the port. Others embarked, including the medical orderly J. Keith Killby, only to fall sick on the voyage. Killby recalls that when they reached Sardinia and the submarine that he was on surfaced, he was just able to climb into one of the rubber landing craft, but then collapsed and had to be carried ashore by his comrades. He was not the only one suffering, and recalls that two of his comrades died on the island from the effects of malaria.

The raid proved in the main to be a disaster, made worse by the fact that they were betrayed by an Italian-American soldier whom they had taken along because he spoke Italian, but who rapidly changed his affiliation once on Sardinia. The section under the command of John Cochrane, including Killby, found themselves surrounded by a much greater force of enemy troops, and had no option but to surrender. Some of the men were in any event in no state to fight. All who landed were eventually captured and shipped off to prison camps on mainland Italy. Poor John Cochrane was one of them. The other ranks were sent to a prison camp at Servigliano, in the Marche, from which they were able to escape after the Italian Armistice was announced on 8 September 1943, but Cochrane, as an officer, was sent to the prison camp at Chieti, which was taken over by the Germans after the Armistice, and he was shipped off to Germany to see out the war. Thus he was not able to see his wife and son until after the European war ended in May 1945.

Chapter 28

Sicily: Operation Chestnut

Appleyard was understandably feeling tired. He had been working endlessly on planning during the day, and was often on operations at night. In a letter home dated 25 June 1943, he told his family that he had been taken off operational duties for the next six months. He found himself 'operationally tired', saying: 'I have been getting jumpy, which I am afraid is rather absurd but, under fire, it is a dangerous sign in the leader of a party, even though I am fully able to control myself.' By now, the SSRF was officially defunct in North Africa as well as England, and it had been subsumed into 2SAS. Even though he was no longer on operational duty, Appleyard remained the Chief of Operational Planning for 2SAS, and therefore was very busy with plans for the invasion of Sicily.

On 10 July 1943, the invasion began and the first Sicilian landings were made. As part of the invasion campaign, it had been intended that a squad of 75 all ranks from 2SAS would be landed on the island behind enemy lines from two submarines, in order to disrupt the enemy's lines of communication. That was the sort of mission with which 2SAS were now very familiar. The operation was given the name Chestnut. With Appleyard in charge of planning, there can be no doubt that his men were well briefed on the operation, and well trained for it. However, for operational reasons the plan was changed at short notice, and it was decided that a smaller number of 2SAS should instead be dropped in by parachute. Although, as Appleyard had said in his letter home a few weeks earlier, 2SAS had almost all now undergone parachute training, this would be their first operational drop, and the vast majority had no experience of dropping into enemy territory as a fighting unit. However, the battle for Sicily was being bitterly fought, and the decision was that 2SAS would be best used in this way.

Appleyard, tired as he was, felt that although he was not allowed to parachute in with his men, he owed it to them to accompany them on the flight to the dropping zone (DZ) on Sicily, to encourage them, and to do his best to ensure that the drop went smoothly. A drop of reinforcements was planned for the following night, and Appleyard also wanted to learn what he could about the drop and the DZ, in order to ensure that the second drop went well. The first part of Operation Chestnut was ordered to fly on the night of 12 July. Two 'sticks' of 2SAS (the name 'stick' was taken from a stick of bombs) were to be dropped behind the German and Italian front line, near Randazzo in Sicily. They were to be flown from Kairoun, the local airfield for 2SAS at Philippeville.

It was a clear night, and visibility was good. A number of Appleyard's friends were on the operation, including Roy Bridgeman-Evans, who was in command of one stick, and Philip Pinckney (still on the roll of the SBS but attached for these purposes to 2SAS) in command of the other. Patrick Dudgeon was to drop as one of Bridgeman-Evans' stick. Appleyard flew on the same plane as Pinckney's stick, nominally as observer and despatcher, but also with the aim of keeping up morale. He had not received any orders to fly with the operational party, it was his choice and within the discretion that he was given by Bill Stirling. He knew that flights over Sicily were hazardous, particularly so two days after the first Allied landings on 10 July. Appleyard, instinctive leader that he was, felt he should be with his men. On the same plane as Appleyard and in a similar role, was Major Lander, the Commanding Officer of 21st Independent Parachute Company, which was also contributing men to the operation.

Two Albemarle aircraft were to take the parachutists to their destination. Geoffrey Appleyard and Pinckney travelled in the first, PMP 1446, piloted by the very experienced Wing Commander May. Roy Bridgeman-Evans went in the second plane. The two planes left from Kairoun Airfield at 2000 hrs on 12 July, for a flight to Sicily that was expected to take about two and a half hours. Thus the aircraft were expected to return at around 0100 hrs on 13 July. It was a clear night, and flying conditions were good. The drop was made successfully by both planes, despite intense anti-aircraft fire from the ground in Sicily, and they turned for home. PMP 1446, however, never arrived back at Kairoun. It simply disappeared, together with Geoffrey Appleyard, Wing Commander May and the other men on board. The rest of the operation went ahead, and reinforcements were dropped in as planned, though it was again cursed by men falling sick with malaria.

The Chestnut operational report records in relation to Appleyard: 'Plane failed to return to base. Unconfirmed report that wreckage and bodies of crew only found. Is accordingly reported missing, believed killed. Awaiting report from 38 Wing on number of bodies found with wrecked plane.' The bodies of the crew were indeed recovered, as was that of Major Lander. They are buried at Catania, on the island of Sicily. Geoffrey Appleyard's body was never recovered.

Appleyard was posted as missing, and then in August as missing believed killed. Despite the hopes of his family and friends, no news came of him or of any other member of the crew being taken prisoner. The true fate of PMP 1446 was never discovered. The investigations in North Africa led to the conclusion that the plane was either shot down over Sicily, or ran out of fuel, perhaps as a result of damage to the fuel tanks. Old comrades of Appleyard were much later to postulate that PMP 1446 might have been brought down by friendly fire, always a danger in time of war, but the author has found no evidence to support that theory. There was intense anti-aircraft fire over Sicily, and the aircraft may well have sustained what eventually proved to be fatal damage, either on the approach to the drop, or as it left the area.

An appendix to the Chestnut operational report comments on the lessons learned: 'This was the first operation carried out by 2SAS from the air, and suffered from the disadvantages that are unavoidable when plans must be made hurriedly, training fundamentally altered or omitted entirely, and the operation carried out by men who, with few exceptions were unaccustomed to conditions obtaining in this particular type of warfare.' Indeed, Appleyard, always a believer in meticulous planning and training, had every reason to be worried about the operation, which is no doubt one reason why he decided to fly with his men and, in the event, sacrificed his life in an attempt to give them a better chance of success.

Albemarle PMP 1446 had been due back at Kairoun at about 0100 hrs. It had dropped its parachutists at about 2230 hrs the previous night. It is therefore impossible to say whether Geoffrey Appleyard died on 12 or 13 July 1943. However, it is an extraordinary coincidence that Appleyard's boyhood friend, Graham Hayes, was shot by the Germans in Paris on 13 July, after many months in captivity. His death must have been within hours of Appleyard's. Both families in Linton on Wharfe, the Appleyards and the Hayes (who lost two sons in the war) took a crumb of comfort from the fact that the two lifelong friends and comrades-in-arms had gone to their graves within hours of each other.

Thus, when dusk fell on 13 July 1943, three of the original four 'James Bonds' had given their lives for their country, each in a different way. Only one remained, the young Dane Anders Lassen.

Chapter 29

Anders Lassen on Crete

Andy Lassen was one of the first two from the SSRF to arrive in North Africa. He signed on to the nominal roll for 1SAS on 22 February 1943. His official SOE record card shows him being transferred to the Holding Battalion, SAS Regiment, on 1 March 1943. When others of 1SSRF arrived, and 1SAS divided and reformed, Lassen joined the section that became Lord Jellicoe's Number 1 Special Boat Squadron (1SBS), as for a time did Philip Pinckney, who had travelled out with him. Both appear on the nominal roll for 1SBS from 24 April 1943. Although it is difficult to draw any clear lines between the various sections of special forces in North Africa, particularly in 1943, it was with the SBS that Lassen spent most of his time. Thus although strictly speaking Lassen's activities after March 1943 are not part of the story of the SSRF or M's Secret Navy, he can fairly be said to have carried the spirit of the Maid Honor Force and the SSRF forward into their natural successor, the SBS. This book and its predecessor have traced the stories of the four men who in composite formed Ian Fleming's licensed to kill Secret Agent, James Bond – Lassen was the last survivor.

For Lassen, whose aim was to kill as many Germans as possible, the Mediterranean and the Aegean were to prove far more profitable hunting grounds than either West Africa or the French Coast and the Channel Islands had been. The headstrong 20-year-old who had joined Gus March-Phillipps and the Maid Honor Force in April 1941 had matured into a very effective commando and a good leader of men. Physically, he had also matured, filling out from quite a slender young man into one who was muscled and physically hardened. He had suffered the loss of a leader he had worshipped, and friends he had cherished, and he had killed a number of Germans. When he arrived in North Africa it was as a lieutenant with an MC to his name (awarded after the Basalt raid). He had been sent there, together with Philip Pinckney, as a training officer in small-scale sea raiding. Lassen got on well with Jellicoe, who developed a soft spot for him, despite once having apparently been on the receiving end of Lassen's fists.

Lassen's first operation with the SBS was in June or July 1943. He was one of a team of 20 men of S Detachment under the command of Major David Sutherland, who left their base at Athlit and embarked at the port of Mersa Metruh. The dates are confused, since according to Lassen's own diary (quoted by his mother) they embarked on 22 June, whereas the 1SBS war diary records that they left Athlit on 5 July. Not until they were at sea did they learn that their objective was to be the German airfields on the island of Crete, as part of preparations for the invasion of Sicily. When Britain had evacuated its troops (including the few who remained of 7 Commando, March-Phillipps' and Appleyard's original Commando regiment) from Crete in 1941, some had been left behind to liaise with the Greek Resistance. The Resistance on the island was active, and with the presence of the British liaison officers the quality of intelligence was good.

Lassen and S Detachment landed successfully on the south coast of Crete, near Cape Kochinoxos. Having made contact with the local British liaison officer and the Cretan partisans, Sutherland divided his force, and assigned to Anders Lassen an attack on the heavily defended airfield of Kastelli Pediada, south of Heraklion. Lassen was to have with him Sergeant Jack Nicholson, a veteran of No. 7 Commando and Anderson Manor, who had himself served on Crete before evacuation in 1941, Corporals Sidney Greaves and Ray Jones, and two radio operators, a Greek interpreter and a local guide.

The Cretans are a hardy people, but Lassen soon won their admiration for his athleticism and endurance. With the assistance of local guides, his party made their way across the Cretan mountains to a point about 10 miles from the airfield. Lassen then went forward to a village near the airfield and stayed with the local people there for some days, gathering as much information as possible. He observed that there were a number of Stuka bombers on the airfield, 5 Junkers 88s and some fighters. He was told that the planes were closely guarded at all times by a guard comprising a mixture of Germans and Italians. Greece (and therefore Crete) was an occupied country, and the Germans were alert to the ever-present danger of attack by Cretan partisans.

Returning to the main body of his men, Lassen informed them of his plan, and briefed them as thoroughly as he could about the layout of the airfield. It was divided in two by the airstrip, which would be extremely difficult to cross covertly. He therefore split the party into two groups. He and Corporal Jones would infiltrate and attack from the west side of the airfield, Sergeant Nicholson and Corporal Greaves would infiltrate and attack from the east side.

After the operation, it was said that Lassen's party had intended to create a diversion for Nicholson's, but Nicholson himself said that the original plan was for both parties to enter the airfield silently and covertly, place their explosives and get out. Both parties would cut the wire and move on to the airfield simultaneously at 2330 hrs on the night of the attack.

The day before, Lassen moved forward to a cave about half an hour's walk from the airfield. Using this as a base, and with the help of his Cretan guide, he carried out further recconnaissance of the airfield, walking more than once in plain clothes close to the wire of its perimeter, and returning to the cave for the night. He sketched a map of the layout of the airfield for Jones. On the night of the attack, at about 2200 hrs, they moved to a vineyard close to the airfield, carryting their explosives, and at 2330 hrs, cut the wire of the fence and crawled on to the airfield itself. Soon after, Lassen was apparently spotted by an Italian sentry, whom he disposed of silently with his knife. Lassen spoke good German (he had German cousins) and believed he would be able to bluff his way past further challenges by pretending to be a German officer. He aimed to reach some of the planes on his side of the airfield and to place the necessary explosives.

Three times he was challenged, and his use of German fooled the guards. A fourth guard was not fooled however, and raised his rifle. Lassen shot him with a pistol that he had ready in his pocket, and was thus forced to give away the advantage of secrecy. There was an immediate reaction from the garrison of the airfield – flares were fired into the air, and the Germans over on the west side of the runway started shouting to each other as they searched for targets to shoot at on the east side. Lassen and Jones, having stirred up a hornets' nest, rapidly retreated through their hole in the fence to the vineyard. On the west side of the runway, Nicholson and Greaves were by now quietly working away fixing their charges to planes and fuel dumps. They remained undisturbed, despite having to freeze whenever a flare went up as a result of the chaos that Lassen and Jones had caused on the other side of the runway.

Having lain quiet for about half an hour outside the wire, and though the guard had been strengthened and were now on full alert, Lassen decided it was time to go in again. He and Jones crept through the same hole, and made their way towards what they hoped would be a quiet part of their side of the airfield. Lassen had actually succeeded in climbing partway into a hangar before he was spotted. He was fired on by one sentry, whom he shot and killed, but then attracted fire from a number of others. Again he and Jones managed to escape into the darkness, but the guards were now so jittery that they were firing at the slightest movement. This time Lassen and Jones could not regain their hole in the fence, but had to cut another way out. Once outside the perimeter, they ran full tilt into a German anti-aircraft battery. Lassen, immediately composing himself, reverted to his earlier role as a German officer and addressed them fluently, explaining that apparently British troops had got inside the perimeter, and ordered them to turn their fire as necessary on the airfield. Whilst the Germans were carrying out his orders, Lassen and Jones faded away into the night.

Such a deception was easier to pull off than one might expect. There were many different German and Italian uniforms worn by Axis troops during the Second World War, and in the dark it would be difficult to make out exactly what an individual was wearing. Frequently, the SAS and SBS would wear a form of 'coverall' which could easily be confused with an Axis uniform, and a confident order given in German would probably discourage any further examination.

Not satisfied with his night's work so far, Lassen decided to go on to the airfield for a third time once the immediate fuss had died down. All remained quiet on the eastern side of the airfield where Nicholson and Greaves were working, but Lassen still wanted to do a bit of damage of his own. He and Jones therefore made their way through the fence again, but this time were spotted almost immediately. The Germans had called out reinforcements, and now turned their full attention, plus searchlights, on the two commandos. Lassen and Jones had no option but to split up, each sprinting for whatever cover he could find. Nonetheless, they somehow managed to find time to place explosive charges on a caterpillar tractor and a petrol dump, and apparently damaged more than one plane.

On their side of the runway Nicholson and Greaves worked on undisturbed, falling flat on their faces every time a flare went up. The explosives they carried were all fused with timers, meaning there was a limit to how long they could stay on the airfield. After the fireworks display caused by Lassen and Jones on the other side, they gave up hope of seeing either of them again. Having placed the last of their charges, Nicholson and Greaves retreated as fast as they could to the hole they had cut in the fence. They had only just crawled through it when the first of their bombs went off, followed immediately by a series of other blasts. The two men rapidly made their way off up the mountainside, freezing whenever a German searchlight swept in their direction.

On his side, Lassen succeeded in finding his way back out through the fence again, and waited at a meeting point earlier agreed with Jones, but Jones did not reappear. According to his mother, who visited Crete after the war, and talked with many of the locals who had helped her son, Lassen now entered the airfield for a fourth time and managed to eavesdrop on the conversation of the Germans long enough to ascertain that they had not taken any prisoners, or killed any intruders. He then melted away and left the airfield for the last time. There was still no sign of Jones, or indeed of any other members of his party.

Lassen tried to put a good distance between himself and the airfield whilst it was still dark, but dawn found him in the middle of a cabbage field, where he had to lie low throughout the day. He travelled again during the following night, but was now lost, and a second dawn again found him in a field, this time full of onions. He had had nothing to eat since the attack except raw cabbage and raw onion. Happily for him, the farmer who owned the field visited it during the day, and when Lassen asked him for help, the Cretan gladly gave it.

That evening Lassen found himself reunited in a nearby village with his guide and with Corporal Jones, who with the guide's help had also made it to safety. Both Lassen and Jones retreated into the mountains, where they met up with the rest of their party and with Major Sutherland. Some days later, Sutherland, Lassen and all but one of their party were successfully lifted off by sea. By that time, in the style of the old SSRF, they had picked up some German prisoners, whom they took home to North Afica with them. The 1SBS war diary records the SBS party as returning to base on 16 July 1943.

The raid on the Kastelli Pediada airfield was regarded as a great success. On 22 July, Anders Lassen was recommended for a Bar to his Military Cross for his part in the raid, and the award was confirmed on 28 July. Jones, Nicholson and Greaves each won the Military Medal. David Sutherland later said of Lassen: 'From that day onwards, Anders never looked back … he was the most outstanding patrol leader I am ever likely to see. Many times I turned to him for advice since he was invariably right. He never failed me, and I hope that I never failed him.'

Sadly, for the Cretan villagers in the vicinity of the airfield there was a tragic price to pay. The German Commandant of Crete selected 52 hostages at random, and shot them all. Knowing that there was a British partisan liaison officer in the mountains, he threatened to shoot another 50 if the local people did not give him up. However, the Cretan partisans refused to allow the British officer in question to surrend himself.

Chapter 30

Anders Lassen on Simi

Not surprisingly, as the Allies fought their way across Sicily and on to the toe of mainland Italy, the Italians lost the will to fight. Mussolini, their Fascist Dictator for over twenty years, was dethroned in late July 1943, and on 3 September an Armistice was signed between the Allies and Italy, which was announced publicly on 8 September. Under its terms, all hostilities between Italy and the Allies would cease, and it was hoped that the Germans would withdraw from Italy. There was also the question of Greece, which was nominally in Italian hands, courtesy of their erstwhile German allies. Unfortunately, the Germans had long foreseen the probability that Italy would sue for peace with the Allies, and after the fall of Mussolini in late July had started to put their own plans in place. Once the Armistice was announced they moved speedily to secure their positions in Italy, Greece and the Dodecanese. The strategically important island of Rhodes was quickly brought under German control, but the Allies simply did not know what was happening on many of the other Greek islands. It was possible that they had also been secured by German troops, or that the Italian garrison was Fascist and did not intend to give them up.

Jellicoe therefore decided to send every vessel he could get his hands on to the Greek islands, to seize as many as possible before the Germans did so. The targets included Simi, Leros and Cos, all of which were close to Rhodes and thus now of strategic importance in themselves. Cos had three landing strips, Leros had a seaplane base, submarine pens and a floating dock. Simi was the least important, but strategically well placed. The Greek islanders would obviously be on the side of the Allies, and it was hoped that the Italian garrisons would be sympathetic also, and would not hand the islands over to the Germans. Even if the islands were already in enemy hands, or could not be held, valuable intelligence could be obtained.

Lassen, now promoted to Captain, had been in hospital in Nazareth with an attack of yellow fever but was determined to go. He duly sailed from Haifa on 12 September 1943, four days after the Armistice was announced, in a task force comprising two motorized fishing boats carrying 40 men under the command of Major Jock Lapraik MC. They were known as X Detachment. The destination was the island of Simi. Their intelligence on Simi was sketchy – they did not know the size of the Italian garrison which they presumed would be there, or whether there were likely to be any Germans on the island.

The town of Simi stretches from one side of the island to the other, connecting two bays across a mountain ridge. Intelligence warned the SBS that there were coastal batteries on either side of the bay that contained the island's main harbour. X Detachment reached the island of Simi on 17 September 1943, five days before Lassen's twenty-third birthday.

By this time, the official Italian position in the war had become complicated. There was now a civil war going on. The Germans had refused to leave, and had sprung Mussolini from his mountain prison and reinstated him as their puppet dictator. Free Italy had joined the Allies in attempting to liberate Italy from the German stranglehold, but the restoration of Mussolini meant that Fascist Italians now again had a focal point to which they could rally. Italy was being ripped apart, and Lapraik and his men could not know what the outlook of any Italians on Simi might be – pro-Mussolini and pro-German, or on the side of free Italy and the Allies.

As was the usual practice, they made their final approach to the harbour in the dark of the night. As they crept in, the only sound they could hear was the tinkling of goat bells on the cliff faces surrounding the bay. The town was blacked out, and they could make out little from on board ship. Lapraik decided to send a scouting party of two men on shore. Lassen and a Sergeant Pomford were selected to paddle a Folbot canoe in to explore the sleeping town. They arrived silently and safely on the shore some distance away, and crept along the south side of the bay into the town itself.

Once in Simi, they found that the town was not asleep after all, but that many inhabitants were still awake and enjoying the relative cool of the night. In the hot summer months, it was the Greek practice to sleep during the afternoon, then stay up late into the night. Lassen, with his experience of the area, expected a sympathetic reception from the local people, but in the event he got rather more than that. He and Pomford were very warmly welcomed, and before long even the church bells began to ring in celebration!

Any hope of surprise had of course been lost. The local people knew that there was a garrison of about 150 Italians on the island, but placed all their faith in the arriving commandos. As the moon rose, the presence of the two SBS ships in the harbour became obvious, and a rumour rapidly spread across the island that a force of 100 Allied commandos had arrived. Happily, this was enough to discourage the Italian commandant from any attempt at resistance. The garrison took no action to prevent the two ships from entering the harbour and docking, which Lassen gave the order for them to do, once he had satisfied himself as to the depth of their intended moorings (his mother later reported that Lassen had done this by jumping into the harbour himself, fully clothed).

Once X Detachment had landed, Major Lapraik divided his men into four patrols and dispersed them through the town. Lassen took his patrol to the highest point, a school building inside an old fort which commanded a view of both the harbour and the bay on the other side of the mountain. On the following morning, Lapraik had a formal meeting with the Italian commandant and it was agreed between them that if the Germans attacked the island, the Italians would fight alongside X Detachment to defend it. It was an important but uncomfortable alliance, since the local inhabitants detested the Italians and, behind closed doors, continually threatened retribution against them once the Allies had gone. However, for the time being the peace was maintained, and Major Jock Lapraik had full control of the island. Cos and Leros were also taken without great trouble.

The next task that the SBS faced was to turn Simi into a base for raids and reconnaissance, in particular on the nearby German-held island of Rhodes. For this purpose, Lapraik gathered together six caiques, crewed by the men of X Detachment and enthusiastic local islanders. Lassen teamed up again with Sergeant Pomford, and with a Greek called Marco Costandi, whose boat they used. They were tasked with reconnoitring three small islands, Piscopi, Alimnia and Calchi, to see if they were inhabited by any Germans, and if so to capture a prisoner or two. Under the cover of Marco's caique, a local fishing vessel, they were able to sail around the islands in broad daylight. No doubt Lassen's mind turned to his days of masquerading as an innocent fishing vessel on board the Q ship *Maid Honor*.

Probably to Lassen's disappointment, they found no Germans on any of the three islands. However, Alimnia turned out to be an abandoned Italian submarine base, and Lassen decided that the island was worth a thorough search in case the Italian military had left anything behind that could be of value to X Detachment on Simi. As it turned out, they had. Lassen and Pomford found a Breda 20mm gun, with its footpiece missing but otherwise in workable condition. Although there is no specific record of it, from the use that the gun was later put to they must also have recovered a quantity of ammunition. They loaded their find on the caique, and sailed it back to Simi, where Lassen commissioned a local blacksmith to create a new footplate. Once complete, Lassen mounted the gun on top of the wall of the old castle on the mountain, outside the school building, so that it commanded the bays on both sides of the mountain.

At some stage during his stay on Simi, Lassen sustained serious burns to the back of his knees. Hank Hancock, an SBS trooper, recalled that they were caused when Lassen tried to sterilize a latrine by pouring petrol into it. He miscalculated what would happen when he dropped a match on the petrol, and the burns were the result. At this time Lassen was probably still suffering to some degree from the yellow fever that had taken him to hospital in Nazareth. He also had what an official report referred to as 'internal trouble', which was probably dysentery. These complaints were causing him increasing pain and discomfort, and the burns in particular refused to heal. X Detachment's medical orderly, an American called Sergeant Porter Jarrell, did his best to treat them, but Lassen took no care of himself, and did little to help Jarrell's ministrations to succeed.

About a week after his visit to Calchi, a native of that island arrived on Simi, with the news that the Germans had landed there. Despite the discomfort he was in, Lassen and a squad of men from X Detachment, including Porter Jarrell, immediately set sail for Calchi with the intention of throwing the Germans off the island and taking a prisoner or two. However, by the time they reached Calchi, the Germans had returned to the island of Rhodes where they were based. Lassen spent some time with the local garrison of carabinieri, encouraging them to resist any further German landings. He also landed supplies and ammunition for the locals, and helped to build defensive positions on the small island. He and his men then returned to Simi.

Lassen's burns were getting worse, not better, and he required treatment from Jarrell both whilst he was on Calchi, and on the voyage back to Simi. He considered asking for evacuation back to their base in North Africa, but in the end decided that there was too much to do. A small party was to be landed on Rhodes to obtain intelligence, and although not landing himself, Lassen went on the raid to ensure that all went well, as Geoffrey Appleyard had done with the SSRF when he was injured. The reconnaissance was successful, although the two men who were landed found themselves quickly discovered and the subject of a hot pursuit before, with the help of locals, they escaped from the island.

It was now early October, and Lapraik had been in command of the island of Simi for two weeks. The Germans were of course aware of the British presence there, and on Cos and Leros. They decided to take decisive action to recapture the islands. On 2 October, backed by overwhelming air support, they attacked and captured the island of Cos. Simi was to be next. Shortly after the fall of

Cos, Lapraik found his own men unexpectedly reinforced. A ship containing about 20 RAF officers and men, intended for the airfields of Cos, sailed into the harbour at Simi. They were apparently an assortment of ground crew and maintenance men, together with a few spare pilots and a doctor, attached to 74 Squadron, Fighter Command. They were unaware that Cos had fallen to the Germans a day or so earlier. Obviously they could not go on, and so they became, temporarily at least, a part of Simi's garrison.

At dawn on 7 October 1943, a German boat sailed into Pedi Bay and landed 120 troops on the island of Simi. Their arrival was not initially identified. According to Hank Hancock, the men of X Detachment were not on guard at the time, having handed those duties over to the RAF for the night. The RAF, inexperienced in the duty that they were performing and knowing little about Simi, did not raise the alarm at the sight of a strange vessel landing men in Pedi Bay, so the Germans went unchallenged. They outnumbered Lapraik's men (including the newly arrived RAF) by two to one, and Lapraik regarded the Italian garrison as unreliable – they might not fight. Once the Germans were on dry ground, they were quickly noticed, and the shooting started. The Italian garrison sent up a series of Verey lights to alert the SBS and the local population. Nevertheless, the Germans quickly established a position on the mountain ridge separating the two valleys and bays of Simi.

At the schoolhouse, Anders Lassen and his patrol were by now fully alerted to what was going on. They divided into four small groups, and set off into the town to reconnoitre, hunting for any Germans who might choose to come down from the mountain ridge. Possibly, the Germans were overconfident, and did not realize that they were facing highly trained Allied commandos, but in any event, having secured high ground, they set out to sweep through the town and mop up any resistance. Simi is a typical small Greek island town, with a labyrinth of small cobbled streets and flights of steps. For a skilled hunter-killer such as Anders Lassen, the opportunities were limitless. Lassen took with him Sean O'Reilly of the Irish Guards, who later gave the opinion that 'he [Lassen] could actually smell Germans.'

Guerrilla warfare took over the streets of Simi as the day progressed. The men of X Detachment had learned the geography of the small town during their stay, the Germans were strangers who had just arrived. X Detachment wore soft-soled boots, the Germans wore hobnailed boots that rattled over the cobbles. Patrol after patrol was ambushed, and the German casualties began to mount. All attempts by the Germans to take the school that was Lassen's headquarters petered out in the twisting alleyways below it. Lassen himself was credited with killing at least three Germans at close range. After a while the Germans called for air cover, which consisted of three Stuka dive-bombers –

they attacked the fort that was Lassen's command post, but did not succeed in dislodging his men.

It became apparent that X Detachment's Italian allies were doing little to help in the fight, so Lapraik despatched Lassen with a small party of men to encourage them, which he did to great effect. An official report of the action records: 'In the afternoon, he [Lassen] himself led the Italian counter attack which finally drove the Germans back.' By 1500 hrs, it was clear that the Germans were evacuating their wounded and beginning their retreat from the town towards the coast. Clearly their commandant had reported back to his headquarters that they were in great difficulty, because at about 1600 hrs, a big German landing craft sailed into the smaller of the two bays, on the opposite side to the harbour, and prepared to disembark substantial reinforcements.

Now came the moment for Lassen to use the Breda 20mm gun that he had rescued from the island of Alimnia. Mounted as it was on the castle wall, and happily undamaged by the Stuka bombers, it commanded a fine view of the small bay as well as the harbour, and was within easy range of the recently arrived German landing craft. Lassen began to fire down on the vessel, eventually scoring hits on its overcrowded deck. The German ship was in danger of being sunk and had no option but to withdraw. It did not land a single man. Deprived of their reinforcements, the remaining Germans evacuated onto their transport and headed out to sea. The German invasion had been repelled.

For his conduct on Simi, Anders Lassen was awarded a second Bar to his Military Cross. The copy of his citation in his SOE personnel file reads as follows:

> This officer, most of the time a sick man, displayed outstanding leadership and gallantry throughout the operations by X Detachment in the Dodecanese, 13 September to 18 October 1943. The heavy repulse of the Germans from Simi on 7 October 1943 was due, in no small measure to his inspiration and leadership on the one hand; and the highest personal example on the other. He himself, crippled with a badly burned leg and internal trouble, stalked and killed at least three Germans at the closest range. At that time the Italians were wavering and their recovery was attributed as due to the personal example and initiative of this officer. He continued to harass and destroy German patrols throughout the morning. In the afternoon he himself led the Italian counter attack which finally drove the Germans back to their caiques with the loss of sixteen killed, thirty-five wounded and seven prisoners, as against a loss on our side of one killed and one wounded.

However, although the battle of 7 October was won, it was inevitable that the Germans would not take the defeat lying down. On the following day, the first of a series of air attacks took place. German bombers flew over the town, and it was gradually reduced to rubble. Many civilians were killed by the bombing and the casualties of X Detachment included Corporal Greaves, who had won the Military Medal on Crete. The medical orderly, Sergeant Porter Jarrell, was later awarded the George Cross for the work he did amongst the victims of the bombing. It became clear that the position on Simi was untenable, and before long, headquarters ordered X Detachment to withdraw. They left on 12 October 1943.

Against the background of such heroism, it seems trite to draw a comparison between Anders Lassen and the fictional character of James Bond. However, Ian Fleming admitted that his James Bond was based on the real-life secret agents he had met, and he had known March-Phillipps, Appleyard, Hayes and Lassen well. By October 1943, Lassen was the only one of the four left alive, and with two bars already to his MC, his courage and daring was widely recognized. Operating as he was amongst the Greek islands, raiding by boat at night, his profile fitted the archetypal Bond-style hero. His role in the defence of Simi reads like part of the script for a James Bond film or an Ian Fleming novel, and of course even though Lassen had by now left M's Secret Service and was with the Special Boat Squadron, Fleming remained in Naval Intelligence, knew Lassen, and would no doubt have had access to all reports of his activities. Lassen was not only the last of the four men who inspired Bond to be left alive, he was also to become the one and only 'James Bond VC'.

Chapter 31

Lake Comacchio

Anders Lassen's war continued throughout 1944, and is well documented both in his mother's book, *Anders Lassen VC, The Story of a Courageous Dane* (1949) and in Mike Langley's later account, *Anders Lassen VC, MC of the SAS* (1988). Judging by his exploits, had he not already won two Bars to his Military Cross by the end of 1943, he would have received further decorations for his actions the following year.

During the first half of 1944, Lassen led a number of raids as part of Operation Cyclades, including on the islands of Thira (8 prisoners taken and 23 enemy casualties) and Paros (26 enemy casualties). On each of those raids his party also knocked out an enemy radio station and captured valuable records and paperwork. As the year progressed, he carried out a number of other raids, in Yugoslavia and the Aegean, including a return to Crete. By the early months of 1945, it seemed that despite his extraordinary reckless bravery, Anders Lassen would be the only one of the original four 'Bond' agents who would survive the war.

Now promoted to major, a rank shared with Lassen's own hero, the late Gus March-Phillipps, and also the late Geoffrey Appleyard, April found Lassen in Italy. At this point the Allied campaign had again stagnated in front of the enemy's Gothic Line, the defensive works in northern Italy that they had eventually fallen back on in August 1944, having abandoned their defence of the Gustav Line (which included Monte Cassino) the previous May. Partly because of the mountainous spine of Italy, the Appenines, which provided so many ideal defensive positions, the Italian campaign had been bitter and long drawn out. The D-Day landings in June 1944 had also absorbed much of the energy, men and equipment that the Allies would otherwise have committed to the Italian campaign. By the beginning of April 1945, it was obvious that Hitler's Germany must lose the war, but there was still much serious fighting to be done – and after Germany, there would still be Japan.

The Gothic line stretched from coast to coast across northern Italy, with its eastern end reaching the sea on the plain of Romagna, at a marshy and heavily fortified area called Lake Comacchio. In early April, the Allies were preparing for their final push against the Gothic line, with US forces concentrating on the western end of the defensive position in the marble mountains above Carrara, and the British and Empire forces focused on the eastern end, which included Lake Comacchio. Comacchio covered an area of about 200 square miles, wet, boggy, and not dissimilar to English fenland. In order to strengthen their position, the Germans had breached the sea defences, flooding further stretches of land. They had built a number of machine-gun posts, and the few causeways that crossed Lake Comacchio were heavily guarded. The fens were crossed by few channels deep enough to take a boat, in most places the water was only a couple of feet deep, although there was plenty of mud. Even a Folbot, which when loaded had a draught of about two feet, would have had difficulty crossing many stretches of the water. Furthermore, the Germans were expecting an attack, and on the alert.

Major Andy Lassen was called to Ravenna at the very end of March with his SBS squadron of 60 men, which was now attached to the Eighth Army. His first task was to reconnoitre the lake and fenland for navigable channels, so that when the 'big push' came, the SBS could attack that way and take the enemy by surprise. He was also to reconnoitre a number of small islands in the lake, and if possible to establish a base on one of them.

Lassen led his men into the fens on the night of 3 April, in Folbot canoes. Corporal Marsden, one of the party, described some of the difficulties they faced: 'We were rowing all the time, but continually got stuck on the mud banks – and had to get out to push the boats free. Then, when we pulled our feet out of the mud to crawl into the boats they nearly capsized. One canoe overturned completely and we lost our rum ration and part of the radio equipment.' Eventually they landed on a small island called Casone Agosta. Having ascertained that the island was not mined, they dug in as best they could and sheltered under camouflage netting all the next day. On the second night, they paddled across to the larger island of Casone Caldirolo, where they expected to find Germans, since there were two houses on the island. On the way they dropped off Captain Stud Stellin with a patrol at another small island. Later that night Stellin's island was visited by four Germans, whom he gratefully took prisoner, enemy prisoners still being of considerable intelligence value.

Lassen led the rest of his squadron on to the island of Casone Caldirolo, where in fact they discovered that the houses were empty, and that no Germans were present. The men dug in a safe distance away from the larger house, since Lassen was worried that the Germans might be tempted to shell the house if they suspected that the commandos had gained a foothold there. Again the day passed without incident, so on the next day Lassen allowed the squadron to move into one of the houses. That night a group of three German boats rowed passed Captain Stellin's island, towards Casone Caldirolo. Once they had passed Stellin's position, and were closing on Lassen's, Stellin opened fire, and the unfortunate Germans were caught in a crossfire between the two islands. Those who could surrendered, and Lassen's squadron took five prisoners.

The following day, a British naval officer called Fison came by boat to the island to liaise with Lassen and his men. No sooner had he arrived than enemy shells suddenly started falling around the house where they had been sheltering. Lassen endeavoured to complete his conference with Fison under a table, but the bombardment continued and before long he and his men, together with Fison and the German prisoners, got out of the house, and made for the trenches where they had sheltered previously. The enemy fire followed them closely. They tried sheltering in the smaller of the two empty houses, but that too came under fire. It was clear that the Germans now had a good observer in position to call down fire on them wherever they went on the island. The shelling continued throughout the day but ceased when dark fell, and Lassen and his men survived a third night on Casone Caldirolo.

The next day, the shelling started again as soon as it was light, and now fire was directed to a number of the other small islands as well. Andy Lassen had no intention of abandoning either of the islands that they had occupied, and at the end of another difficult day he called for reinforcements. They came, travelling on the fourth night and arriving just before sunrise on 8 April. During the night, Lassen had also sent a reconnaissance party to try to discover the lie of the land on the German side of the water, but it failed to bring back anything of any value.

The island was again shelled during the day of the 8th, but with a relieving force now present, Lassen and his men were available for an attack on the Germans who had been giving them such a difficult time. In the course of the afternoon, he received a telegram from Second Commando Brigade, stating that attacks on the enemy positions must take place that night, 8 April. The telegram added: 'Every reasonable risk must be taken. These military operations are vital to the completion of present plans.' Unfortunately, because the attempt at reconnaissance the previous night had failed, Lassen had little idea of where and what the enemy positions would be, or what to expect. The attack would be blind, but the order was unequivocal. Lassen's squadron was to cross the remainder of the lake, and to land south-east of the town of Comacchio that stood on the edge of the lake. It would then proceed towards the town itself.

Lassen divided his squadron into three patrols. Two would go with him, his own and a second under the command of Lieutenant G. W. Turnbull; while a third patrol under Captain 'Stud' Stellin would land further to the north-west about 20 minutes later. They would carry as many fused bombs as possible, in order to create a substantial series of explosions suggestive of a major attack. The aim was to cause maximum confusion behind enemy lines, and to create the impression that a far greater force had landed. This was intended to distract the enemy's attention from the main attack on the Gothic line, which was imminent, and give it a greater chance of success.

Lassen, with the first two patrols, successfully crossed the lake and landed on a dyke dividing two stretches of water, along which the road leading to the town of Comacchio ran. The road was about five yards wide, with little room either side. Lassen's patrol took the lead, with Turnbull's bringing up the rear. They moved forward in the dark. It was now that the lack of a reconnaissance really made a difference. They did not know who or what they might meet on or beside the road. The story is best picked up in the citation for Lassen's VC:

> On the night of 8–9 April 1945, Major Lassen was ordered to take out a patrol ... to raid the north shore of Lake Comacchio. His tasks were to cause as many casualties and as much confusion as possible, to give the impression of a major landing, and to capture prisoners. No previous reconnaissance was possible, and the party found itself on a narrow road flanked on both sides by water. Preceded by two scouts, Major Lassen led his men along the road towards the town. They were challenged after approximately five hundred yards from a position on the side of the road. An attempt to allay suspicion by answering that they were fishermen returning home failed, for when moving forward again to overpower the sentry, machine gun fire started from the position, and also from two other blockhouses to the rear. Major Lassen then himself attacked with grenades, and annihilated, the first position containing four Germans and two machine guns. Ignoring the hail of bullets sweeping the road from three enemy positions, an additional one having come into action from three hundred yards down the road, he raced forward to engage the second position under covering fire from the remainder of the force. Throwing in more grenades he silenced this position, which was then overrun by his patrol. Two enemy were killed, two captured and two more machine guns silenced.
>
> By this time the force had suffered casualties and its firepower was very considerably reduced. Still under a heavy cone of fire Major Lassen rallied and reorganized his force and brought his fire to bear on the third

position. Moving forward himself he flung in more grenades, which produced a cry of 'Kamerad'. He went forward to within three or four yards of the position to order the enemy outside and to take their surrender. Whilst shouting the order to them to come out he was hit with a burst of Spandau fire from the left of the position and he fell mortally wounded, but even whilst falling he flung a grenade, wounding some of the occupants and enabling his patrol to dash in and capture this final position. Major Lassen refused to be evacuated as he said it would impede the withdrawal and endanger further lives, and as ammunition was nearly exhausted, the force had to withdraw.

By his magnificent leadership and complete disregard for his own safety, Major Lassen had, in the face of overwhelming superiority, achieved his objects. Three positions were wiped out, accounting for six machine guns, killing eight and wounding others of the enemy, and two prisoners were taken. The high sense of devotion to duty and the esteem in which he was held by the men he led, added to his own magnificent courage, enabled Major Lassen to carry out all the tasks he had been given with complete success.

Lieutenant Turnbull, commanding the rear patrol, explained in his operational report: 'Each block house was slightly larger than the one in front, so they could fire over the top of the position ahead ... after the capture of the second position, the two remaining positions were continuing with heavy fire of machine guns down the road, sweeping the banks and sending up illuminating flares.'

Sergeant Les Stephenson had been with Lassen when the firing started. After Lassen had taken out the first two machine-gun posts, Stephenson found himself crouching beside him as he assessed the situation. According to Stephenson, after a period of intensive firing, the shooting died down for a while as the enemy tried to sort out who and what they were fighting, and where they were. Stephenson said of Lassen that 'he was a grenade man ... very fond of grenades. Some people hardly used them, but he had a good throw, and could put a grenade where he wanted. He said: "Have you any grenades Steve?" so I passed him mine which I had been keeping in reserve... . He shouted to the pill-box in German to surrender. Although a ruthless man, he wasn't brutal, and on occasions would offer an opportunity to surrender. Somebody shouted "Kamerad", so he stood up from behind the small rise in the road that we had been using for cover. He told the rest of us to stay put while he went across in the darkness; as he neared the pill-box, there was a burst of machine-gun fire and then silence.'

Stephenson found Lassen moments later, lying by the right-hand side of the pillbox entrance, mortally wounded. According to Stephenson, Lassen said to him, 'Steve, I am wounded, I am going to die', and then when Stephenson tried to give him morphine and said they would get him back to the boats, Lassen said: 'It's no use Steve, I am dying and it's been a poor show. Don't go any further with it. Get the others out.' Moments later, Lassen was dead.

His last order was passed back to Lieutenant Turnbull who was with the rear party, and was now in command. Turnbull fired the red flare to indicate that they should all withdraw. Retreating to the boats, the survivors of the attack and their prisoners successfully made their way back to the island of Casone Caldirolo. Lassen's patrol had been virtually wiped out: five were dead, three wounded and one missing. The following day, the Germans retaliated with pinpoint shelling of the islands held by the SBS and the commandos who had reinforced them. However, what many of Lassen's comrades and friends regarded as a suicide mission was declared by High Command to have been successful. The Germans were duped into believing that there was a far larger force attacking from the islands in the lake than was the case, and diverted valuable resources to the area. It was not long before the Allies' final push succeeded, and by the end of April the war in Italy was effectively over.

Anders Lassen was the last of the 'James Bond' figures to die. Undoubtedly, his death was the most in keeping with the character of the secret agent whom Ian Fleming was to create eight years later. Fleming never did kill off James Bond – he was very much the goose that laid the golden egg – but if he had, he would surely have given him the sort of heroic end that Anders Lassen had, killed with his guns blazing, in an action that would merit the Victoria Cross.

Appendix A

Leslie W. 'Red' Wright – the Man Who Was Not There

Those who have fought and risked their lives for their country deserve our considerable respect. Those who have been decorated for valour stand rightly on a pedestal, however modest they may choose to be about their achievements. In contrast there is nothing worse than a man who claims to be a decorated hero, but is in fact a simple fraud. Having spent more than forty years working regularly in criminal courtrooms, I have heard many lies told, and have encountered numerous fraudsmen and confidence tricksters. Lying is far easier than is generally believed, and many people are able to lie convincingly, at least for a little while.

Historians, like criminal lawyers, are always aware of the dangers of an untruthful witness. As I commented in a previous book, *SAS in Tuscany*, it is surprising how old soldiers' stories can distort what actually happened, usually without a shred of malice, because either it makes the story sound better on retelling, or else the memory is beginning to fade or play tricks. Any historian has to do his best to check what he is told by an eye witness and even contemporaneous accounts may be misleading.

The most dangerous source of all, however, is a witness who is deliberately making things up and is trying to distort history for his own purposes or his own glorification. In my researches for this book and its predecessor, one of the potential sources that I encountered was the late Leslie W. 'Red' Wright. Wright was interviewed during the latter years of his life by a number of eminent historians and authors, and his accounts of Maid Honor Force and the Small Scale Raiding Force, both of which he claimed to have served with, have appeared in a number of publications. I am particularly grateful to Chris Rooney, son of 'Mickey' Rooney, who was one of many with whom Wright claimed to have served, for documents that he sent me from his father's collection, and to Mike Langley for the fact that he had the good sense to record a lengthy interview that he conducted with Wright. As a result of that material, Leslie 'Red' Wright does not appear anywhere in either of my books – until now.

Wright claimed to have served in the Royal Marines, to have been selected for the Maid Honor Force, to have sailed out on the *Maid Honor* to West Africa as a sixth member of the crew, and to have been an active member of the Small Scale Raiding Force. He told various historians that he had taken part in the raid on Dieppe, on Sark (Operation Basalt), and various other operations. The earliest accounts of Wright's exploits appear in Charles Messenger's excellent book, *The Commandos 1940–1946*, published in 1985. Charles Messenger is an experienced and professional historian. An article in *The Times* from 22 March 1984 also added credibility to Wright's claims to have served in Maid Honor Force. Mike Langley, in his book, *Anders Lassen VC, MC, of the SAS* (1988), quotes Wright extensively. The French authors Gerard Fournier and André Heintz, in their very helpful and well-researched book, *If I must die ... from Postmaster to Aquatint*, published as recently as 2006, also drew heavily upon Wright's accounts. It seems that towards the end of his life, Wright was feted in a number of circles, particularly in France, as a veteran of Maid Honor Force and the SSRF.

Wright could certainly tell a tale. His account to Mike Langley of how he came to be recruited to the Maid Honor Force is a typical example. Wright claimed that, whilst serving as a Royal Marine (in what must have been at the latest the early summer of 1941), he had caught a sheep in a field near his barracks, and had killed it with a knife. He then took it back to his mess so that it might be used to supplement his unit's rations, but news of what he had done leaked out, and he was hauled before his CO. There, he found himself in the presence of two officers of Maid Honor Force, Prout and Pinckney, who recruited him because he had been prepared to use his knife on the sheep. It made a good story, and of course echoed what Lassen had done, stalking a deer and killing it with his knife. However, the dates do not stand up. This would have had to have taken place in the early summer of 1941, when the Maid Honor Force was based in Poole. It left for West Africa in August 1941. Captain Philip Pinckney did not join the SSRF until late September of 1942, and was never in the Maid Honor Force. More significantly, it seems that Wright did not even join the Royal Marines until 1942, after the Maid Honor Force had been disbanded.

I have listened to the recording made by Mike Langley of an interview he had with Wright in the late 1980s or early 1990s. Wright had lunch with

Langley at a pub, and Jan Naysmith, who been a genuine member of Maid Honor Force in its early days was also present. Naysmith had left the Maid Honor Force before they departed for West Africa, to take compassionate leave when his father was dying. Langley interviewed the two of them together, well over forty years after the events that he was asking them to recall. Listening to the interview with the practised ear of the criminal lawyer, Wright's technique is clear. When Langley asks a detailed question, Wright waits until Naysmith answers it and then agrees with his answer, hoovering up the details and repeating them. When he thinks that Naysmith won't be able to contradict him, he volunteers information, but he often gets a fact wrong, and Naysmith picks him up on it – for instance when describing Appleyard's hair, or how the mainsail of the *Maid Honor* got damaged. It is, of course, always difficult forty or fifty years after an event to remember details accurately. Witnesses often disagree. When I came across the reported accounts of what Wright had said, I was inclined at first to accept that they were roughly correct. Other historians more eminent than I had accepted his accounts as long ago as 1985, albeit perhaps with a pinch of salt since they seemed at times to be exaggerated.

Whilst I was researching for both this book and its predecessor, *Ian Fleming and SOE's Operation Postmaster*, Chris Rooney kindly sent me copies of some of his father's papers. They included a letter written to Major 'Mickey' Rooney on 4 March 1989, by Henry Brown, then the Honorary Treasurer (but previously for forty years the General Secretary) of the Commando Association, more formally known as the Old Comrades Association of the Army Commandos (which stood down in 2005). By 1989, both Charles Messenger's book and Mike Langley's had been published, and it seems that Wright was now confidently putting himself forward as a much decorated war hero. Members of the Commando Association had taken exception to this, and an investigation had begun. Henry Brown's letter reads as follows:

> Official Royal Marine records confirm his [Wright's] Royal Marine service from 17 June 1942, and say that he is only entitled to the War Medal. [Wright] has in his possession a DSM [Distinguished Service Medal] stamped on the rim 'L. W. Wright, RM, SSRF' but to date official channels say that they can find no gazette entry for this award. The man has said that the late General Gubbins handed it to him at Anderson Manor ... The covering letter from Buckingham Palace this man holds with the same medal does not contain his regimental particulars, in fact what particulars were on the letter is blanked out!!
>
> ... He states having been on the Sark operation (code-name Basalt) with the SSRF detachment and that whilst covering the withdrawal he lost two

fingers. He is in fact two fingers short, but an entry in his RM Medical History sheet states that he lost them when a detonator exploded at a training centre. He has also been seen wearing several medals including the Atlantic Star and the France and Germany which were never issued to one individual ... Needless to say this man is extremely plausible and many comrades have approached me in recent years saying that in conversation ... many things he stated did not ring true. Also last year when I asked him to sign a statement adding his national insurance number, he refused to sign.

'Mickey' Rooney replied replied speedily, and although I have not seen a copy of his reply, it evoked the response from Henry Brown: 'Your comments will greatly help the people dealing with the case in question.' Not long afterwards, Wright's membership of the Commando Association was cancelled, but sadly that did not stop him from continuing to deceive those who did not know the truth of his military record.

It is clear that Leslie W. 'Red' Wright stored up other people's information and experiences, as all good confidence tricksters do, and represented them as his own. When he thought that he could get away with it, he simply made things up. He was entitled, of course, to attend Royal Marine reunions, because he had served with them, though it seems that he never left England. Wright appears also to have befriended and duped Tom Winter towards the end of Winter's life. Winter had been born in 1904, and was therefore in his eighties by the time Messenger's book came out. He returned to St Laurent-sur-Mer, the scene of Operation Aquatint with Wright in 1994, at the age of ninety.

Even today, Leslie Wright's false stories can be found on at least one Internet website. The French Omaha Beach website includes several pages of his memoirs (*Souvenirs de Leslie Wright*). There Wright claims to have been recruited into the SSRF (or Maid Honor Force?) at the end of January or early February 1941, initially by two officers including 'John' Pinckney (*Philip Pinckney did not join the SSRF from 12 Commando until September 1942*), and sent directly to Anderson Manor (*Anderson Manor was not acquired by March-Phillipps until the very end of March 1942*).

Thereafter Wright mixes everything up. He carries out raids on MTB 344 between March and August 1941 (*it wasn't yet built*), with a force including the Ogden Smiths and 'John' Pinckney (*none of whom joined until 1942*). He does not go off to Africa with the Maid Honor Force until the end of 1941 (*cf August*), and spends Christmas in Freetown, Sierra Leone (*cf Lagos, Nigeria*). That Operation (Postmaster), Wright says, was organized by Lord Louis Mountbatten (*it was in fact exclusively an SOE operation*). He returns to

England, rejoins MTB 344, and becomes busy again raiding across the Channel. He takes part in the raid on Dieppe (*there is no evidence that the SSRF were ever a part of the Dieppe raid on 17 August 1942*), and then Sark, where he speaks of rescuing a Polish SOE agent who had been horribly tortured by the Gestapo (*totally at odds with all other reports*). He carries on into 1943, and lands in Nomandy in 1944, managing to be at Pegasus Bridge on 5/6 June. He was apparently then badly wounded, and hospitalized for the rest of the war.

As a result of what I have learned about Wright, I have made no mention of him in either of my books about Maid Honor Force and the SSRF. He has no place in their history, and deserves no credit for their achievements. However, the books in which he has appeared are referred to in the bibliography of each of my books and, inevitably, serious historians who read those books will stumble across him, and may believe the tales he told. Thus I believe it necessary to include this appendix, with a careful examination of what he has said. Leslie Wright did not serve with the Maid Honor Force or with the SSRF. He did not sail on the *Maid Honor* to West Africa. He did not take any part in the ill-fated raid on Dieppe, or the raid upon Sark that had such dreadful consequences. He ranks alongside those fantasists whom one all too frequently meets in a crowded pub who claim to have served in the SAS and obviously have not – the 'Walter Mitty' syndrome. If all the stories of him are true, he even went so far as to acquire and wear medals to which he was not entitled. History can, and must, do without such men. If their falsehoods are not corrected, later generations may take them to be true and history becomes distorted.

Appendix B

Captain J. E. O. Evans

A historian's duty is to present the facts as clearly as possible, and to inform the reader of his sources. Sometimes, we record the recollections of those who were there; sometimes we rely on contemporaneous documents or reports. All are open to error, and need to be cross-checked and corroborated wherever possible. In the sad and intriguing case of Jack Evans, a member of SOE and the Small Scale Raiding Force, I did not find myself able to include his account in the main text for the reasons below. However, in justice to a brave young man who appears to have paid a heavy price for his wartime activities, I will record what I have learned of him in this appendix.

After the first draft of my manuscript had been completed, my attention was drawn by a friend and fellow historian, Wesley Richards, to a book published in 1957 called *Confessions of a Secret Agent*. The book was said to reproduce a manuscript written by Captain Jack Evans, and to have been given by him to one Ernest Dudley, who sold it to the publishers, Robert Hale, in late 1955 or early 1956, ten years after the war. The story was of Evans's recruitment, well under age, into SOE, and his subsequent service with the Small Scale Raiding Force and, later, SOE's Brandon Mission in North Africa, where he was captured behind enemy lines and sent eventually to Stalag Luft III prisoner-of-war camp at Sagan – the camp famed for the Wooden Horse and the Great Escapes. At the end of the war Evans was liberated and returned eventually to London, where the effects of what we nowadays call Post Traumatic Stress Disorder began to substantially affect him, and his life went downhill. He suffered a series of flashbacks to traumatic moments in wartime, as well as constant nightmares, all of which led to a failed suicide attempt.

Evans's book was a dramatic account which undoubtedly drove a coach and horses through the Official Secrets Act – one reason, I initially suspected, why it was submitted for publication not by Evans himself, but by an intermediary. By 1955, relatively little had been published about the workings of SOE in this country. However, *Geoffrey*, a book published in 1946 by Geoffrey Appleyard's father, contained many details of the activities of Maid Honor Force and the Small Scale Raiding Force. Anyone who read that would have learned quite a lot about what the SSRF had achieved, and who had been involved. Initially, I considered the possibility that Captain Jack Evans was a fake.

My task was to read Evans's account, and to assess, so far as I could, whether it was true. Evans said that he was the son of a Welsh father and a French mother, and that his father had worked for the War Graves Commission at the Somme. He had grown up in France, and spoke perfect French. He had been sent to study at Cambridge Grammar School in 1939. When France fell, he claimed to have been still 'in his early teens' (born in 1925), and therefore well under age to sign up to the armed forces. Despite this, by lying about his age, he joined the RAF in 1940. Given a desk job with the RAF, he claimed then to have joined SOE in late 1940 (aged just 15) and later, in early 1942, to have been recruited by March-Phillipps and Appleyard personally, following a clandestine meeting at an SOE flat in London. Obviously, if Evans was half-French, he would have been attractive to SOE, and if March-Phillipps, who had already taken 17-year-old Buzz Perkins into Maid Honor Force, felt that he was a suitable candidate, the man's young age would not have put him off.

There were two central questions for me to answer: (a) was Jack Evans a real person (or perhaps another Leslie Wright), and (b) if so, had he been a member of the SSRF? If the answer to both was yes, then a third question arose: could the account that he had written in 1955 be relied upon? Upon examination I found many significant differences between it and the evidence that I had already gathered. There were a number of colourful features in what Evans said which I would have loved to include in my main text, but I eventually concluded that I could not rely on their accuracy, and that therefore the only appropriate place to record them was this appendix.

One of the difficulties is that there appears to be no nominal roll of the members of the SSRF at any particular time. After the disaster of Operation Aquatint, the membership of the SSRF became larger and more fluid, as members of 12 Commando, the SBS and others joined in. However, even before that it is difficult to find any comprehensive list. Jack Evans purported to have been a member of the SSRF from its very early days. The only hard evidence as to who was a member of the SSRF that I have been able to find (others may do better) comes from two different files at the National Archives. The first is the Combined Operations Planning File for Operation Fathom. Fathom never actually took place – it was one of many operations either lost to the weather or to competing interests in the Channel. It was intended to go ahead between 20 and 23 June 1942, to be mounted by two Motor Launches (ML), ML347 and ML297, and there is a nominal roll in the file for the 24 men of the SSRF who were to be employed on the operation. They would be landed in three boats:

No. 1 Landing Craft: Lieutenant Vann, cox, Private Perkins, bowman, Major March-Phillipps, OC force, Captain Appleyard, 2nd i/c force, Captain Hayes, Captain Howard, Second Lieutenant Lassen, Second Lieutenant Desgranges, Sergeant Winter, Private Mitchell, Private Maher.

No. 2 Landing Craft: Second Lieutenant Young, cox, Private Hellings, bowman, Captain Ogden Smith, Sergeant Williams, Private Orr, Private Lenart [Leonard], Captain Dudgeon, Corporal Edgar, Rifleman Roe.

No. 3 Landing Craft: Sub Lieutenant Laming, cox, Private Ogden Smith, bowman, Captain Torrance, 3rd i/c force, Lieutenant Hall, Second Lieutenant Reynolds, Second Lieutenant Evans, Captain Burton, Captain Kemp, Second Lieutenant Warren.

The planning officer, Major Gwynne, was to be in radio contact with *ML347*. This nominal roll, although no doubt not a complete list of all those then serving with the SSRF at that time, is the earliest list of members that I have been able to find, and it includes a Second Lieutenant Evans in No. 3 Landing Craft. Contrastingly, a list of the British officers on the strength of the SSRF on 20 August 1942, which appears in Tony Hall's personnel file, does not include any officer called Evans – it is as follows:

> March-Phillipps, Gwynne, Appleyard, P. F. Bodvan-Griffiths, Burton, Dudgeon, Hall, Hayes, Howard, Kemp, R. S. Langlands, Lassen, C Ogden-Smith, Prout, Reynolds, Torrance, Warren and Young.

There is, however, an SOE personnel file, in the name of Jack Emile Olive [sic] Evans, born allegedly on 11 May 1921, which, if true, would have made him 18 when war broke out in 1939 – a plausible lie if he was in fact some years younger. The mixture of British and French Christian names is also consistent with a Welsh father and a French mother. This file remains closed until the year 2022. Of course, if Jack Evans was born in 1921 (or 1925) he could well be with us still, and it is entirely right that his personnel file should not be open.

Surprisingly, I have been unable to find any officer called J. E. O. Evans on the General List of Officers in the Army Lists for the years 1940–45.

There is other evidence. Jack Evans talks in his book of meeting in Stalag Luft III with Flight Lieutenant Waddington, who had earlier been in the Fresnes Prison with Graham Hayes. In Hayes's SOE personnel file, there is a reference to the return of a Captain J. E. O. Evans from France in June 1945. Evans had telephoned in to SOE while making his way to Barry Island in Wales, reporting that at Stalag Luft III he had heard something of Hayes from Waddington. Evans also contacted the Hayes family, and eventually Waddington was traced and told what he knew. One obvious reason why Waddington and Evans might have talked about Graham Hayes in Stalag Luft III would have been if Evans had served with him in the SSRF. In my opinion, the entries in the Hayes file confirm that Captain Jack Evans, the author of the book, was in fact J. E. O. Evans – and the personnel file proves that J. E. O. Evans did indeed serve with SOE.

For that reason, it is right that Evans's account of the SSRF should have its place in this book. His description of the mental anguish that he suffered after the war must, however, be taken into account when assessing the accuracy of his story, as must the official records. Evans describes how his wartime experiences had substantially changed him, and how he did not feel after the war that he could meet his parents again. He found his life falling apart. The flashbacks dogged him, and may well have led to the disordered account of events in his book. If what he says is true, and he was a soldier and member of SOE between the ages of 16 and 20, his mental deterioration is not surprising. Eventually he turned to religion, and entered a seminary at Amiens, in France. When that failed to provide him with what he needed from life, at the age of 30 he joined up as a First Lieutenant in the French Foreign Legion, feeling that soldiering was his natural calling.

In the book, Evans describes his training when first recruited into SOE, and how he learned to jump by parachute in preparation for an operation into France. Upon completing the training, he was granted a commission as a Second Lieutenant, General List. However, he did not in the end go on the French operation because SOE discovered that he was under age. Later, he was recruited, following a meeting in a soundproofed room, by March-Phillipps and Appleyard, who did not mind about his age. If what Evans says is true he would then have been 16 or 17. He was sent to Anderson Manor. His description of training there is similar to that of others. Evans says, however, that the owner of Anderson Manor was a woman in her sixties, who remained in the house and shut herself away, so the SSRF only occasionally glimpsed her. He describes what clearly would have been MTB344, but says it was an old torpedo boat (it was in fact brand new), and that it was armed with only one light machine gun. He says that Lieutenant Van [sic] commanded the MTB, and makes no mention at all of Lieutenant Bourne.

The first operation Evans records appears to be Operation Barricade. However, he describes it as an attack on a Nazi marine battery manned by 300 marines. Having landed on the beach, on the blowing of a hunting horn by March-Phillipps, all ten men of the raiding party threw two grenades apiece at the defensive wire and the German guards behind it, inflicting substantial casualties. The SSRF then retreated to their boat and paddled out to sea, as all hell broke loose behind them. They could not find the MTB in the dark until Van took the risk of briefly turning its lights on. As firing from the shore broke out, the SSRF scrambled aboard the MTB, and it took off before the enemy guns could find their range.

Two weeks later was the Casquets raid, Operation Dryad. Evans claims to have gone on the raid, but describes it differently to everyone else, though he does confirm the taking of seven prisoners without a shot being fired. Peter Kemp lists all ten of the SSRF who carried out the Casquets rock raid, and the sections that they were assigned to: Evans was not one of them. I prefer Kemp's account, and have relied upon it in my main text.

Evans then describes an operation on the Cherbourg coast which appears to me to be an amalgamation of Operations Dryad, Fahrenheit and Aquatint. Following this, Evans says that he began to work with Major 'Y', clearly a reference to Major Gwynne, on what appears to have been Operation Facsimile, a raid on an enemy airfield in France. For the purpose of this raid, Evans says that he and two others went off for another six weeks' training, returning before Operation Aquatint. Since Dryad was on the night of 2/3 September 1942, and Aquatint ten days later, Evans's account cannot be right. Furthermore, Evans gives a detailed account of how he, Gwynne and two others whom he names as Paddy and Fichell actually carried out a successful attack on an airfield in France (Operation Facsimile), and describes rather colourfully his escape through Marseilles – where he was sheltered in a brothel – into Lisbon in neutral Portugal. From there he was able to return to London.

Both Appleyard's operational report, and the Combined Operations War Diary, record that the Facsimile operation never took place. In the author's opinion, it is likely to be true that Evans was one of those designated and briefed for it. He was very suitable, being half-French and fluent in the language. But the only records I have been able to find clearly state that the operation was not carried out. This is the most troubling part of Evans's account, since if the raid did not take place, it is pure invention. If I have missed something, I can only apologize.

Evans says that upon his return he was granted two weeks' leave. He describes a state of increasing mental turmoil. He was then posted down to one of the new SSRF bases near Redruth, Cornwall (which would have been Scorries House), with Major Gwynne (Y) as his Commanding Officer. He apparently arrived there in November. Very early in January, Evans says he was posted to North Africa, together with Major Gwynne. Gwynne's personnel file confirms that he, Gwynne, was transferred to join Brandon Mission, leaving on 3 February 1943. Evans says that he was still 18, which tallies if his true year of birth was 1925. It is certainly right that Gwynne was posted to Brandon Mission in North Africa in early 1943 and Evans, again valuable as a French speaker, may well have gone with him.

Promoted to captain early in 1943, Evans then records being captured after a parachute drop behind enemy lines. The remainder of his tale is intriguing, as he describes life as an inmate in Stalag Luft III, his contact with Flight Lieutenant Waddington there, the Long March (also experienced by 'Adam Orr') and the concentration camps. That part of his story has no relevance to this book, except for the Waddington connection, which I have already dealt with.

In 2022, when J. E. O. Evans's personnel file is opened (or earlier if his death is established), more will be known. I hope that I have done him no injustice here. He and Peter Kemp are the only two survivors of the SSRF whom I know to have written of their experiences within 10–15 years of the end of the war. Interestingly, Peter Kemp's *No Colours or Crest* was published in 1958, just a year after Evans's *Confessions of a Special Agent*. However, Kemp makes absolutely no mention of Jack Evans, probably deliberately. Certainly, he is categoric in his account that Evans was not on the Casquets/Dryad raid.

Whatever the case, Jack Evans is in a totally different category to Leslie W. Wright. Wright was a fraud. Evans was a very brave, very young man who was truly a member of the SSRF and SOE, and who undoubtedly suffered extreme anguish as a result of his war experiences. There can be no doubt that he was promoted to the rank of captain at a very young age, and it seems clear that he was captured behind enemy lines in 1943. His Post Traumatic Stress Disorder (PTSD) subsequently went untreated at a time when such a condition was not properly understood. His courage and audacity is not to be doubted, but his accuracy once he had fallen on hard times and was suffering from PTSD does not stand up to scrutiny. This again is one of the problems that historians will always face.

Acknowledgements

I pay tribute to those who serve and have served in our Armed Forces, and who are prepared to make the ultimate sacrifice for their fellow countrymen. The price that they and their families sometimes have to pay is too high, and they all deserve our unswerving support, admiration and funding.

It is high time that I publicly expressed my thanks to those who have been of such help to me during the writing of the three books that I have now had published by Pen & Sword. Jan Chamier, my editor for all three books, has been consistently charming, constructive and helpful. The team at Pen & Sword, in particular Laura Lawton and Matt Jones, have put up with both my good days and my bad, and always provide youthful inspiration amongst the trials and tribulations of the modern publishing world. Lastly, my thanks go to Brigadier Henry Wilson, Pen & Sword's commissioning editor, for the faith that he has had in my writing, albeit he has never encouraged me to give up my day job! Henry, one day we must walk over some mountains together.

I have previously expressed my love for and thanks to my wife Angela, who has been very supportive of my efforts over the last few years. My thanks too go to my children, Julian, Robin, Stephanie and Toby, who have greeted my endless comments about James Bond with amused tolerance. Finally, within the family I must thank my sister Valerie, who has proved more than once to be the world's best proof-reader. Any errors and mistakes that have crept into the first print runs of any of my books have preceded her careful inspections.

My research has been significantly helped by friends and fellow historians, amongst whom I mention Wesley Richards, Chris Rooney and Steven Kippax. My thanks go to them and many others. I am also indebted to those authors who have previously dealt with the topics that I have covered, in particular Geoffrey Appleyard's father, J. E. Appleyard, and Anders Lassen's mother,

Suzanne Lassen. They each suffered the loss of a child, of course had intimate knowledge of them, and had the advantage of speaking to many eye witnesses to the events described in this book, not long after those events had occurred. I have already paid tribute to Charles Messenger's excellent work, *The Commandos*, and Mike Langley's rewrite of Suzanne Lassen's book, which included many fascinating later interviews with those who had been involved (and in Leslie Wright's case one who hadn't). I am also indebted to the French authors, Gerard Fournier and André Heintz, for the excellent research that they performed over many years in order to produce their book, *If I must die....* For others, I refer the reader to the bibliography.

Any historian, particularly an amateur like myself, can only strive for accuracy. I have done my best to achieve that in all three books that I have written, relying on primary evidence wherever it is available. If I have failed to do justice to my subject, I can only apologise.

Brian Lett
Somerset
2013

Sources

A. The National Archives, Kew

There is a vast quantity of material now available at Kew that touches upon the various subjects of this book. The individual contents of the files are rarely indexed, but simply run in chronological order. The author sets out what are, in his view, the most important files, and attempts simply to reference the relevant topic or topics that each deals with. This list is not exhaustive, but will provide a researcher with all of the core information. A number of obviously relevant files (particularly SOE personnel files) still remain closed.

ADM 116/5112	Admiralty records re SSRF November 1942-April 1943
ADM 179/227	Operation Aquatint
ADM 223/480	Naval File on SOE, includes Fleming's 'intimate knowledge' of SOE
AVIA 11/23	Operation Performance
AVIA 22/1588	SOE's special gadgets department.
DEFE 2/2-5	Combined Operations War Diaries
DEFE 2/9	Report from Lt Cdr Curtis re Bill Stirling 17/3/43
DEFE 2/66	Operation Witticism
DEFE 2/99	Operation Batman
DEFE 2/109	Standing orders, and Operations Barricade, Dryad, Branford, Aquatint, Basalt, Facsimile, Fahrenheit, Batman, honours and awards
DEFE 2/198	Operation Fahrenheit
DEFE 2/201	Operation Fathom
DEFE 2/264	Operations Huckaback and Backchat
DEFE 2/433	German War Crime report on Graham Hayes, Winter's report on Aquatint

DEFE 2/523	Operation Pussyfoot
DEFE 2/622	Operation Witticism
DEFE 2/957	Further operations intended for the SSRF in 1943
DEFE 2/1093	Planning of SSRF from October 1942
FO 837/850	Operation Performance
HS 2/179	Operation Frodesley
HS 6/304	Operation Huckaback
HS 7/23	SOE boats, comment on Welman
HS 7/27	Full history of SOE's gadgets department under Newitt, and many of their inventions, and reports on their work in progress
HS 7/47	SOE's catalogue of special devices
HS 7/169	History of Massingham Mission
HS 7/210	SOE's instructions on how to fake illnesses and deal with the doctor's questions
HS 7/236-7 SOE	Massingham North Africa War Diaries 1943
HS 8/115	SOE/OSS liaison
HS 8/785	Operation Frodesley
HS 8/793	Welman miniature submarines
HS 8/797	Welman miniature submarines
HS 8/801	Welman miniature submarines (includes photographs)
HS 8/818 and 9	Liaison between SOE and Combined Operations
HS 9/48/1	Appleyard's personnel file
HS 9/210/7	Brinkgreve's personnel file
HS 9/394/5	Darby's personnel file
HS 9/426/8	Desgranges' personnel file
HS 9/630/8	Gubbins' personnel file
HS 9/640/1	Gwynne's personnel file
HS 9/647/2	Tony Hall's personnel file
HS 9/680/5	Hayes' personnel file
HS 9/705/5	Lord Howard's personnel file
HS 9/888/2	Lassen's personnel file
HS 9/907/5	Lehniger/Leonard's personnel file
HS 9/1183/2	March-Phillipps' personnel file
HS 9/1215/1	Leslie Prout's personnel file
HS 9/1250/5	Reynolds/Bingham's personnel file
HS 9/1377/2	Colin Ogden Smith's personnel file
HS 9/1418/6	Bill Stirling's personnel file
PREM 3/409/1	The beginnings of SOE
WO 106/4117	Early planning of the SSRF

WO 218/7   Setting up of 7 Commando, 1940
WO 218/41   12 Commando War Diary for 1942
WO 218/57   12 Commando War Diary for 1943
WO 218/97   1SAS War Diary
WO 218/98   Operation Chestnut
WO 218/103   Early days of SBS, formed 2/5/42
WO 218/104   2SBS War Diary 1943
WO 218/106   M Detachment SBS/SAS War Diary 1943
WO 218/112   1 SBS War Diary 1944, Operation Cyclades, Lassen
WO 218/174   Operation Hawthorn
WO 218/175   Operation Cesnut
WO 379/116   SBS Records

B. The Imperial War Museum
Documents:
12618 Gubbins Collection Box 04/29/8
14857 Major March-Phillips Collection Box 06/103/2
17255 Major Leslie Prout collection
19040 John Cochrane collection
90/1785 Peter Kemp Collection
Audio Recordings:
Lady Marjorie Marling: 12306
Herbert Maurice Roe: 12666
Lieutenant Freddie Bourne RN 11721

C. Bibliography
Appleyard, J. E., *Geoffrey*, Blandford Press, 1946
Beevor, J. G., *SOE Recollections and Reflections*, The Bodley Head, 1981
Boyce, Fredric and Everett, Douglas, *SOE – The Scientific Secrets*, Sutton Publishing, 2005
Butler, Ewan, *Amateur Agent*, George Harrap, 1963
Butler, Rupert, *Hand of Steel*, Hamlyn Paperbacks, 1980
Evans, Jack and Dudley, Ernest: *Confessions of a Special Agent*, Robert Hale, 1957
Fournier, G. and Heintz, A., *If I Must Die...* , Orep, 2006
Guillou, Michel, *Operation Farenheit*, Dartmouth History Research Group, 1996
Kemp, P., *No Colours or Crest*, Cassell, 1958
Killby, J, Keith, *In Combat, Unarmed*, Monte San Martino Trust, 2013

Langley, Mike, *Anders Lassen V.C., M.C., of the SAS*, New English Library, 1988
Lassen, Suzanne, *Anders Lassen VC*, English edition, Frederick Muller, 1965
Messenger, C., *The Commandos*, Wm. Kimber, 1985
Ramsey, Winston G., *The War in the Channel Islands*, After the Battle Publications, 1981
www.spiritofcanada.com *Memoir of Flying Officer Winston Churchill Parker, RCAF*
Wilkinson, Peter and Astley, Joan Bright, *Gubbins and SOE*, Leo Cooper, 1993

D. Personal interviews
Mr Malcolm Paul Hayes (nephew of Captain Graham Hayes MC)
Mrs Irene Walters (daughter of Private Richard Lehniger)
Mr Jerry Appleyard (nephew of Major Geoffrey Appleyard DSO, MC)
Mr John Appleyard (brother of Major Geoffrey Appleyard DSO, MC)
Mr Derek West (nephew of Sergeant Allan Williams)

In addition to the above, I had the great pleasure in December 2012 of interviewing my long-term friend Cavaliere Ufficiale J. Keith Killby, OBE, about malaria and the problems it caused on Operation Hawthorn.

Index

No. 4 Commando, 128, 147
No. 7 Commando, B Troop, 13, 28, 31, 35, 36, 42, 68, 177
No. 12 Commando, E Troop, 42, 102, 105, 106, 108, 129, 131–3, 142, 149, 152
No. 45 Royal Marine Commando, 128
The French Commando, 128
1 SAS Regiment 30, 153–5, 157, 160, 176
2 SAS Regiment, A or No. 1 Squadron, 155, 160, 162–4, 167, 168, 17–4
1 SBS, 171, 172, 176, 177
1 SBS 'S' Detachment, 177, 180
1 SBS 'X' Detachment, 182–7
2 SBS, 150
11 SAS Battalion, 28
74 Squadron, Fighter Command, RAF, 185
The Pioneer Corps, 20, 37, 83

Abel, German soldier, 64
Admiral von Tirpitz, 17, 18, 43–7
AFH, Allied Force Headquarters, 156, 157, 159
Albermarle PMP 1446, 174, 175
Alderney, 56, 57, 65, 67–70, 73
Alexander, Field Marshal Sir Harold R. L. G., DSO, MC, 154
Alimnia Island, 183, 186
Ampleforth College, 12, 128
Anderson, Lieutenant General Sir Kenneth, 154
Anderson Manor (Station 62), 21–3, 24, 28, 29, 34–6, 39, 40, 42, 48, 49, 51, 54, 57–9, 66, 68, 71, 73, 74, 79, 101–5, 108,
118, 129, 131, 137, 140, 144, 146, 148, 152, 154–7, 161, 165, 177, 196, 197, 202
Antelope Hotel, 21
Appleyard, Major Geoffrey 'Apple', DSO, MC, 1–3, 5, 11–15, 17–19, 21, 24, 25, 27, 30–3, 36, 38–40, 42–5, 49–51, 56–64, 66–74, 76, 77, 79, 85, 90, 93, 97, 98, 101–3, 105–18, 121, 122, 125–8, 130, 132, 134, 137, 139–44, 146, 147, 150–2, 154, 156–71, 173–5, 177, 184, 187, 188, 196, 200–2
Arisaig, 26
Asnières-en-Bessin, Château d'Asnières, 88, 90

Baker Street, 3, 11, 17–19, 97
Baleine Bay, Sark, 108
Balga, Leutnant, 117
Barker, William George, 57, 58, 68
Barkworth, Captain, 155, 156
Barry, Sergeant Joe, 132, 135–8
Belvoir House and Beach, Herm, 148, 149
Benn, Major A. A., 49
Bingham, Brian *see* Reynolds, Sylvanus Brian
Bismark, 43
Bleicher, Sergeant Hugo 'Paul', 92, 94
Bleyer, Gefreiter, 114, 118
Boddington, Commander Nicholas, 90
Bodvan-Griffiths, Captain P. F., 201
Bond, James, 1–3, 5–8, 10, 27, 160, 166, 175, 176, 187, 188, 193
Bootham School, 13

Bourne, Lieutenant Freddie, DSC, RNVR, 41, 42, 50, 51, 53, 54, 59, 68, 73, 74, 76, 77, 79, 101, 103, 107, 108, 117, 132, 134, 137, 139, 141, 142, 147, 148, 150, 165, 203
Brandon Mission, 127, 153, 154, 157–9, 199, 204
Bridgeman-Evans, Roy, 161, 163, 165–7, 171, 174
Brinkgreve, Lieutenant Henk, 35, 58, 59, 62, 63, 152
Broderson, Sergeant Sam, 132, 133, 137
Bromsgrove School, 129
Brown, Henry, 196, 197
Brooke, General Sir Alan, 118
Bruce, Robert the, 11
Buckmaster, Colonel Maurice, OBE, 90
Burhou Island, 67–70
Burton-Burton, Captain John Langthorne, 19, 30, 31, 49, 50, 58, 59, 62, 63, 72, 78, 79, 81, 82, 90, 101, 103, 201
Butler, Ewan, 5, 6

Cadman, Company Sergeant Major, 86
Calchi Island, 183, 184
Casone Agosta, Lake Comacchio, 189
Casone Caldirolo, Lake Comacchio, 189, 190
Casquets Rock, Lighthouse, 48, 56–60, 63–6, 70, 105, 108, 109, 114, 147, 203, 204
Cheltenham College, 9
Chieti, PG 21, 172
Cholmondeley, Hugh, 22, 24
Churchill, Sir Winston, 4, 5, 10, 14, 65, 118, 128, 140
Club, Private Forbes, 86
Cochrane, Lieutenant John 40, 161, 162, 168–72
Collins, Lieutenant Colonel Ian, 101, 102, 105
Comacchio, Lake, 188, 189, 191
Combined Operations, 16, 18–20, 23, 35, 48, 49, 58, 118, 140, 142, 145, 152, 154–7, 159, 203
Cos, 181, 183–5
Costandi, Marco, 183
Cotter, Lance Corporal Percy, 132, 136, 137, 139

Crete, 31, 5, 36, 176, 177, 179, 188
Curtis, Lieutenant Commander, 159

Daily Mirror, 121
Daily Telegraph, 120, 121
Dalton, Dr Hugh, 4, 5, 10
Darby, Captain Sam, 85, 129, 134, 139, 140
Davidson, Mrs Winifrid, 92–5
de Brunville, Paul, 88
de Brunville, Olivier, 88, 89
de Wiart, General, 10
Dembowy, wireless telegrapher, 64
Derrible Bay, Sark, 107–9, 112, 117
Desgranges, Maître Quartier André Jules Marcel, CGM, 28, 72, 78, 80, 81, 97–9, 201
DFS – Direction Finding Station, 49–52, 54
Dieppe raid, 120, 121, 146, 195, 198
Dismore, Lieutenant Colonel 'Dizzy', Legion d'Honneur, Croix de Guerre, US Medal of Freedom, 98, 100
Dixcart Bay, Sark, 108, 109, 111, 112, 117
Dixcart Hotel and annexe, 113–17, 119, 122
Dornier DO 17, 54
Downside School, 32
Drake, Sir Francis, 11, 22–3
Dreyer, Jane, DZ.41; 93–5
Duchessa d'Aosta, 29
Duckett, Miss, 119
Dudgeon, Captain Patrick, MC, 32, 58–60, 62, 64, 106, 115, 116, 118, 124, 146, 155, 160, 174, 201
Dudley, Ernest, 199
Dunkirk, 4, 12, 13, 27, 30, 34, 36, 49, 66, 67, 101, 131

Eden, Sir Anthony, 14
Edgar, Corporal, 69, 201
Eisenhower, General Dwight D., 153, 154, 156
Eleonora Maersk, 26
Esslinger, Gefreiter, 114, 118
Eton College, 4, 34
Evans, Captain J. E. O., 199–204
Evans, Lance Sergeant Sid, 132, 136, 137
Evison, Sergeant Ernest, 29

Farran, Major Roy, DSO, MC, 162
Felix, Leo, 23, 73
Felsted School, 34
Fernando Po, 11, 67, 91
Fionia, 26
Fison, Naval Officer, 190
Fleming, Commander Ian, 1–6, 8, 11, 14, 18, 19, 26, 43, 128, 160, 176, 187, 193
Fleming, Peter, 128
Flint, Corporal, 106
Fournier, Gerard, 195
Frager, Jacques Henri 'Paul', 90
Franco, General, 30
Fresnes Prison, Paris, 94–6, 202
Fyfield (codename), 20

Gairdner, Lieutenant General Sir Charles, 159
Garches, 92
General List, Army, 26, 32, 202
Geneva Convention, 120–3
Gestapo, 82, 84, 98–100, 120, 198
Giffard, General Sir George, KCB, DSO, 33
Gilchrist, Lieutenant, 129, 131, 141, 142
Godfrey, Admiral John, 11, 14, 19, 43
Gothic Line, 188, 189
Goubeau, Robert 'Bob', 92, 94, 96
grain race, Australia to England, 25
Greaves, Corporal Sidney, MM, 177–80, 187
Gubbins, Major General Sir Colin McVean, DSO, MC, *see* 'M'
Guernsey, 119, 139, 146
Guernsey Star, 119
Gustav Line (Monte Cassino), 188
Gwynne, Major John, 19, 34, 58, 73, 125–7, 154, 157, 201, 203, 204

Halifax, Lord, 4
Hall, Captain Thomas Anthony Inglis, 'Tony', 24, 32, 72, 74–76, 78, 81, 90
Hambro, Sir Charles, 10, 156
Hancock, Trooper Hank, 184, 185
Hannau, Julius, 'Caesar', 1
Haydon, Major General, 155
Hayes, Captain Graham, MC, 1, 2, 25–8, 33, 58, 61, 63, 72, 78, 79, 85, 87–97, 99, 100, 101, 160, 187, 201, 202

Hayes, Dennis, 95, 175
Hautechaud, Dr Paul, 90, 91, 94
Heintz, André, 195
Hellings, Private Jan Eire, 35, 72, 78, 79, 81, 82, 84, 85, 90, 97, 101, 103, 120, 201
Herdt, Oberleutnant, 106, 117, 119
Herm Island, 146–8, 151
Herstell, Trooper, 168, 170, 171
Hewitt, Captain W., 147–9
Hichens, Lieutenant Commander Robert, DSO, DSC, RNVR, 143, 144
Hitler, Adolf, 'Fuehrer', 12, 30, 65, 72, 96, 119, 120, 123, 124, 188
Hitler's Commando Order, 123
Hoare, Sir Samuel, 30
Hog's Back, Sark, 108, 110, 111, 115–17, 119, 122
Hornet, HMS, 50
Horning, Major, 156, 157
Horse Guards, Room 98; 33, 161
Howard, Captain the Lord Francis Philip of Penrith, 32, 39, 58, 59, 62, 72, 74, 76, 78, 80, 81, 201
Howells, Corporal Ellis, 132, 137, 139
Humann, Septime, 88–90

Inchmery House, Exbury, Hampshire, 128
Inter Services Research Bureau (ISRB) – *see* SOE

Jarrell, Sergeant Porter, GC, 184, 187
Jellicoe, Lord George, 155, 160, 163, 176, 177, 181
Jones, Corporal Ray, MM, 177–80
Just, Gefreiter, 114, 118

Kairoun, 174, 175
Kastelli Pediada airfield, Crete, 177, 180
Kieffer, Robert 'Raoul', 91, 92, 94, 96
Kemp, Major Peter, DSO, MC, Cruz de Guerra and bar, 7, 8, 19, 29–32, 35, 38, 49, 50, 58–60, 62–4, 66, 72, 102, 103, 125, 128–40, 146, 152, 156, 201, 203, 204
Kepp, German soldier, 64
Kharkov War Crimes Trial, 95
Killby, Cavaliere Ufficiale J. Keith, OBE, 171, 172

214 The Small Scale Raiding Force

King's College School, Wimbledon, 27
Klatwitter, German soldier, 64
Klotz, Gefreiter, 114, 117–19
Kowalski, Private, 75
Kraemer, wireless telegrapher, 64

La Galite, 165, 167
La Jespellaire, Sark, 111–13, 115
Laming, Sub Lieutenant, 201
Lampedusa, 167
Lander, Major, 174, 175
Langlands, R. S., Lieutenant, 201
Langley, Mike, 195, 196
Lapraik, Major Jock, MC, 182–6
Lassen, Major Anders, VC, MC and two bars, 1, 2, 19, 26, 27, 32, 39, 40, 68, 69, 72, 102, 106, 109, 110, 113–16, 118, 146, 154–6, 158, 160, 175–93, 195, 201
Lehniger, Richard (alias Leonard), 23, 37, 39, 40, 72–74, 78, 80, 83, 103, 201
Lehniger, Irene, 37, 38, 104
Lehniger, Julia 'Lilly', *née* Dorfler, 37, 40, 73, 104
Leigh, Sergeant, 168, 171
Lemasson, Marcel, 88
Le Pin, 88–92
Leros, 181, 183, 184
Lett, Major Gordon, DSO, 1
Lochailort, 30
Lovatt, Lord, 155
Lumley Beach, Freetown, 33, 162
Lupton House, near Paignton, Devon, 128, 134

'M', Major General Sir Colin McVean Gubbins, DSO, MC, 1 ,2, 3, 5–6, 9–13, 17–21, 26, 30, 31, 34, 35, 44–6, 83, 94, 95, 98, 100, 101, 105, 107, 108, 129, 140, 145, 152, 154, 156–64, 176, 187, 196
MI5, 98–100
MI9, 64, 81, 97, 98–100, 118, 123, 140
McClair, Second Lieutenant, 150
Maher, Private, 201
Maid Honor, Maid Honor Force, 7, 10, 11, 13–15, 17–22, 24, 26–29, 33, 40–2, 44, 46, 48–50, 58, 73, 78, 80, 89, 91, 94, 97, 100, 121, 158, 160, 162, 176, 183, 194, 195, 197, 198, 200
Malta, 167, 168, 171

March-Phillipps, Major Gus, DSO, MBE, 1–3, 5, 7, 11 –24, 26–36, 38–45, 48–64, 66–78, 80, 87, 90, 91, 93, 97, 101–4, 107, 114, 125, 128, 144, 146, 160, 161, 163, 176, 177, 187, 188, 200–3
March-Phillipps, Henrietta, 104
Marsden, Corporal, 189
Mary Celeste, 65
Massingham Mission, 97, 98, 153, 154, 156–9
May, Wing Commander, 174
Mayne, Lieutenant Colonel Paddy, 160
Meerut, 12
Messenger, Charles, 195
Mill Hill School, 35
Mitchell, Private, 201
Mountbatten, Lord Louis, 16–19, 23, 58, 71, 105, 118, 125, 143, 145, 152, 154, 155, 159, 197
MTB 344 – the 'Little Pisser', 41, 42, 48, 50, 51, 53, 54, 56, 58–64, 66–70, 73, 74, 76, 77, 79, 90, 101, 107, 108, 113, 117, 126, 129, 132, 134, 137, 139–43, 145–8, 150, 151, 154, 165, 197, 198, 202
Mullins, Reginald, 22
Mundt, Chief Petty Officer, 62, 64
Murray, Major Neville, 84, 85
Mussolini, Benito, 'Il Duce', 32, 181, 182

Naysmith, Jan, 196
Nelson, Sir Frank, 5, 10, 43
Nelson, Admiral Lord Horatio, 56
News of the World, 122
Newton, 34, 35
Nicholson, Sergeant Jack, DCM, MM, 36, 129, 132, 133, 136–8, 177–80

Ogden-Smith, Captain (later Major) Colin Malcolm, 31, 35, 68–70, 72, 106, 131, 141, 142, 152, 197, 201
Ogden-Smith, Private (later Sergeant) Bruce, DCM, MM, 31, 106, 197, 201
Operations
  Aquatint, 72, 73, 90, 101, 102, 104, 106, 109, 113, 117, 129, 133, 142, 197, 200, 203
  Backchat, 145–7, 149, 150, 151
  Barricade, 48, 49, 54, 56, 58, 59, 64, 66, 149, 203

Index

Basalt, 96, 105, 106, 118–20, 122, 124–7, 130, 132, 142, 144, 147, 166, 176, 195, 196
Batman, 131, 133, 141
Branford, 67, 68
Catswhiskers, 151
Chestnut, 173–5
Cyclades, 188
Dryad, 48, 49, 56–9, 64, 66, 67, 118, 203, 204
Facsimile, 125, 203
Fahrenheit, 130, 131, 134, 141, 142, 203
Fathom, 200
Frodesley, 43, 45, 46
Hawthorn, 172
Huckaback, 145–7, 149, 150
Husky, 160
Inhibit, 146, 147
Kleptomania, 151
Performance, 34
Postmaster, 1, 2, 4, 6, 11, 13–15, 17, 18, 24, 27, 29, 33, 43, 50, 87, 90, 91, 93, 98, 158, 197
Pussyfoot, 145, 151
Ramification, 15, 18, 19, 25
Savannah, 13
Snapdragon, 168
Torch, 153, 159
Witticism, 142–4
Opoczynski, Abram (alias Adam Orr), 36–7, 58–60, 62, 64, 72, 78, 79, 81–6, 90, 101, 103, 120, 201, 204
Opoczynski, Hersz, 83
O'Reilly, Trooper Sean, 185
Orr, Adam, *see* Opoczynski, Abram
Orr, Charles, 83–5
Ortet, Jean-Louis 'Armand', 92–4, 96
Oswald, Obergefreiter Peter, 114, 118
Oundle School, 32

Page, Miss, 119
Pantelleria, 167, 168, 171
Paros, 188
Perkins, Frank 'Buzz', 28, 200, 201
Perry, Sir Percival, 147
Petit Dixcart, 110, 111, 113
Philippeville, 162, 165, 172, 174
Pinckney, Captain Philip, 105, 106, 111, 115, 116, 124, 129, 142, 146, 149, 152, 155, 156, 160, 174, 176, 195, 197
Piscopi, 183
Pittard, Mrs Frances, *née* Mardon, 112, 113, 119, 121
Pointe Château, Sark, 108, 109, 112, 113, 117, 122
Pointe de Plouezec, 131, 132, 134–6, 139
Pomford, Sergeant, 182, 183
Pommern, 89
Poole, Poole Harbour, 17, 18, 21, 22, 39, 48
Porteous, Captain Pat, VC, 146–9, 151
Pritchard, Captain A. Hesketh, 147
Prout, Major Leslie Ewart, 21, 27, 28, 33, 85, 99, 100, 146, 195, 201
'Q' – Professor Dudley M Newitt, MC, 6–8, 44

Raleigh, Sir Walter, 11
Randazzo (Sicily), 174
Ramsay, Winston G., 105, 117
RDF, 142, 146
Redbourn, Bombadier, 42, 105–7, 111, 113–15
Reineck, wireless telegrapher, 64, 105, 111
Reynolds, Second Lieutenant Sylvanus Brian John, alias Bingham, 34, 35, 58–60, 62, 63, 102, 103, 129, 132, 133, 135, 139, 152, 201
Rhodes, 181, 183, 184
Richards, Wesley, 199
Ringway Parachute School, Manchester, 19, 104
Robb, Lieutenant, MC, 166
Roberts, Lance Corporal Ronald, 132, 137
Robinet, Claude (alias Rivière), 131
Rooney, Major Oswald Basil 'Mickey' Rooney, 129–40, 142, 152, 194, 196, 197
Rooney, Chris, 194, 196
Rowe, Rifleman Herbert Maurice, 36, 201
Rudellat, Yvonne, 90

St Laurent sur Mer, 75, 80, 82, 90, 93, 101, 197
St Nazaire raid, 36, 105
St Peter Port, Guernsey, 143, 144
Santa Isabel, 11, 14, 91, 94
Saracen, HMS, 172
Sardinia, 172

Sark, 80, 102, 105–9, 112, 114, 116, 119–22, 195, 196
Scorries House, Redruth, 128, 204
Sedbergh School, 32
Servigliano, PG 59, 172
Severn, HMS, 172
Septaux, Suzanne, 88–92, 94
Seton-Watson, Professor G. H. N., 5–6
Shell Beach, Herm, 148, 149
Sicily, 160, 167, 171, 173–5, 177, 181
Simi, 181–7
SIS – the Secret Intelligence Service, MI6, 13, 145
sleeve gun, 8
Smee, Lieutenant, 150
SOE – the Special Operations Executive, alias the ISRB, 1–14, 16–20, 23, 26, 28, 29, 31–7, 41, 43, 44, 46, 48, 57, 58, 81, 83–7, 90, 93–5, 97–9, 101, 103, 105, 128, 129, 140, 145, 152, 153, 156, 160, 163, 167, 176, 186, 199, 201, 204
Spiro, Leopold, 83–5
SSRF – the Small Scale Raiding Force, or 62 Commando, 2, 10–11, 16–18, 20–5, 27–32, 34–42, 48–67, 69–76, 78–81, 83, 85, 97, 100–2, 105–12, 114, 116–18, 122, 125–8, 130, 131, 133–8, 140–50, 152–8, 160–9, 171, 173, 176, 180, 184, 194–204
Stalag VIIB (later Stalag 344), 82, 84, 86, 120
Stalag Luft III, 199, 204
Station IX, The Frythe, 7, 44, 45
Station 62 – *see* Anderson Manor
Stellin, Captain 'Stud', 189–91
Stella, SS, 56
Stephenson, Sergeant Les, 192, 193
Stewart, Marjorie, later March-Phillipps, 11, 17, 19, 24, 31, 73, 104, 107
Stirling, Lieutenant Colonel David, 30, 128, 153–5, 157, 160
Stirling, Lieutenant Colonel William 'Bill', 30, 32, 128, 129, 133, 134, 136, 139, 140–2, 146, 151–60, 162, 163, 174
Stock's Hotel, Sark, 113, 115, 116
Stokes, Horace Leonard 'Stokey', 105, 106
Street, Major V. W., 155
Sutherland, Major David, 177, 180
Swatko, Jadwiga, 83

Taylor, W M, 'Jock' 'Haggis', 29
Thackerthwaite, Major, 99, 100
Thira, 188
Thompson, Lieutenant, 147–9
Thorneycroft, Lieutenant Roger, 41
thumb knife, 8
Tigris, HMS, 167
Times, The, 195
Truant, HMS, 30, 128
Todd, Lance Corporal Arthur, 86
Torrance, Captain Hamish, MBE, 31, 102, 103, 201
Tottenham, Denis, 29, 46
Turnbull, Lieutenant G W, 191–3

Unshaken, HMS, 168, 169, 171

Vann, Lieutenant, RNVR, 147, 150, 151, 201, 203
Victory, HMS, 56
Vulcan, 27

Waddington, Flight Lieutenant Peter, 95, 96, 202, 204
Warre, Captain, 108
Warren, Lieutenant Ian 'Bunny' Warren, 27, 33, 34, 40, 58, 60, 61, 100, 118, 144, 201
Weinrich, Obergefreiter, 114–16, 118
Welpen/Welpipe/Welwoodbine/Welcheroot, 8
Welman submarine, 46
Whitton, Lieutenant Jack, RN, 168
Wichert, Corporal, 75
Williams, Sergeant Allan Marcus, 36, 72, 78, 80, 201
Winchester College, 129
Winter, Company Sergeant Major Thomas William, DCM, 28, 41, 58, 59, 62, 63, 72, 75–7, 80–2, 84, 97, 85, 90, 103, 120, 197, 201
Wraxall Manor, near Dorchester, 128
Wright, Leslie W. 'Red', 194–8, 200, 204

YAK mission, 128
Young, Captain Graham Salter, 35, 106, 109, 115, 117, 147
Young, Lieutenant Colonel, 153, 154, 158, 159, 201